Reality Rules II

Recent Titles in
Genreflecting Advisory Series

Diana Tixier Herald, Series Editor

Reality Rules II

A Guide to Teen Nonfiction Reading Interests

Elizabeth Fraser

Genreflecting Advisory Series

Diana Tixier Herald, Series Editor

LIBRARIES UNLIMITED

AN IMPRINT OF ABC-CLIO, LLC
Santa Barbara, California • Denver, Colorado • Oxford, England

Library of Congress Cataloging-in-Publication Data

Fraser, Elizabeth, 1970–
    Reality rules II : a guide to teen nonfiction reading interests / Elizabeth Fraser.
        pages cm. — (Genreflecting advisory series)
    Includes bibliographical references and indexes.
    ISBN 978-1-59884-790-1 (cloth) — ISBN 978-1-61069-292-2 (ebook)
  1. Teenagers—Books and reading—United States.   2. Young adult literature—Stories, plots, etc.
3. Young adult literature--Bibliography.   I. Title.   II. Title: Reality rules 2.   III. Title:
Reality rules two.
    Z1037.F8433   2012
    028.5'5—dc23   2012020232

ISBN: 978-1-59884-790-1
EISBN: 978-1-61069-292-2

16 15 14 13 12   1 2 3 4 5

This book is also available on the World Wide Web as an eBook.
Visit www.abc-clio.com for details.

Libraries Unlimited
An Imprint of ABC-CLIO, LLC

ABC-CLIO, LLC
130 Cremona Drive, P.O. Box 1911
Santa Barbara, California 93116-1911

This book is printed on acid-free paper ∞
Manufactured in the United States of America

Contents

Part 1: Nonfiction Genres

Part 2: Life Stories

Part 3: Nonfiction Subject Interests

Acknowledgments

This volume would not have been possible without the support and advice of my friend and editor, Diana Tixier Herald, or the wonderful opportunity afforded me by the Young Adult Library Services Association in allowing me to serve on not only the 2008 Michael L. Printz award committee but also its first committee for the YALSA Award for Excellence in Nonfiction for Young Adults, whose members were very valuable allies in promoting and recognizing quality nonfiction. I would also like to thank the publishers that sent me review copies of the books annotated in this volume, many of which found their way to the shelves of my library system.

Introduction

Since the publication of the first volume of *Reality Rules* (Libraries Unlimited, 2008), nonfiction has garnered quite a bit of attention. In 2009 the Young Adult Library Association (YALSA) added an award specifically to recognize the best nonfiction published for young adults; the award was conferred for the first time in January 2010 and proved to be the cap of a phenomenal year of publishing, including three of five finalists for the National Book Award, a Newbery Honor winner, the Coretta Scott King Author Award, and a Michael L. Printz Honor, in addition to the Award for Excellence in Nonfiction winners. Teachers, librarians, and media specialists looking at the Common Core State Standards will acknowledge that a recognition of research, evidence, and understanding other perspectives highlights the importance of nonfiction in the Standards of English Language and History and Social Studies. A *School Library Journal* article by Rebecca Hill considers that the emphasis on reading across the curriculum with the Common Core and posits that "informational texts will soon take center stage" (2012, 26). Elizabeth Partridge, in a recent *Horn Book Magazine* issue dedicated to nonfiction, points out the strengths of narrative nonfiction, which "uses all of the best techniques of fiction writing: plot, character development, voice, and theme" (2011, 69). Her article discusses two examples of award-winning nonfiction, demonstrating how Deborah Heiligman and Philip Hoose use research to turn ideas into mouth-watering literary gems.

Definition

As pointed out by Sarah Statz Cords, author of *The Real Story* (Libraries Unlimited, 2006), nonfiction is the "only literary genre, or collection defined by what it is *not* (fiction)." The *Oxford English Dictionary* defines nonfiction as prose writing other than fiction, concerned with the narrative of factual events. That definition has been broadened in this guide to include titles that are either purely informational or in other ways not fictional, such as poetry or guidebooks. This allows for the inclusion of a wider variety of formats that still have nonfiction content. Readers will find graphic nonfiction, which conveys a story in a graphic format. Poetry is considered nonfiction, as by definition it is not prose. In those cases where verse is used to tell a narrative story, it is categorized as fiction or nonfiction depending on whether the story it is telling is fictional or biographical.

Trends in Young Adult Nonfiction

Nonfiction has been providing readers with a number of alternative formats and variations for some years, from literary fiction to photo biographies to graphic novels. While award-winning author Elizabeth Partridge (2011) discusses the strengths of literary nonfiction, teacher and reviewer Kathleen Isaacs (2011) offers the changes in illustration and design, the wide variety of subject matter, and the importance of back matter as some of the changes in the genre in recent years. Readers opening a copy of Nic Bishop's *Spiders* (2007) are treated to an up-close view that they would never have in life—a blessing for most people—along with the facts that are needed to stimulate their interest and lure them to any of Bishop's other books. Libraries and schools now have the opportunity to provide appealing books with interesting subject matter, at a wide variety of reading levels. Books that are highly illustrated and well designed may be very useful for a broad range of readers, providing material that can appeal to reluctant and English as a Second Language (ESL) readers, while still providing reliable, authoritative information that can be useful in schools and public libraries. Poetry and verse is often used to convey information to readers beyond a particular subject or form; it may be found in several subgenres, including one devoted to verse biographies. As Ms. Isaacs concludes, "These books stretch our understanding of informational books for young readers. As they do, they invite more readers in" (2010, 10).

Purpose, Scope, and Selection Criteria

While a practical and valid use for a readers' advisory guide is to lead a reader to a title similar to one he or she has already enjoyed, other potential uses for this guide with young adult and school librarians include collection development, ideas for programming, training, and bibliotherapy. Guides are meant to help when dealing with this important segment of our customer base, especially considering the wide variety of materials available in the nonfiction range. There are readers who genuinely prefer to read nonfiction; this book is meant to serve as a tool for those serving that population.

The books covered in this guide have been published since 2007 and were not included in *Reality Rules*; thus this book can be seen as a companion to, rather than replacement of, that book. The main selection criteria have not changed since the completion of the first volume; the author has taken into consideration the authority, organization, style, design, and illustrations of each book. Popularity has been considered. The included genres remain popular for recreational reading. This is reflected in the number of titles that have been chosen for selection lists such as the Quick Picks for Reluctant Readers and Popular Paperbacks. Books used exclusively for schoolwork and those that have largely been supplanted by online sources, such as dictionaries and encyclopedias, have not been included.

Organization and Features

Each chapter includes a definition of the genre or literature type, a description of subgenres and themes within it, and annotations for each title. Someone trying to find a new title may start with the author/title index of this book to locate a specific book's listing or with the subject index to find relevant titles or genre areas. The author has read and reviewed each individual title. Where a series has been included, selected titles from the series have been reviewed.

The book is divided into three major parts, "Nonfiction Genres," "Life Stories," and "Nonfiction Subject Interests." Part 1 focuses on two exciting and fast-paced genres, "True Adventure" (chapter 1) and "True Crime" (chapter 2). Part 2, "Life Stories," includes both "Memoirs and Autobiographies" (chapter 3) and "Biographies" (chapter 4). The last part includes the popular subject interests "History" (chapter 5); "Science, Math, and the Environment" (chapter 6); and "Sports" (chapter 7), all of which have continued to be popular areas in publishing over the last few years.

Chapter 8, "All About You," contains nonfiction titles of interest to teens developing their own identities. This chapter covers a wide variety of subjects, such as teen identity, health, nutrition, self-improvement, career development, and lighter personal interests. Chapter 9, "How To," contains a wide range of books for both genders, varying from general crafts to cooking, fashion, technology, drawing, and transportation. Chapter 10, "The Arts," examines visual arts, music, film, and literature. The final chapter, "Understanding and Changing the World," lists books about teenagers and their place in the world. Topics in this area include the media and consumer culture, social concerns, and religions.

The Entries

The entries in each section are arranged alphabetically by the authors' last names. Exceptions to this are books in a series that have been written by more than one author, which are listed in series order under the series title. Each entry includes the book's author, title, publisher, publication date, number of pages, and ISBN. Each annotated book has also been assigned a suggested reading level:

- **M**   middle school (grades 6–8)
- **J**   junior high school (grades 7–9)
- **H**   high school (grades 10–12)

These are suggested guidelines only, based on reviews, publishers' recommendations, and personal experience. Some books published for adult audiences that teens will enjoy have also been included.

The following symbols also appear on the entries:

🏵   title has won award(s)

A/YA   books that both teens and adults enjoy

RR   suitable for reluctant readers

GN   graphic nonfiction

The annotations provide enough information about the content and style of the book to help answer a readers' advisory question. Awards won are indicated at the end of annotations for applicable titles, using the following acronyms or short forms:

AENYA or AENYA Honor	Award for Excellence in Nonfiction for Young Adults or Honor
ALA	Association for Library Services to Children Notable Books for Children
Alex	Alex Award
BBYA	Best Books for Young Adults (discontinued in 2009)
BG-HB or BG-HB Honor	Boston Globe-Horn Book Award or Honor
CSK or CSK Honor	Coretta Scott King Award or Honor
IRA	International Reading Association Teachers' Choice list
NBA	National Book Award Winner or Finalist
Norma Fleck	Norma Fleck Award or Honor
OP or OP Honor	Orbis Pictus Nonfiction Award or Honor
PP	YALSA Popular Paperbacks
Printz or Printz Honor	Michael L. Printz Award or Honor
QP	YALSA Quick Picks
Red Maple	Ontario Forest of Reading Red Maple Award
Sibert or Sibert Honor	Robert F. Sibert Informational Book Award or Honor

A list of keywords follows each annotation. These are intended to help users identify similar reads. In addition, approximately 10 percent of the entries have "Now Try" suggestions, read-alikes that share authors, subjects, themes, or common styles with the main entry. Nonfiction titles do not afford an avid reader the same luxury that fiction titles do; there simply aren't that many available series and subject headings to provide librarians with comparable titles. These features are intended to help make those connections.

"Consider Starting with . . ." and Fiction Read-Alike Sections

Two additional sections are provided at the end of each chapter. "Consider Starting with . . ." lists a selected number of popular, highly accessible titles from the chapter. The books listed have been chosen as great starting points for people who would like more information about a certain genre. They may also be considered suggestions for displays or booklists. The titles listed in the "Fiction Read-Alikes" sections offer additional possibilities for readers interested in particular genres, themes, or subjects.

References

Cords, Sarah Statz. 2006. *The Real Story: A Guide to Nonfiction Reading Interests.* Westport, CT: Libraries Unlimited.

Hill, Rebecca. "All Aboard!." *School Library Journal* 58.4 (April 2012): 26

Isaacs, Kathleen T. 2011. "The Facts of the Matter: Children's Nonfiction, from Then to Now." *Horn Book Magazine* (March 1): 10.

National Governors Association Center for Best Practices, Council of Chief State School Officers. 2010. Common Core State Standards (English Language Arts Standards). Washington, DC: National Governors Association Center for Best Practices, Council of Chief State School Officers.

Partridge, Elizabeth. 2011. "Narrative Nonfiction: Kicking Ass at Last." *Horn Book Magazine* (March 1): 69.

Part 1

Nonfiction Genres

Chapter 1

True Adventure

Definition

A common misconception about adventure fiction is that the cover will have a rugged-looking male with a large gun or another weapon facing an overt threat, with some kind of military vehicle, plane, or force looming in the distance. Though it is stereotypical, there remains a kernel of truth to this cliché. Nonfiction books in this category, more than any in other genre, have parallels to their fictional counterparts, in that the protagonists face the same challenges, demonstrating remarkable courage, endurance, and fortitude, which may be more attractive given the veracity of the story. Books in these subgenres include survival and disaster stories, war stories, and sports stories.

Appeal

Adventure is the genre in nonfiction that is most geared toward escapist reading. It is assumed that it will appeal more to male readers, as there remains a persistent stereotype that there "are male brains and female brains, and never the twain shall meet" (Barnett and Rivers, 2011, 23). Books in these subgenres tend to be fast-paced and give readers narratives in which people are struggling to survive, compete with, or hide from their enemies, as well as more leisurely paced travels. This provides librarians with an opportunity: readers who might not otherwise think about picking up a book could be interested in finding out how miners were rescued from 2,000 feet underground in Marc Aronson's *Trapped*, or readers who have seen the movie but aren't really football fans (or vice versa) might be willing to try *The Blind Side*.

Chapter Organization

The first subgenre presented in this chapter is the section "Survival and Disaster Stories." These are harrowing tales of near calamities and the people who work to avert them. Survival stories are followed by the section "Sports Adventures," which includes a variety of stories, from a book by YouTube sensation "J-Mac" McElwain to two vastly different tales of endurance: Brian Boyle's recovery from a devastating car crash and Simon Whitfield's long Olympic journey. The next section, "War Stories," contains titles that show war's effects on people as well as the lengths to which people will go to survive during times of war, emphasizing courage and endurance. The final subgenre section, "Explorations, Travel, and Historical Adventures," contains tales of interesting voyages and some opportunities for armchair travelling.

Survival and Disaster Stories

The popularity of survival and disaster stories crosses both age and gender. Reading about difficult and harrowing experiences allows readers to vicariously share the experiences of natural disasters and death-defying trips that are more exciting than armchair travel, with the added benefit of their being true. Readers may already have a surface familiarity with some of the stories recounted in these books, which isn't surprising given the extensive media coverage at the time devoted to, for example, the riveting story recounted in Marc Aronson's *Trapped: How the World Rescued Three Miners from 2,000 Feet Below the Chilean Desert*, which should whet readers' appetites for the real story. These books fill in the blanks by giving accurate, detailed information about what actually happened before, during, and after an event, adding pertinent historical information and giving further resources. With their fast pace and atmosphere of imminent danger, these tales keep readers on the edges of their seats. Readers get the opportunity to relive the pulse-pounding moments and try to decide what they would do if they found themselves in the same horrible circumstances as the men and women in the stories found here. Those who prefer to learn what to do in the event of a disaster should check the "Survival Skills" section of chapter 9.

Aronson, Marc.

Trapped: How the World Rescued Thirty-Three Miners from 2,000 Feet Below the Chilean Desert. New York: Simon & Schuster, 2011. 134p. ISBN 9781416913979. **J H**

The San Jose Mine in Chile has been a small part of Chile's long-standing copper mining business for over a century, but it was unknown to the world at large until a mine collapse left a huge amount of rock between thirty-three men and their anxious families and countrymen, 2,300 feet above them. The story of the teamwork and endurance that allowed them to survive, while the rest of the world watched, while crews from various nations used the combined expertise, equipment, and resources contributed by outside agencies such as NASA to rescue them, will intrigue readers. Additional resources include photographs, a timeline, suggested Web sites, and the captivating first note sent up by the miners, as well as a discussion about the historical importance of mining that will make this a valuable book for reports.

Keywords: Copper mining • Mine accidents • Mine rescues

Thompson, Kalee.

Deadliest Sea: The Untold Story Behind the Greatest Rescue in Coast Guard History. New York: HarperCollins, 2010. 309p. ISBN 9780545997904. **H** **A/YA**

Early on Easter morning in 2008 the fishing vessel *Alaska Ranger* began to take on water in the frigid Bering Sea, putting all forty-seven people on board at imminent risk of dying and setting in motion the single largest Coast Guard cold water rescue in history. The training needed to undertake a Coast Guard rescue by sea or air, whether swimming or flying, is intense. The reason becomes understandable when contemplating the vast resources needed to undertake this mission. No part of this "rescue" was easy: the crew lost one of the life rafts when attempting to abandon ship; many of the men had difficulties finding the life rafts, boarding the helicopter, or being offloaded on one of the rescue trawlers; and some of the men were unable to get to medical help in time. Thompson is able to impart several breathless moments. This book will appeal to readers who enjoy fast-paced stories of adventure, survival, or sports and combinations of all three.

Keywords: Coast Guard • Fishing • Rescues

Verstraete, Larry.

At the Edge: Daring Acts in Desperate Times. Toronto: Scholastic Canada, 2009. 154p. ISBN 9780545997904. **M**

When faced with a life-or-death decision and with only moments in which to make it, what would you do? Readers are presented with true tales of momentous and critical choices, divided into four sections: the first section, at the edge of disaster, includes stories in which choices saved lives; the second looks at moments of terror such as facing oxygen deprivation in the "Death Zone" climbing Mount Everest; the third examines instances of injustice; and the final section presents impossible choices, including what to do when you don't have any viable options. Readers will find this a gripping book that can be browsed or read straight through.

Keywords: Choice • Decision making • Survival

Sports Adventures

The characters in these books exhibit an athlete's most admirable qualities, such as mental and physical endurance, fighting to the finish as an underdog, and determination to overcome all obstacles between oneself and the finish line. These books may give readers a chance to experience adventures vicariously, often in a sport that interests them, as well as developing empathy for the protagonists' battles. A good example of this is Jason "J-Mac" McElwain's short but very successful basketball career, in which he scored twenty points in the last four minutes of his senior high basketball game. The game can still be seen on YouTube and is described in his book, *The Game of My Life: A True Story of Challenge, Triumph, and Growing Up Autistic.*

Boyle, Brian, with Bill Katovsky.

Iron Heart: The True Story of How I Came Back from the Dead. New York: Skyhorse Publishing, 2009. 249p. ISBN 9781602397712. **H**

> Brian Boyle was an eighteen-year-old swimmer when a near fatal car crash with a dump truck resulted in his losing 60 percent of his blood volume, injured every one of his internal organs, and required his doctors to induce a coma and operate fourteen times to repair the damage. He was not expected to survive or to regain his mobility. Boyle narrates the story of his long and painful recovery, from his initial vegetative state, through his subsequent determination to become a competitive athlete, to the point of his participation in the Ironman Triathlon. Readers will find this journey both compelling and inspiring.
>
> **Keywords:** Bodybuilding • Boyle, Brian • Triathlon

Lewis, Michael.

🎖 *The Blind Side: Evolution of a Game.* New York: W.W. Norton and Company, 2006. 299p. ISBN 9780393061239. **H**

> The production of a movie loosely based on this book has made Michael Oher a household name, but this book is much more. It was released before Oher was drafted by the NFL, and its focus is more on the importance of the left tackle position, using Oher's admittedly amazing and inspirational story as an example rather than as the centre of the book. Both sports and history buffs will be drawn to the stories about great NFL players and the history and insights about how the game itself has changed. **Alex**
>
> **Keywords:** Football • Football players • NFL • Oher, Michael
>
> **Now Try:** Sports fans and film buffs alike will enjoy Michael Oher's memoir, in which he clarifies misconceptions presented in Hollywood's take on his story and reiterates that "Cinderella didn't get her happy ending without lifting a finger." *I Beat the Odds: From Homelessness to "The Blind Side"* provides him with a forum in which to point out the dismal statistics for kids in foster care and encourage not only foster kids but other people to do what they can to help kids in the system, while also thanking the people who helped him.

McElwain, Jason, with Daniel Paisner.

The Game of My Life: A True Story of Challenge, Triumph, and Growing Up Autistic. New York: New American Library, 2008. 243p. ISBN 9780451223012. **H**

> As a young boy, Jason "J-Mac" McElwain was diagnosed with severe autism. By high school he had come farther than his mother ever dreamed, serving as the team manager for the JV basketball team. The coach even let him dress for the last game of the JV season, for which he was serving as the team manager, and put him in to play during the final minutes of the game. Coach Johnson was just as

happy and astounded as the rest of the crowd when J-Mac was called for a foul and managed to sink three free throws in a row. That game became a driving force for the next year of his life, until the real life-changing minutes actually happened, when he was put into the final four minutes of the last game of his senior year and scored twenty points. He became a poster boy for achievement in the autism community and went on to win an ESPY award. This book appeals not only to basketball fans, but also to readers who appreciate stories about individuals who are determined to keep trying and know that doing their best at all times is an important part of life.

Keywords: Autism • Basketball • McElwain, Jason

Whitfield, Simon, and Clive Dheensaw.

Simon Says Gold: Simon Whitfield's Pursuit of Athletic Excellence. Victoria, BC: Orca Book Publishers, 2009. 118p. ISBN 9781554691418. **M**

Simon Whitfield was an unknown quantity when he won the gold medal at triathlon's Olympic debut at the Sydney games in 2000, but although he started the race with a world ranking of only 26th, he quickly became a Canadian national hero and proof of how inspiring the Olympics can be. Readers are given a thorough understanding of an Olympic athlete's ongoing training. Simon's path to the Sydney games was followed by continuing efforts to overcome injuries and a series of highs and lows at the Commonwealth games and World Championships on his way to the Athens and Beijing Olympics. His story is one of commitment and perseverance, demonstrating the drive necessary to the athlete who wants another chance at an Olympic podium.

Keywords: Athletics • Olympic athletes • Olympics • Triathlon

War Stories

Adventures with a backdrop of warfare often show the lengths to which people will go to survive during combat, and they emphasize endurance, courage, and strength. It is these characteristics that separate these stories from the books in the "Human Cruelties" subsection of chapter 5.

Axe, David.

War Is Boring: Bored Stiff, Scared to Death in the World's Worst War Zones. Illustrated by Matt Bors. New York: Penguin Books, 2010. 125p. ISBN 9780451230119. **H** **GN**

David Axe takes readers along with him as he travels to one war zone after another as a war correspondent, happier in these risky areas than in the United States, and even cutting himself off from his publishers when they order him to return from an area that they feel to be too dangerous. The view that readers are given of his journey shows how he ended up at the Iridimi Refugee Camp in Chad, also stopping in on a number of conflicts around the world. Along the way Axe contemplates the tedium that many feel when faced with war every day and presents his struggle about deciding what to do when confronted with that tedium.

Keywords: Graphic nonfiction • War correspondents • War zones

Folman, Ari.

Waltz with Bashir: A Lebanon War Story. Illustrated by David Polonsky. New York: Henry Holt & Company, 2009. 119p. ISBN 9780805088922. **H**

Ari Folman was an Israeli soldier during the 1982 invasion of Lebanon who suppressed the memories of what he had witnessed until a friend told him about a recurring dream in which he appeared. Readers gain a greater understanding of the horrors and dehumanization of war through the story of the Sabra and Shitala massacre as Ari recovers his memories and finds he was one of the Israeli soldiers who witnessed the massacre by the Lebanese Christian Militia of unarmed civilians. This graphic novel is a powerful adaptation of the author's documentary.

Keywords: Graphic nonfiction • Lebanon • War

Guibert, Emmanuel, Didier Lefèvre, Frédéric Lemercier, and Alexis Siegel.

The Photographer. Translated by Alexis Siegel. New York: First Second, 2009. 267p. ISBN 9781596433755. **H GN**

In 1986 Didier Lefèvre undertook his first major mission as a photojournalist, accompanying a Doctors Without Borders (MSF) mission into Northern Afghanistan. He didn't know what to expect, and the beautiful but rough country, which was in the middle of a war with the Soviet Union, took its toll upon him both mentally and physically. This graphic novel, supplemented by Lefèvre's photographs, provides an inside look not only at the war in Afghanistan but also at the remarkable humanitarian efforts undertaken and dangers faced daily by the MSF.

Keywords: Afghanistan • Doctors Without Borders • Graphic nonfiction • Lefèvre, Didier

Now Try: Rafal Gerszak gives readers a comprehensive picture of life in Afghanistan, starting during wartime, when he embedded with Polish troops in order to deploy with the U.S. military, in *Beyond Bullets: A Photo Journal of Afghanistan.* Gerszak spent a year in Afghanistan with the military, photographing the people and seeing the country, and came to the conclusion that he would need to go back to see the other side of the story and talk to the people of Afghanistan. The book presents both his time with the military and his time speaking to Afghans, from people in hospitals to prisoners. The result is a remarkable achievement and a picture of a country in flux, one that has come to mean a great deal to Gerszak and to which he says he will "keep going back."

Hillenbrand, Laura.

Unbroken: A World War II Story of Survival, Resilience, and Redemption. New York: Random House, 2010. 473p. ISBN 9781400064168. **H** **A/YA**

After a surprisingly effective showing at the 1936 Berlin Olympics, college miler Louis Zamperini was understandably disappointed when world events caused the cancellation of the 1940 games, although the drama of his subsequent war story dwarfs any possible sports triumph. Readers find out how lucky Louis was to survive at every stage. His story starts with the numbers of pilots who were lost in the Pacific before introducing several narrow escapes he had while serving as a bombardier on a B-24, then moving on to a heart-pounding account of the forty-seven days he and two members of his crew spent on a raft after their plane was shot down, before they were captured and transferred to the first of several Japanese POW camps, where they received increasingly worse treatment. Hillenbrand's description of the management of the POWs by the Japanese drives the final part of the book, in which Louis, who has been haunted by one soldier at a time when PTSD has not been identified or treated, seeks a method for forgiveness, enabling him to recover from alcoholism and return to Japan several times.

Keywords: Japan • Prisoners of war • World War II • Zamperini, Louis

Kramer, Clara, and Stephen Glantz.

Clara's War: A Young Girl's True Story of Miraculous Survival Under the Nazis. Toronto: McClelland & Stewart, 2008. 352p. ISBN 9780771095832. **H**

Clara Kramer's survival in World War II was highly improbable: she was only twelve years old in 1939 when the Hitler–Stalin pact divided up Poland. She was also one of the 50,000 Jews living in Zolkiew. The story of how an anti-Semitic neighbor hid her family in a bunker while the town and their own home were occupied by Nazis makes for a gripping and painful read. By the time the Soviets liberated Zolkiew, there were only 50 Jews left of the original 50,000.

Keywords: Holocaust • Kramer, Clara • World War II

McClafferty, Carla Killough.

In Defiance of Hitler: The Secret Mission of Varian Fry. New York: Farrar, Straus and Giroux, 2008. 196p. ISBN 9780374382049. **M** **J** **H**

Varian Fry was a thin, unassuming journalist inspired to join the Emergency Rescue Commission when he witnessed an uprising in pre–World War II Germany. He was subsequently sent to Marseilles in 1940, where he was supposed to spend two weeks organizing papers for artists, writers, and scientists trapped by the Vichy government to help them escape. He ended up spending over a year there. The large numbers of refugees required that he create a refugee center to deal with the demand for papers, which in turn increased the amount of attention paid him by the Gestapo. This gripping story recounts how Fry and his staff rescued more than 2,000 people before he was forced to return to the United States, although he lost both his job and his wife in the process.

Keywords: Emergency Rescue Commission • Fry, Varian • Holocaust

Rubin, Susan Goldman.

The Anne Frank Case: Simon Wiesenthal's Search for the Truth. Illustrated by Bill Farnsworth. New York: Holiday House, 2009. 40p. ISBN 9780823421091. **M J**

In 1959 Simon Wiesenthal was called to an Austrian theatre, where a performance of the play based on Anne Frank's diary had been interrupted by teenaged neo-Nazis, who believed that the Holocaust was a fraud. He asked the youths what it would take to make them change their minds. He was a Holocaust survivor who had dedicated himself to gathering information about the whereabouts of Nazi war criminals in order to bring them to justice. He was determined to devote himself to finding the Gestapo officer who had arrested the Frank family in order to prove that Anne's diary was not a fake. This book describes not only the horrors of Wiesenthal's life, from ghetto to concentration camp, but also the extraordinary detective work that he undertook, making this a book that is a natural and great supplement to Anne's diary.

Keywords: Frank, Anne • Holocaust • Wiesenthal, Simon • World War II

Seiple, Samantha.

Ghosts in the Fog: The Untold Story of Alaska's World War II Invasion. New York: Scholastic Press, 2011. 224p. ISBN 9780545296540. **M J**

In May 1942, just five months and two weeks after the attack on Pearl Harbor that precipitated the U.S. entry into World War II, a cryptanalyst in Hawaii tasked with trying to determine the Japanese forces' next target decoded a message with the words "invasion force." The book gives a complete recounting of the subsequent invasion of Alaska's Aleutian Islands as well as the difficulties experienced by the Aleuts, who were evacuated from their homes and placed in rundown and abandoned camps, and then found upon returning home that their residences had been vandalized and stripped of everything of worth. Few civilian detainees taken to Japan survived. In 1981 the Aleuts were issued a formal apology for their suffering by the U.S. government .

Keywords: Aleutians • Japanese in World War II • World War II

Explorations, Travel, and Historical Adventures

These titles provide readers with a wealth of exciting possibilities—from journeying with both experienced and novice travelers to searching for new frontiers alongside the people who were sent to find them. They give readers a chance to gain an understanding of new places, cultures, and historical periods. Readers will find out what it took to make long trips in the Middle East hundreds of years ago and see how those trips opened up trade routes, and have the chance to compare a round-the-world trip taken as a vacation with earlier, exploratory trips.

Galloway, Patricia, with Dawn Hunter.

Adventures on the Ancient Silk Road. Toronto: Annick Press, 2009. 164p. ISBN 9781554511983. **M** **J**

> This book tells the stories of three travelers who made long journeys between India, China, and Egypt, helping to pave the way for the trade routes that would become the "Silk Road." These brave and fascinating men, who lived centuries apart, changed the world that came after them. Xuanzang, a Chinese Buddhist monk, spent sixteen years both instructing and learning from the people with whom he came into contact. Genghis Khan, born as Temujin, greatly expanded the Mongol Empire in his short life. Marco Polo began his long adventures accompanying his merchant family to trade in China as a teenager. The narratives in this book are engaging and vivid and will provide a wealth of information about both the subjects and their times. The book includes a long list of further reading.
>
> **Keywords:** Khan, Genghis • Polo, Marco • Silk Road • Temujin • Xuanzang

Ross, Stewart.

Into the Unknown: How Great Explorers Found Their Way by Land, Sea, and Air. Illustrated by Stephen Biesty. Somerville, MA: Candlewick Press, 2011. 89p. ISBN 9780763749487. **M** **J**

> Over the course of history brave men have set off to learn what lies beyond the horizon. From the 340 BC voyage of Pytheas from Greece to the Arctic Circle without so much as a compass to the first trip to the moon in 1969, readers will find introductions to some of the world's most intrepid explorers and their journeys. Each voyage, from Zheng He's treasure fleet to Cook's circumnavigation of the globe, is accompanied by colorful sidebars and foldout pages with further illustrations, maps of the trips, and Stephen Biesty's cross-sections. Supplementary information in this inviting book includes sources and a glossary. **ALA**
>
> **Keywords:** Exploration • Explorers

Scieszka, Casey.

To Timbuktu: Nine Countries, Two People, One True Story. Illustrated by Steven Weinberg. New York: Roaring Brook Press, 2011. Unpaged. ISBN 9781596435278. **H**

> Casey Scieszka and Steven Weinberg met while studying abroad in college and ended up applying for grants that would let them travel and work together overseas as part of "Their Future Together." Casey's narrative, accompanied by Steven's illustrations, follows them as they live and work

in Beijing, Shanghai, Vietnam, Laos, Thailand, and Mali. Readers will find the couple very pleasant and witty travelling companions indeed.

Keywords: Overseas travel • Scieszka, Casey • Weinberg, Steven • World travel

Steinberger, Aimee

 Japan Ai: A Tall Girl's Adventures in Japan. Agoura Hills, CA: Go!Comi, 2007. 183p. ISBN 9781933617831. **H GN**

Six-foot-tall professional animator Aimee Steinberger jumped at the chance to visit Japan. As a longtime fan of cosplay and a devotee of Volks, a company known for its Dollfie dolls, she couldn't wait to visit the company's Japanese store. Accompanied by two of her friends, she took full advantage of any opportunity to examine Japan's popular culture, shown here in manga-style drawings highlighted with bright colors. Readers will appreciate the extremes of Steinberger's fish-out-of-water position, exacerbated not only by the language barrier, but also by her height and interests. **PP, QP**

Keywords: Cosplay • Graphic nonfiction • Japan • Travel • Volks

Willems, Mo.

You Can Never Find a Rickshaw When It Monsoons: The World on One Cartoon a Day. New York: Hyperion Paperbacks, 2006. 393p. ISBN 0786837470. **H**

After he graduated from college, Mo Willems took an around-the-world trip, capturing his journey in cartoons that encapsulated the things that best caught for him the places he visited. Fifteen years later he revisited the journal, inserting editorial comments about the pictures that add a narrative to the whole and help make this unique and quirky travelogue accessible.

Keywords: Cartooning • Cartoonists • Travel • World travel

Consider Starting with . . .

Aronson, Marc. *Trapped: How the World Rescued Three Miners from 2,000 Feet Below the Chilean Desert.*

Lewis, Michael. *The Blind Side: Evolution of a Game.*

McClafferty, Carla Killough. *In Defiance of Hitler: The Secret Mission of Varian Fry.*

McElwain, Jason, with Daniel Paisner. *The Game of My Life: A True Story of Challenge, Triumph, and Growing Up Autistic.*

Ross, Stewart. *Into the Unknown: How Great Explorers Found Their Way by Land, Sea, and Air.*

Rubin, Susan Goldman. *The Anne Frank Case: Simon Wiesenthal's Search for the Truth.*

Scieszka, Casey, and Steven Weinberg. *To Timbuktu: Nine Countries, Two People, One True Story.*

Steinberger, Aimee. *Japan Ai: A Tall Girl's Adventures in Japan.*

Thompson, Kalee. *Deadliest Sea: The Untold Story Behind the Greatest Rescue in Coast Guard History.*

Fiction Read-Alikes

- **Bertozzi, Nick.** *Lewis & Clark.* Nick Bertozzi presents a graphic account of the momentous 1804 expedition led by Meriwether Lewis and William Clark to find a water route from the Missouri River to the Pacific. The men were determined to accomplish their goal and faced innumerable difficulties. This reimagining of an epic adventure allows Bertozzi to ponder the points of view of the various people encountered along the way, as well as of the explorers. *Lewis & Clark* also provides readers with information about what happened to the explorers after they returned from the expedition.

- **De Vries, Maggie**. *Hunger Journeys.* Teenagers Lena and Sophie, along with their families, are starving during the final winter of World War II in Amsterdam. In order to survive, the people have to make dangerous "hunger journeys" into the countryside to find or barter for enough food to feed themselves, while evading the Nazis who are guarding the town. The girls decide to go farther afield on one such journey, with very poorly forged identity papers, setting in motion events that could get food for their families, throw them straight into the path of the enemy, or both.

- **McCaughrean, Geraldine.** *The White Darkness.* In Geraldine McCaughrean's Printz-award-winning book, Symone knows everything there is to know about the Antarctic, although the only people who appreciate that fact are a family friend, Uncle Victor, and Captain Lawrence "Titus" Oates, her closest friend. Titus is a perfect conversationalist and Sym's closest friend, and knows as much about the Antarctic as she does, which would make him perfect for her, if only he hadn't died on Robert Scott's failed expedition to Antarctica over a hundred years before. When Uncle Victor's weekend trip to Paris actually turns into a trip to Antarctica, Sym has no idea that her dream is about to turn into her worst nightmare, especially when she will only have herself—and Titus—to rely on.

- **Phelan, Matt.** *Around the World. Around the World* presents readers with three narratives from the award-winning graphic novelist, in which intrepid souls find themselves inspired by Jules Verne's *Around the World in Eighty Days* to make remarkable journeys. The first finds coal miner Thomas Stevens cycling long before bicycles were commonplace or safe; the second follows reporter Nellie Bly, a journalist at a time when women were neither encouraged to pursue nor believed capable of pursuing that occupation; and the last follows Captain Joshua Slocum on his solo sailing voyage around the world.

- **Reedy, Trent**. *Words in the Dust.* Based on a true story, in *Words in the Dust* Zulaikha only remembers a few of the words that her mother taught her. Her mother had loved poetry before the Taliban killed her. Now the only women in the house are her father's second wife, Malehkah, and her older sister, Zeynab; Malehkah, is always finding fault with her, beyond the forward-facing teeth and cleft lip that cause everyone to stare at her and the boys in town to call her donkey-face. Americans arriving in town bring changes to Zulaikha's family, first bringing work to Zulaikha's father, then a potential husband for Zeynab, and finally introducing Zulaikha to a doctor who says that he can fix her lip and teeth. Zulaikha happens upon a friend of her mother's who offers to teach her the reading and poetry that her mother had loved, introducing her to an even wider world of possibilities.

- **Watts, Irene.** *No Moon.* In this fast-paced novel, Louisa Gardener always knew that the drowning death of her younger brother in the sea in 1902 was her fault. The accident left her with persistent nightmares and a lifelong fear of the water. She has also always been overprotective of her younger brothers and sisters, and she works hard at her position as a nursemaid in Lord and Lady Milton's household. When her diligence results in her taking the nanny's position and accompanying the family on the *Titanic*, she overcomes her fears and nightmares to be where the children and Lady Milton need her. Middle grade girls will enjoy Louisa's search for her place in the world, along with a touch of romance and her adventure on the doomed ship.

Reference

Barnett, Rosalind, and Caryl Rivers. 2011. "No Blank Slates." *Women's Review of Books* 28. no. 3: 23. MasterFILE Premier/Web (accessed February 23, 2012).

Chapter 2

True Crime

Definition

True crime books focus on a real event, usually a crime, solved or unsolved, and present the events, following through the investigations and providing a picture of the people involved. The enduring popularity of television shows such as *CSI* and the *Law and Order* and *NCIS* franchises bears witness to the appeal of this genre.

Appeal

True crime, much like true adventure, is escapist reading. There is an inherent desire to see criminals punished for the crimes they commit, and arduous investigations offer readers a fast-paced, adrenaline-filled story with satisfying conclusions. Many also offer readers stories that ponder criminals' motives, which is necessary to determine how to catch them. Readers are also shown how investigations take place. Espionage titles provide a larger scale look at crimes than the average person generally sees, involving events that affect battles, wars, countries, and even history itself.

Chapter Organization

The chapter starts with "Cons and Crimes: Solved and Unsolved," contemplating both recent and historical accounts of scams, crooks, and the men and women who tried (and perhaps failed) to catch them. The section "Crime Science," containing books about forensics, is next. The final section, "Intrigue and Espionage," looks at spies and spying.

Cons and Crimes: Solved and Unsolved

This section comprises true accounts of crimes and scams, many of which are historical, along with descriptions of the work undertaken by law enforcement agencies to investigate them. Both narrative and graphic nonfiction are included, with material that appeals to a wide age range and both genders. Books that focus on the sentencing of convicted criminals and provide case studies on teen cyberbullying provide opportunities for discussion and debate.

Alphin, Elaine Marie.

An Unspeakable Crime: The Prosecution and Persecution of Leo Frank. Minneapolis, MN: Carolrhoda Books, 2010. 152p. ISBN 9780825589440. **H**

> The murder of a teenaged factory worker in 1913 in Atlanta, Georgia, was greeted with shock and horror. The determination on the part of the police to find the perpetrator led them to focus solely on Leo Frank, the factory's superintendant. Frank, who was both a northerner and a Jew, was an easy target for the community's prejudices, which were constantly fed by the media and dubious prosecutorial practices. His prosecution for the crime, despite evidence proving his innocence, is made even more horrifying by Frank's subsequent kidnapping and lynching by men who went on to reestablish the Ku Klux Klan in the Marietta area. This case led to the formation of the American Anti-Defamation League.
>
> **Keywords:** Frank, Leo • Lynching • Murder • True crime
>
> **Now Try:** Elaine Marie Alphin gives readers a different sort of murder mystery that ties into the Leo Frank case in her novel *One Perfect Shot*. Brian is having a hard time coping with his girlfriend's murder and isn't sure he believes the popular theory that her father did it, especially as he saw a jogger in the area. When he is assigned a school project to study the prosecution of Leo Frank for a murder he hadn't committed, Brian sees undeniable parallels to his own situation and must decide whether or not to come forward, especially when readers can empathize with the dangers that Brian has already faced.

Barton, Chris.

Can I See Your I.D.: True Stories of False Identities. Illustrations by Paul Hoppe. New York: Dial Books/Penguin Group (USA), 2011. 129p. ISBN 9780803733107. **J H**

> The ten cases profiled in this book are brief accounts of people taking on alternate identities. In a few wartime cases, the individuals might be seen as particularly brave, dangerous, or daring: for example, the young woman who disguised herself as a man to fight in the Civil War or Solomon Perel, a teenaged Jew trying to survive during World War II, who posed as a member of the Hitler Youth. Other stories include the more famous cases of the fraudster and now security consultant Frank Abagnale Jr., which has inspired a feature film and a musical; and Forrest Carter, best-selling author of *The Education of Little Tree*, who was long dead by the time he was also revealed to be segregationist Ace Carter. These stories provide fodder for discussion and debate, as well as interesting reading material.
>
> **Keywords:** Case studies • False personalities • Imposters • Imposture

Busby, Cylin, and John Busby.

The Year We Disappeared: A Father-Daughter Memoir. New York: Blooms-bury, 2008. 329p. ISBN 9781599901411. **H** **A/YA**

> In 1979 Cylin Busby was a normal, Muppet-loving nine-year-old, and John Busby was a police officer working the night shift in Falmouth, Massachusetts. Then John was shot in the head. The story that follows is told by the two of them in alternating chapters as John began the series of reconstructive surgeries necessary to rebuild his jaw and face. The Busby family was faced with not only the ongoing frustrations of stalled investigations, but also the dangers associated with being survivors and witnesses to such a brutal crime and the lengthy difficulties associated with witness relocation.
>
> **Keywords:** Busby, Cylin • Busby, John • Memoir • Shooting • True crime

Dobyns, Jay, and Nils Johnson-Shelton.

No Angel: My Harrowing Undercover Journey to the Inner Circle of the Hells Angels. New York: Crown, 2009. 328p. ISBN 9780307405852. **H** **A/YA**

> Jay Dobyns, an officer with the Bureau of Alcohol, Tobacco and Firearms, spent two years as an undercover agent successfully infiltrating the Arizona chapter of the Hells Angels. His transformation from Jay Dobyns to Jay "Bird" Davis gave him a firsthand look at both the Hells Angels and the effect that such a successful transformation could have on his life.
>
> **Keywords:** Crime • Hells Angels • Undercover operations

Geary, Rick.

Famous Players: The Mysterious Death of William Desmond Taylor. New York : NBM Comics Lit, 2009. Unpaged. A Treasury of XXth Century Murder. ISBN 9781561635559. **H** **A/YA**

> By the beginning of the 1920s, Famous Players was the most important studio in Hollywood, with important stars and directors such as Cecil B. DeMille and William Desmond Taylor. So on Thursday, February 22, 1922, Hollywood was rocked when Taylor's valet found him dead, setting in motion an investigation that would uncover a secret life, scandals among the leading ladies, and a mystery that would remain unsolved. The distinctive artwork in Geary's true crime graphic novels immerses readers in the setting while presenting them with an involving story with multiple suspects and ample motives and opportunities.
>
> **Keywords:** Graphic nonfiction • Murder • Taylor, William Desmond • Unsolved crimes

The Lindbergh Child: The Atrocious Kidnapping and Murder of the Infant Son of America's Hero, Col. Charles A. Lindbergh. A Treasury of XXth Century Murder. New York: NBM, 2008. Unpaged. ISBN 9781561635290. **H** **A/YA**

> The kidnapping-turned-murder case of Charles Lindbergh Jr. was one of the first to be avidly followed by the media, because of Lindbergh's celebrity, and was a shambles from the beginning. Geary presents it here from the beginning, laying out all the evidence and showing why Bruno Hauptman, who was found guilty of and executed for the crime, may not in fact have been the sole person responsible for it.
>
> **Keywords:** Graphic nonfiction • Kidnapping • Lindbergh, Charles • Murder

The Saga of the Bloody Benders: The Infamous Homicidal Family of Labette County, Kansas. A Treasury of Victorian Murder. New York: NBM, 2007. Unpaged. ISBN 9781561634999. **H** **A/YA**

> This volume in Rick Geary's series introduces readers to the two John Benders, Senior and Junior, who set up house in 1870 in preparation for the women of the family to join them in 1871, then throughout 1872, either made use of or capitalized on the medical skills of Katie Bender to solicit or entice victims for their murderous passions. The Benders escaped when it looked like the townsfolk were becoming overly suspicious, and a chapter at the end ponders what might have happened to them.
>
> **Keywords:** Benders • Graphic nonfiction • Murder • Murderers • Unsolved crimes

Haugen, Brenda.

🎗 *The Zodiac Killer: Terror and Mystery.* True Crime. Mankato, MN: Compass Point Books/Capstone Press, 2011. 96p. ISBN 9780756543570. **J**

> There is something inherently frightening about a serial killer. The case of the Zodiac Killer, who is known to have killed at least five people in the late 1960s and whose identity still remains unknown, is presented here, along with the letters that he sent to the newspapers taunting the police and the public and the stories of the victims and the survivors of his attacks. This title was chosen as a top ten Quick Pick. **QP**
>
> **Keywords:** Crimes • Serial killers • Zodiac Killer

Hoshowsky, Robert J.

Unsolved: True Canadian Cold Cases. Toronto: Dundurn, 2010. 218p. ISBN 9781554887392. **H** **A/YA**

> The loss of a loved one is never easy; families who must deal with losing a family member to murder or having a missing person, when the crimes remain unsolved, find that they are unable to find any relief from their pain. There can be no moving on when there is no understanding why someone was killed or the police have not identified the perpetrator. Robert Hoshowsky presents twelve of Canada's cold cases in their entirety, such as the well-known and truly horrifying 1983 murder of nine-year-old Sharin' Morningstar Keenan as well as the murders of tourists Domenic and Nancy Ianiero in the Mayan Riviera in 2006. Sharin'

Keenan's murder led to an international manhunt that has been going ever since. All of the stories provide fascinating information about how police work, as well as how the authorities in Canada, notably the Ontario Provincial Police, update their information about cold cases and continue to work to solve these crimes.

Keywords: Cold cases • Crimes • Unsolved crimes

Jacobs, Thomas A.

Teen Cyberbullying Investigated: Where Do Your Rights End and Consequences Begin? Minneapolis, MN: Free Spirit Press, 2010. 195p. ISBN 9781575423395. **J** **H**

This recounting and evaluation by a former judge of court cases involving teenagers serves as a valuable and timely reminder of the potential consequences of posting personal information on the Internet. Each chapter offers a number of related cases that demonstrate that not every country, state, or indeed court operates under the same rules or will render the same verdict. Chapters also provide a list of further resources and ask readers to reflect on what their decision would be in cases that range from posting comments, to creating Web sites with graphic or profane content, to cases of cyberbullying and harassment.

Keywords: Computer crimes • Cyberbullying • Cyberharassment • Law

Macleod, Elizabeth.

🎗 *Royal Murder: Deadly Intrigue of Ten Sovereigns.* Toronto: Annick Press, 2008. 128p. ISBN 9781554511280. **M** **J**

The life of a royal is not automatically one of power and luxury; occasionally the position and authority associated with royalty have brought with them danger, plots, and outright assassination. Such is the case in these stories, which range from the many deaths in the twisted tale of the Ptolemies, Cleopatra's family, to the grisly story of Vlad Tepes, to the complicated relationship between Elizabeth I and Mary, Queen of Scots, to the more modern tale of the Romanovs, including both their assassination and the outrageous, almost unbelievable account of Rasputin's murder. The many sidebars provide some fascinating information and are highlighted by a large number of photographs. The information may be browsed or read sequentially. **Norma Fleck, Red Maple**

Keywords: Assassination • Attempted murders • Cleopatra • Elizabeth I • Kings and rulers • Mary I • Mary Queen of Scots • Rasputin • Richard III • Romanovs • Vlad Tepes

Schroeder, Andreas.

Duped! True Stories of the World's Greatest Intrigues. Illustrated by Rémy Simard. It Actually Happened. Toronto: Annick Press, 2011. 157p. ISBN 9781554513505. **M** **J**

Long before the Nigerian letter scam started appearing on the Internet, offering people a percentage of a potential fortune for their help and then stringing them along for one administrative fee after another without any recompense, people have been fooled by both outrageous acts and devious swindles. This book provides fact-based accounts of eight of the most unbelievable cons in history, most of which had ramifications that spanned a country, if not the globe. The cases, which may be browsed or read straight through and will appeal to readers of either crime fiction or historical fiction, range from Orson Welles's 1938 broadcast of *The War of the* Worlds, which caused mass hysteria across the country, to Operation Bernhard, an incredible German counterfeiting operation that remains unique in the history of counterfeiting. Each story includes a background, an explanation of the events as well as a summary of the aftermath, and cartoon-style illustrations and sidebars with pertinent information. Readers interested in these cases will find suggestions for further reading.

Keywords: Fraud • Hoaxes • Scams • Swindles

Swanson, James L.

Chasing Lincoln's Killer. New York: Scholastic Press, 2009. 194p. ISBN 9780439903547. **J H**

James Swanson's enthusiasm for his subject shines through in this gripping account of Lincoln's assassination and the twelve-day search for his killer that followed. The incredible amount of detail and liberal use of quotations helps to give readers a sense of immediacy, whether at the original murder scene at Ford's Theatre or when Booth's accomplices were trying to kill the secretary of state. **BBYA, AENYA Honor**

Keywords: Assassination • Booth, John Wilkes • Lincoln, Abraham • True crime

Crime Science

Demonstrating what forensic sciences contribute to criminal investigations has remained a very popular topic in the past few years. Many of the following titles are aimed specifically at reluctant readers.

Ballard, Carol.

At the Crime Scene! Collecting Clues and Evidence. Solve That Crime. Berkeley Heights, NJ: Enslow Publishers, 2009. 48p. ISBN 9780766033733. **M J**

Fans of procedural crime shows such as *CSI* know that when a criminal act is committed, the perpetrator often leaves evidence behind. This may come in many forms, from foot- or fingerprints to physical evidence such as blood, fibres from clothing or other fabrics, and hair. Carol Ballard explains how forensic officers and investigators search for, process, and use this critical proof to help solve crimes, and she includes a supplement discussing what it would be like to have a career in forensics, as well as further resources on the subject.

Keywords: Crime sciences • Forensic sciences

Crime under the Microscope! In the Forensics Lab. <u>Solve That Crime</u>. Berkeley Heights, NJ: Enslow Publishers, 2009. 48p. ISBN 9780766033740. **M**

> Forensic laboratories must be able to run many different types of tests. Carol Ballard explains the science behind the techniques used to examine various kinds of evidence, including fingerprints, fibres, chemical evidence, DNA, pathology, and ballistics. Sidebars include case studies of true crimes solved by the use of forensic evidence.
>
> **Keywords:** Crime sciences • DNA • Fingerprint evidence • Forensic sciences

Biegert, Melissa Langley.

Crime Solvers. **RR**

> The four volumes in the <u>Crime Solvers</u> series look at different aspects of criminal investigation and their importance in the legal process. Officers are shown investigating crime scenes and gathering evidence; scientists are shown processing the evidence in labs. All four volumes are highly illustrated and include a list of further resources and a link to facthound. com, where readers will find related, recommended Web sites.

> *Determining the Cause of Death*. Mankato, MN: Capstone Press, 2010. 32p. ISBN 9781429633758. **M**
>
> > Though there may be several reasons for a sudden death, it is the job of police officers to investigate the cause and manner of death to determine whether it was natural. Investigators will process the scene of the crime, evidence will be taken to the lab, and the body will be delivered to the medical examiner. The ME works to determine the official cause and manner of death through an autopsy.
> >
> > **Keywords:** Autopsy • Criminal investigation • Forensic pathology • Forensics

> *Finding the Murder Weapon*. Mankato, MN: Capstone Press, 2010. 32p. ISBN 9781429633741. **M**
>
> > To determine the guilt or innocence of a murder suspect, it is necessary for investigators to find the murder weapon. This short volume looks at investigative techniques used to discover how a victim was killed and what kind of weapon was used to commit the crime, which can in turn help find the murderer and be used to convict criminals in court.
> >
> > **Keywords:** Criminal investigation • Evidence • Murder • Weapons

> *Gathering Blood Evidence*. Mankato, MN: Capstone Press, 2010. 32p. ISBN 9781429633734. **M**
>
> > When detectives find blood evidence, they know that it can help them figure out who committed a crime and how that crime was carried out. Not only can blood evidence explain where victims were when they were attacked, but it also is difficult to remove and can be gathered with special chemicals years after a crime occurred.
> >
> > **Keywords:** Blood evidence • Criminal investigation • Forensics

1
2
3
4
5
6
7
8
9
10
11

Looking for Fingerprints. Mankato, MN: Capstone Press, 2010. 32p. ISBN 9781429633727. **M**

This volume of the <u>Crime Solvers</u> series looks at the methods used by experts to recover the fingerprints that criminals leave behind at the scene of a crime. Readers are shown the three different kinds of fingerprints and the different patterns that help make every fingerprint unique.

Keywords: Criminal investigation • Evidence • Fingerprints • Forensics

Martin, Russell, and Lydia Nibley.

The Mysteries of Beethoven's Hair. Watertown, MA: Charlesbridge. 2009. 120p. ISBN 9781570917141. **M** **J**

At the time of Beethoven's death in 1827, it was common for survivors to keep a memento of the dead. This explains not only the plaster mask made of Beethoven but also the permission given to his student, Frederick Hiller, to cut a lock of Beethoven's hair. Where the mysteries in the book come in are the amazing strands of the stories of how the lock of hair managed to stay intact as it passed through generation after generation of a family that escaped from Germany during World War II and what the hair revealed during forensic testing over 175 years later. Would it be determined to be Beethoven's? And if so, would it be able to tell shed any light on his cause of death?

Keywords: Beethoven, Ludwig van • Forensic sciences • Relics

Intrigue and Espionage

These books offer a fascinating look at the business of spying to provide readers with an understanding of how espionage works and give them an inside look at how history has been affected by spies. It is also not surprising that in the age of Wikileaks there is a book on failures in the world of espionage.

Allen, Thomas B.

Declassified: 50 Top Secret Documents That Changed History. Washington, DC: National Geographic Society, 2008. 320p. ISBN 97814262022223. **H** **A/YA**

Readers are presented with fifty secret documents and the evidence of the effects they had. The cases vary widely, from the 1780 letter in which Benedict Arnold offered to surrender West Point to the British to the 1980 warning delivered to President Carter by the Soviet Union that it was about to impose martial law on Poland. In all cases, these documents provide a window into the covert and hidden intrigues behind politics and make history a fascinating subject.

Keywords: Covert operations • Espionage

Bowers, Rick.

🏅 *Spies of Mississippi: The True Story of the Spy Network That Tried to Destroy the Civil Rights Movement.* Washington, DC: National Geographic, 2010. 120p. ISBN 9781426305955. **M** **J**

Bowers provides readers with an introduction to the Mississippi State Sovereignty Commission, created in 1956 and used through much of the 1960s as a clandestine investigative tool of the state government to preserve segregation and derail the National Association for the Advancement of Colored People. Historical events of note during the period include the forcible integration of 'Ole Miss and the Freedom Rides. **AENYA**

Keywords: Civil rights • Mississippi State Sovereignty Commission • Segregation

Earnest, Peter, and Suzanne Harper, in association with the International Spy Museum.

The Real Spy's Guide to Becoming a Spy. New York: Abrams Books for Young Readers, 2009. 144p. ISBN 9780810983298. **M** **J**

It is an old adage that one should write about what one knows, but in this case it is very true: as a former CIA operations officer and the founder of the International Spy Museum, Peter Earnest is the perfect person to introduce readers to the concept of spies.

This guide is divided into seven very readable chapters that cover the history of spying, what spies do, how one becomes a spy, as well as information about the training a spy will undergo, with some suggested activities and a mention of the need for spying in the future. An abundance of additional information, including a glossary entitled "Spy Speak," quizzes, and spy stories are sprinkled liberally throughout the text. Appendices include suggestions for additional reading, Web sites, and information about organizations in the spying community.

Keywords: Espionage • Spies • Spying

Gilbert, Adrian.

Codes and Ciphers. Spy Files. Buffalo, NY; Richmond Hill, ON: Firefly Books, 2008. 32p. ISBN 9781554075737. **M**

This volume in the Spy Files series introduces readers to the various methods used by spies to encrypt information. Gilbert also includes information about famous spies such as Lord Robert Baden Powell, whose guise as a butterfly collector allowed him to collect information about enemy forts and hide them in his drawings, and a number of different methods for creating and breaking codes. Readers will enjoy Gilbert's suggestions for making up their own codes and ciphers.

Keywords: Ciphers • Codes • Espionage

Secret Agent. <u>Spy Files</u>. Buffalo, NY; Richmond Hill, ON: Firefly Books, 2008. 32p. ISBN 9781554075744. **M**

> This history of espionage points out that leaders as far back as Chinese emperors and the Egyptian pharaohs had spies, which have become a common, useful, and necessary tool for governments. Readers are given explanations and examples of a number of different sorts of spies: spies in wartime, female spies, U.S. secret services, Soviet secret services, and British secret services. The author then delves into spy writers before dealing with what happens when spies are caught by governments, in spy catching, and traded back to their countries, in spy swaps.
>
> **Keywords:** Espionage • Spies • Spying

Spy School. <u>Spy Files</u>. Buffalo, NY; Richmond Hill, ON: Firefly Books, 2008. 32p. ISBN 9781554075751. **M**

> This slim volume lets readers in on some interesting information about what it takes to be a spy, including language and height requirements, as well as the day-to-day activities that spies undertake. The author illustrates these with examples of famous spies, double agents, and notorious uses of spying in history that demonstrate the importance of espionage.
>
> **Keywords:** Spies • Spying

Top Technology. <u>Spy Files</u>. Buffalo, NY; Richmond Hill, ON: Firefly Books, 2008. 32p. ISBN 9781554075768. **M**

> This introduction to the many weapons in a spy's arsenal goes beyond the tools a spy can use to listen in on, watch, hide from, and variously spy on others, from individuals to nations. It also includes descriptions of the various forms of counterintelligence used to avoid those methods, from invisible powder and lie detectors to breaking and entering and assassination.
>
> **Keywords:** Counterintelligence • Spies • Spying • Technology

Holdcroft, Tina.

Spy, Spy Again: True Tales of Failed Espionage. Toronto: Annick Press, 2011. 110p. ISBN 9781554512232. **M** **J** **RR**

> Tales of failed attempts at spying are divided into five categories: bad luck, wherein things could not always be controlled or helped; miscommunication of information; overconfidence; sheer incompetence; and betrayal. Each category contains four stories, with some basic historical background preceding a colorful and appealing graphical presentation of the story itself. Vocabulary is integrated into the text and used to illustrate not only why espionage is not a glamorous profession but also how it has been used politically since 323 BC, commenting on the repercussions of failed missions. The list of sources includes Web sites.
>
> **Keywords:** Espionage • Spies • Traitors

Melton, H. Keith.

Ultimate Spy: Inside the Secret World of Espionage. New York: DK Publishing, 2009. 224p. ISBN 9780756655761. **H**

This thorough and complete introduction to the world of espionage is broken roughly into thirds that deal with famous spying operations; equipment and techniques; and how to be a spy, a section that looks at training, recruitment, spy networks, and spying in the future. Forewords from a former director of the CIA and a former head of the HVA, the East German Foreign Intelligence Service, illustrate the amount of material about espionage available to the public that would have been unheard of during the Cold War.

Keywords: Espionage • Spies • Spying

Consider Starting with . . .

Alphin, Elaine Marie. *An Unspeakable Crime: The Prosecution and Persecution of Leo Frank.*

Earnest, Peter, and Suzanne Harper, in association with the International Spy Museum. *The Real Spy's Guide to Becoming a Spy.*

Geary, Rick. *Famous Players: The Mysterious Death of William Desmond Taylor.*

Jacobs, Thomas A. *Teen Cyberbullying Investigated: Where Do Your Rights End and Consequences Begin?*

Melton, H. Keith. *Ultimate Spy: Inside the Secret World of Espionage.*

Swanson, James L. *Chasing Lincoln's Killer.*

Fiction Read-Alikes

- **Carter, Ally. <u>Heist Society</u>.** The girls attending the Gallagher Academy for Exceptional Young Women certainly receive an unusual education. To the outside world, they are ordinary schoolgirls; only they know that they are spies in training, whose schooling includes chemical warfare, code breaking, and martial arts. Cammie Morgan and the other girls' exploits are introduced in *I'd Tell You I Love You, But Then I'd Have to Kill You* and continue in *Cross My Heart and Hope to Spy, Don't Judge a Girl by Her Cover, Only the Good Spy Young,* and *Uncommon Criminals.*

- **Hooper, Mary. *Newes from the Dead*.** This historical novel is based on the true story of Anne Green, a seventeenth-century serving girl who became pregnant with the child of her employer's grandson, something simply not done in Victorian England. When the baby was stillborn, Anne was convicted of murder and sentenced to hang. After the sentence was carried out her body was taken for study by New College and the reader is brought to the start of the story, which is told from the dual points of view of Anne, which fills in her history, and the doctors, particularly Robert Mathews, the medical student who first notices that the hanging did not kill her.

- **McClintock, Norah.** *Dooley Takes the Fall.* The first book in a projected trilogy finds a boy named Mark Everson taking the initial fall, plummeting over a bridge to his death in a ravine. Dooley (as Ryan Dooley prefers to be called) is the first person on the scene and the only witness to Mark's death. He knows instantly that with his history this experience is going to bring him grief. He's right: the police are suspicious of his convenient appearance, and it would be so easy if he were involved. At the same time, Dooley's interest in Mark's sister, Beth, who's unaware that her brother was a jerk, leads Dooley to start investigating to please her as well as to protect himself from false police charges, leading him deeper and deeper into a complicated web of deception, corruption, and betrayal.

- **McNamee, Graham.** *Acceleration.* In this BBYA and QP title, Duncan is spending the summer in the Toronto Transit Commission's Lost and Found department, working off a punishment for breaking into a show home, when he comes across a diary that appears to have been written by a serial killer. Initially Duncan is not sure what to do with the diary, because he does not think the police will take seriously a complaint from a guy who was caught stealing a toilet.

- **Metter, Christian.** *Shutter Island.* When U.S. Marshal Teddy Daniels travels to Shutter Island with his partner Chuck Aule, he knows that he is being sent to find a mass murderer who has escaped from Ashecliffe Hospital, the island's hospital for the criminally insane. What the men find, in this graphic version of Dennis Lehane's novel, is an obscure puzzle that seemingly leads nowhere. The two men, stranded on the island due to an approaching hurricane and determined to solve the mystery of the missing woman and with baggage of their own, follow a dangerous path that threatens not only their lives but also their sanity.

- **Sala, Richard.** *Cat Burglar Black?* When K finds herself in the Bellsong Academy, she is told it is because an aunt has taken an interest in her care. Raised in an orphanage that had actually been a headquarters for a gang of thieves, K finds out that she has gone from the frying pan into the fire when the head of the academy tells her that the students there are actually working for a secret organization called The Obtainers, and she will fit right in with them. Will K leave her past behind, or will she pull off the art heists?

Part 2

Life Stories

Chapter 3

Memoirs and Autobiographies

Definition

Memoirs and autobiographies, which have both remained popular genres in the last few years, differ significantly from each other. In a recent article for *Library Journal*, Rosalind Reisner posited that an autobiography is a "reflective, often detailed account of a person's life," whereas a memoir covers a "memorable or meaningful portion of the author's life, often in the context of the times" (2010, 41). This helps to distinguish the two.

Memoirs generally rely on an author's memory of an event and frequently do not have the supplementary material and secondary sources that one finds in an autobiography. At the same time, a reader is given a greater impression of the author's own emotions and viewpoint.

Appeal

As with biographies, the books in this category allow readers to learn from other people's experiences and explore other lives. Memoirs are usually presented in the first person point of view and range from tragic to hilarious. They allow readers to experience events that are completely foreign to them and range far from the obvious celebrity or noteworthy subject, providing topics and subjects to which readers can relate on a personal level.

Chapter Organization

Memoirs come in a wide variety. In the section "Coming-of-Age" the authors deal with difficult and emotional times that helped them become who they are today, whether dealing with a medical trauma and a horrible home life or waiting to leave a homeland ruled by a dictator. This is followed by the section "Overcoming Adversity," in which the stories deal with adversity and triumph, such as Mariatu

Kamara's experiences during and after Sierra Leone's civil war. The section "Working Life Memoirs" includes authors' tales about their experiences in the workforce at home and abroad and offers insight into such novel professions as cartoonists, tattoo artists, and ice road truckers. The final section, "Humorous Memoirs," offers some books to be enjoyed, with possibilities for reading aloud. A Quick Pick title that arose from a challenge to compose a memoir in six words may challenge readers to write their own such memoirs.

Coming-of-Age

The books in this category deal with the authors' childhoods and early lives and the events that occurred during those times that helped them become the people they are today. There haven't been a great many titles published in this subgenre in the past few years, but there has been one standout title in the genre, David Small's graphic memoir *Stitches*, which illustrates his miserable teenaged years, his relationship with a psychiatrist, and his discovery of art. The book won both critical and popular acclaim.

Calcines, Eduardo F.

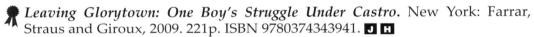 *Leaving Glorytown: One Boy's Struggle Under Castro*. New York: Farrar, Straus and Giroux, 2009. 221p. ISBN 9780374343941. **J H**

Eduardo Calcines's life in Cuba under the rule of dictator Fidel Castro in the 1950s and 1960s was vastly different from anything experienced by a teenager today. Applying for exit visas in 1959 brought his family to the attention of the government: all of them faced hardships, from being cut off from family to Eduardo's father's arrest and the knowledge that Eduardo would have to report to the army if their papers did not come through in time. This book shows themes of family and love of country and provides readers with insight into a subject seldom dealt with for teens.

Keywords: Calcines, Eduardo • Cuba • Memoir

Small, David.

Stitches: A Memoir. New York: W.W. Norton & Company, 2009. 329p. ISBN 9780393068573. **H A/YA GN**

Caldecott Award–winning illustrator David Small's memoir packs a real punch. David was a chronically ill child, treated with X-rays for a sinus condition by his father, a radiologist. When he was ten he developed a cyst on his throat that he was told eventually would need minor surgery to correct. As it turns out, he was the only person who didn't know that the massive doses of radiation used to treat him as a child had given him cancer, and he wasn't expected to survive his surgery. He awoke from the "minor surgeries" he underwent when he was fourteen with one vocal cord and no ability to speak. A psychiatrist who helped him find his voice in an unbelievably dysfunctional family is portrayed here as the white rabbit in Small's wonderland. The book then takes readers on an incredible journey as David discovers his art and begins to truly recover his voice. **Alex, BBYA**

Keywords: Cancer • Graphic nonfiction • Memoir • Radiation • Small, David

Smithson, Ryan.

🎖 *Ghosts of War: The True Story of a 19-Year-Old GI.* New York: Harper Collins, 2009. 321p. ISBN 9780061664700. **H**

Ryan Smithson first thought about entering the military as a high school student after witnessing the events of 9/11. He entered the Army Reserves at the age of seventeen and was deployed to Iraq two years later. Smithson thoughtfully and completely recounts his time in boot camp, learning to become an equipment operator, and overseas as an army engineer; he participated in missions that later caused his night terrors. Upon his return to the United States he went back to school and therapy for PTSD, which led to his writing. Readers learn about the good and bad of war in this unique portrayal of one young soldier's experiences overseas.

Keywords: Iraq • Military and wars • Smithson, Ryan

Overcoming Adversity

These books, with their subject matter of remembered pain, turbulent pasts, and overcoming difficulties, are popular with teenagers. Several address subjects that are graphic, including depictions of disease, death, depression, war, and various forms of abuse, which makes them more appropriate for older readers. Nevertheless, the consistent appearance of these titles on readers' choice lists is a testament to how their readers are moved and inspired by them.

Readers who enjoy fiction about these subjects may well also enjoy reading about real people overcoming the various things described in these titles.

Kamara, Mariatu, with Susan McClelland.

🎖 *The Bite of the Mango.* Toronto: Annick Press, 2008. 216p. ISBN 9781554511594. **H** **A/YA**

Mariatu Kamara's experiences as a twelve-year-old child during Sierra Leone's civil war were beyond brutal: she was raped, her town was attacked by rebels, and as a reminder to everyone who would see her, the attackers cut off her hand. She was able to escape to a hospital in a nearby town. In the years after the attack, her time was spent first begging, then subsisting in refugee camps, and eventually as an immigrant in Toronto, where she now lives. Her tale progresses from a painful to a triumphant story, as it becomes one of hope and forgiveness. **Norma Fleck, Red Maple**

Keywords: Amputees • Child soldiers • Kamara, Mariatu • Sierra Leone • War • War victims

Now Try: Readers interested in the conflict in Sierra Leone may be drawn to a BBYA and Alex award-winning title that shows them the conflict from a male perspective, Ishmael Beah's *A Long Way Gone: Memoirs of a Boy Soldier*. Beah chronicles his life from the time he was turned into a solder at the age of thirteen through several difficult years of war until his flight to the United States.

Kor, Eva Mozes, with Lisa Rojany Buccieri.

Surviving the Angel of Death: The Story of a Mengele Twin in Auschwitz. Terre Haute, IN: Tanglewood Press, 2009. 141p. ISBN 978193318286. **H**

This is a young adult version of Eva Mozes Kor's account of the atrocities to which she and her sister were subjected as "Mengele's twins" in Auschwitz. Eva's determination to survive is matched only by her astounding capacity to make sure that young people remember what happened and learn from it; her decisions to not only start a museum but also to return to Auschwitz and to forgive Mengele provide some very valuable lessons.

Keywords: Holocaust (1939–1945) • Jewish children in the Holocaust • Kor, Eva Mozes

Renn, Crystal, with Marjorie Ingall.

🏵 *Hungry*. New York: Simon & Schuster, 2009. 231p. ISBN 9781439101230. **H** **A/YA**

Crystal Renn was fifteen when a modeling scout told her that she could make a living as a fashion model. All she needed to do was lose some weight. She was only sixteen when she signed a contract and moved to Manhattan, starting an odyssey on which she lost seventy pounds and reached size 0. Crystal shares with readers her struggles to become a successful fashion model while also managing her anorexia before she had the epiphany that saved her life, reshaping her body and her career, making her one of the most successful plus-size models working today and, as proven by the included pictures, absolutely stunning. **QP**

Keywords: Modeling • Modeling industry • Models • Renn, Crystal

Now Try: Cheryl Diamond initially tried her luck at modeling in New York at the age of fourteen. Though she had the proper proportions and found an agency that liked her look, she wasn't quite tall enough and was stymied when the agency went out of business after 9/11. After growing a few inches, she tried again at the age of sixteen. After signing with an agency she found herself prepared to do whatever it would take to become a successful model, while remaining cynical in an industry ripe with corruption, eventually rising to walk in Fashion Week and modeling for Clairol. Diamond's *Model: A Memoir* is a story of triumph as well as a testament to the power of a teenager able to stand up for herself.

Telgemeier, Raina.

🏵 *Smile*. New York: Graphix, 2010. 214p. ISBN 9780545132053. **M** **J** **GN**

Raina Telgemeier's graphic memoir, presented in bold, visually appealing colors, starts with a traumatic but endurable event: her orthodontic appointment to be fitted with the braces that were to correct her overbite. While she is teased by her sister about her impending status as a "metal-mouth," her friends comfort her. She never expects the accident in which her two front teeth are knocked out, setting her on a traumatic orthodontic odyssey involving a root canal, braces, headgear, and successive retainers with fake front teeth while her own teeth are moved into the gap. At the same time she is undergoing the same journey as other girls her age, juggling thoughts of friends and boys while trying to deal with what they must think of her strange appearance. This title was an honor book for the Boston-Globe Horn Book Award and chosen as a Top Ten title in the 2011 Great Graphic Novels for Teens List.

Keywords: Adolescence • Braces • Dentists • Graphic nonfiction • Orthodontists

Welch, Diana, Liz Welch, Amanda Welch, and Dan Welch.

The Kids Are All Right: A Memoir. New York: Harmony Books, 2009. 334p. ISBN 9780307396044. **H** **A/YA**

The four Welch siblings faced a number of traumas in 1983, including their father's death and their actress mother's initial cancer diagnosis. This was followed within a few years by crumbling family finances and their mother's death. While the eldest, Amanda, was old enough to attend college and be handed the bills from her parents' estates, she was not named the guardian of her youngest sister, Diana. This memoir presents readers with the four Welch siblings' turbulent versions of their lives after their parents' deaths. The alternating points of view both illustrate that the same event can be seen in a different light when being remembered by more than one person and let readers know that the Welch kids were, in the end, all right. **Alex**

Keywords: Adolescence • Memoir • Orphans

Working Life Memoirs

These authors use their work to offer a view into new worlds. Readers may gain insight on professions, cultures, and places. This genre offers readers the possibility to cross not only borders, but also formats, as demonstrated in the graphic novel remembrances of Guy Delisle's time in Burma.

Delisle, Guy.

Burma Chronicles. Montreal: Drawn & Quarterly, 2008. 208p. ISBN 9781897299500. **H**

Guy Delisle's third graphic memoir reflects on the fourteen months his family spent in the dictatorship of Burma, recognized as Myanmar by the United Nations although not by the United States, Canada, the United Kingdom, or Australia, among other countries. This volume introduces readers to the country, its politics, and its denizens from a different perspective, as Guy and his baby accompanied his wife to Burma for her Doctors Without Borders posting.

Keywords: Burma • Cartoonists • Delisle, Guy • Doctors Without Borders • Graphic nonfiction • Myanmar

Johnson Jeff.

Tattoo Machine: Tall Tales, True Stories, and My Life in Ink. New York: Spiegel & Grau, 2009. 249p. ISBN 9780385530521. **H** **A/YA**

True tales from a veteran tattoo artist provide an illuminating look at the tattooing life. Readers will find stories that impart customer service tips and warnings culled from Johnson's experience with his shop, explanations of the different kinds of art, a glossary of the accompanying jargon, and many stories about the incredibly wide variety of people who want tattoos and the artists who provide them.

Keywords: Tattoo artists • Tattooing • Tattoos

Rowland, Hugh, with Michael Lent.

On Thin Ice: Breakdowns, Whiteouts, and Surviving on the World's Deadliest Roads. New York: Hyperion, 2010. 235p. ISBN 9781401323684. **H** **A/YA**

Hugh Rowland, the best-known "character" from the reality television show *Ice Road Truckers*, gives readers a closer look at what makes him tick, as well as the very real dangers that go along with his profession and what has kept him at it for thirty years. He comes across as an able, knowledgeable, and likeable person, whether describing his wife and colleagues or the many difficult situations they have endured while driving the ice roads of Yellowknife.

Keywords: Ice driving • Ice roads • Rowland, Hugh

Humorous Memoirs

Memoirs are occasionally simple stories to be enjoyed. Some authors are able to reminisce in such a way that their stories make one smile while reading, whether or not lessons are imparted. This is never difficult for Jon Scieszka, and was initially a challenge imparted to the writers contributing to *Not Quite What I Was Planning*, who were asked to write their own memoirs in six words.

Bryson, Bill.

The Life and Times of the Thunderbolt Kid: A Memoir. New York: Broadway Books, 2006. 270p. ISBN 9780767919364. **H** **A/YA**

Bryson introduces readers to a more leisurely time for growing up, Des Moines in the 1950s. This will be a completely unfamiliar world, in which although everything from candy to toys left much to be desired, "pretty much everything was good for you," in an age when doctors advertised cigarettes. Bryson reflects on his upbringing, remembering with pride the accomplishments of a father who was "the best baseball writer of his generation." This introduction to Bryson's teenaged years and the changes that both he and Iowa underwent is amusing and bittersweet.

Keywords: Bryson, Bill • Des Moines • Humor

Hershleiser, Rachel, and Larry Smith, eds.

Not Quite What I Was Planning: Six Word Memoirs by Writers Famous and Obscure. New York: HarperPerennial, 2008. 225p. ISBN 9780061374050. **J** **H** **RR**

While it was Shakespeare who first wrote about men of few words, and Hemingway who wrote the six-word short story, it took *Smith Magazine* to challenge memoirists to sum up their lives in six words. The lives portrayed run the gamut from instantly recognizable and assured, such as Mario Batali's "Brought it to a boil, often" and Stephen Colbert's "Well, I thought it was funny," to the tragic or sad. The index of subjects, which vary from cancer to food to siblings, makes this a great book for browsing or reading straight through and may inspire readers to come up with their own versions. **QP**

Keywords: Humor • Memoirs • Writing

Now Try: Readers who like the concept of a six-word short story or epitaph will enjoy the other books in the series. The editors created a volume of six-word memoirs just by teenagers entitled *I Can't Keep My Own Secrets: Six Word Memoirs by Teens Famous and Obscure* that serves as a great introduction to the series for middle and junior high school students. The teens in the book concentrate on the matters that affect them, making this book both pertinent and interesting to them and an apt choice for the Quick Picks for Reluctant Readers list.

Scieszka, Jon.

Knucklehead: Tall Tales and Mostly True Stories of Growing Up Scieszka. New York: Viking Children's Books, c2008. 106p. ISBN 9780670011063. **M** **J** **RR**

Jon Scieszka's memoir may be the funniest book of its year. It will appeal to reluctant readers and boys in equal measure. Readers will learn many things about Mr. Scieszka, including how to say his name correctly, that he is one of six brothers, that being one of the older brothers in a large family has many advantages, and that you never want to be one of six in the back of a car when the cat gets sick. The chapters are short and humorous, advocate reading, and will be a good step up for Gary Paulsen's *How Angel Peterson Got His Name: And Other Tales about Extreme Sports.* **ALA**

Keywords: Authors • Humorist • Scieszka, Jon

Consider Starting with . . .

Delisle, Guy. *Burma Chronicles.*

Kamara, Mariatu, with Susan McClelland. *The Bite of the Mango.*

Renn, Crystal, with Marjorie Ingall. *Hungry.*

Scieszka, Jon. *Knucklehead: Tall Tales and Mostly True Stories of Growing Up Scieszka.*

Small, David. *Stitches: A Memoir.*

Telgemeier, Raina. *Smile.*

Fiction Read-Alikes

- **Boyce, Frank Cottrell.** *The Unforgotten Coat.* Julie comes across a Polaroid picture and reflects on a friendship that transformed her view of her town, other people, and cultures. Two new boys, Chingis and Nurgui, in her sixth-grade class are certainly unusual: for one thing, they arrived in the summer term wearing identical heavy coats with fur linings; for another, only Chingis was to be in Julie's class. The boys tell Julie that they are from Mongolia and that she will be their "Good Guide." Julie finds out that the boys have their own fears, and in helping them to hide from the "Vanisher" learns about the beauty of Mongolia and Bootle, as well as gaining new friends.

- **Conkling, Winifred.** *Sylvia & Aki.* A dual point of view is used to tell the stories of Sylvia and Aki in this moving historical novel. Sylvia Mendez moves into Aki Munemitsu's room in 1941. Aki's family has been sent to an internment camp, although she and her siblings are American; Sylvia ends up at the center of a lawsuit when she is told that she and her siblings must go to the "Mexican" school. This novelization of their stories, and the case that set the stage for *Brown v. Board of Education,* is still relevant today.

- **Cross, Gillian.** *Where I Belong.* Khadija is sent thousands of miles from her own family in Somalia to keep her safe. When Sandy Dennis, a world-famous designer who is working on a Somali-inspired collection, offers her a veritable fortune to model the upcoming collection, Khadija can't bring herself to refuse, especially when Sandy tells her to keep her identity a secret and labels her Qarsoon, the hidden one. So where can she go for help in London when someone discovers her connection to Sandy and kidnaps her brother in Somalia? Gillian Cross treats readers to fashion, adventure, and mystery.

- **Gantos, Jack.** *Dead End in Norvelt.* Jack Gantos presents a fictionalized account of his twelfth summer in Norvelt, Pennsylvania. A young Jack tries to avoid anything shocking, scary, or troublesome while grounded, as they exacerbate his "nose problem" and cause his nose to start spurting blood. His only respite is his work acting as the hands for his neighbor, the frightening-amusing Miss Volker, who takes her duties to the town's namesake, Eleanor Roosevelt, very seriously. This funny novel develops several subplots, including suspicious deaths and a failed hunting trip, which will delight readers of history and humor. Gantos was honored with both the Newbery medal and the Scott O'Dell Historical Fiction award.

- **Jimenez, Francisco.** *Reaching Out.* In his third autobiographical novel, Francisco Jimenez describes his college years at Santa Clara University. The book starts with him arriving at school for his freshman year in 1962, afraid to let people know that he was born in Mexico and is in the country illegally. Readers follow him through his years at Santa Clara, as he both grows into a student capable of earning a national fellowship and demonstrates a strong moral and social conscience, consistently sending money to his family, mourning President Kennedy, and making arrangements to miss school in order to support Cesar Chavez's strike. This title was chosen as an ALA Notable Book.

- **Little, Jean.** *Exiles from The War: The War Guests Diary of Charlotte Mary Twiss.* Charlotte chronicles her twelfth year in a 1940 journal, during which time her family hosts war guests and siblings Sam and Jane. Charlotte needs the diary to keep her busy, as her thoughts tend to stray to her brother, who is off fighting. Jean Little's entry in the <u>Dear Canada</u> series was an honor book for the Geoffrey Bilson Award for Historical Fiction for Young People in 2011.

- **Myers, Walter Dean.** *Sunrise over Fallujah.* Robin Perry's choice to join the army during his senior year in high school was a reaction to 9/11: he wanted to stand up for his country. He then found himself becoming part of the initial U.S. deployment in 2003 to the second Iraq war. His letters are used as a lens to present the war and his place in it, even as he tries to protect his family back home from the dangers that he faces every day.

- **Scieszka, Jon, ed.** *Guys Read: Funny Business.* While humor is often a matter of opinion, readers are guaranteed to find a story to tickle their funny bone among the ten stories in this anthology. The stories include tales of outright sibling rivalry, life-changing correspondence between a student and teacher, and the event that gave Eoin Colfer the idea for Artemis Fowl.

- **Selvadurai, Shyam.** *Swimming in the Monsoon Sea.* This book features a lovely Sri Lankan setting, family secrets, and Naresh, a Canadian relative who finds that he can't fit into his own family's culture while complicating the life of the fourteen-year-old protagonist Amrith, who falls in love with him and must come to terms with his homosexuality. This title was chosen as the winner of the Canadian Library Association's Young Adult Book of the Year and as a Best Book for Young Adults.

Reference

Reisner, Rosalind. "Listen to My Life's Story." *Library Journal* (October 1, 2010): 41.

Chapter 4

Biography

Definition

A biography is a history of an individual's life. The term, which comes from the Greek *bios* (meaning life) and *graph* (meaning writing), had its first recorded English usage in Dryden's *Life of Plutarch* in 1663. Historians and biographers who compile information to write a biography make sure that the events recorded are factual, verifiable, and as complete as possible, using both primary and secondary sources. Unlike memoirs, biographies and autobiographies share someone's whole life, rather than focusing on part of it.

Appeal

People continue to be fascinated with other people. There is an inherent appeal in looking at how others live. Biographies provide the clearest window into another time, place, and perspective. Readers who do not enjoy any other type of nonfiction are often drawn to biographies because of an interest in the person or the subject. An interest in dance may lead someone to open *Alicia Alonso* or *Dynamic Women Dancers*; the inspiring nature of the subjects' actions, inherent bravery, and a window into different times could lead readers to *Claudette Colvin: Twice Toward Justice* or *Almost Astronauts: 13 Women Who Dared to Dream*.

Biographies also continue to provide a wide variety of reading experiences for readers. As Marc Aronson so compellingly remarked, "[E]very biography should have a freshness, a creativity, an interesting tension that makes it different from every other one" (2003, 69–72). Readers may be shown how people with whom they have a cursory familiarity actually faced and dealt with difficult decisions, as in Deborah Heiligman's stunning and award-winning *Charles and Emma*, which considered not only Charles Darwin's life, but also the scientist's relationship with his very religious wife. Biographies are readily available in diverse formats. Reluctant readers will be very happy with graphic nonfiction, photo biographies, and picture-book biographies.

Readers will also find biographies in alternative formats listed in the section "Sports Biographies" in chapter 7 and biographies written in verse in the poetry section of chapter 10.

The copious supplementary materials contained in biographies make them good resources for schoolwork as well as recreational reading. These may include source notes, Web sites, photographs, and other historical illustrations. Readers new to the genre are often surprised at the quality of the narrative.

Chapter Organization

The first section in this chapter, "American Presidents and Other Political Leaders," covers some of the most influential people in our history. These continue to be popular subjects; not only have books been published in recent years on America's newest president, there is also a new title devoted to George Washington. The following sections are grouped into the categories for which the subjects are best remembered. The first is "Outstanding in Their Fields: Professional Biographies," containing the life stories of people associated with science and their career. The next section, "Change-Makers and Activists," includes those remembered for a lifetime of trying to make a difference socially and politically. The books in "Historical Biography" provide unique pictures of individuals and the times in which they lived.

This section is followed by "Partner and Group Biographies," which includes stories told by or about more than one individual, such as the compelling and intertwined narrative of two men relayed in Judith St. George's *The Duel: The Parallel Lives of Alexander Hamilton & Aaron Burr*. There is no doubt that there is an innate fascination with famous people, as reflected in the next section, "The Creative Life: Entertainers," which is concerned with people in the public eye. The final section, "Biography Collections," covers titles that tell the stories of a number of people.

American Presidents and Other Political Leaders

Many readers are fascinated by the lives of the people who run their country. Teachers like students to know about decisions that shape our lives and our history. These interests make a good match with books that focus on national or world leaders. This subgenre provides not only the details of the time and someone's part in it, but also a sense of how people in power got there and how they affected the countries they led. These books also provide readers with a reliable source of information. Readers may also look under "Biography Collections" for titles about more than one person in this category and in the "Change-Makers and Social Activists" section for more political heavyweights.

Abramson, Jill.

Obama: The Historic Journey. New York: Callaway, 2009. 96p. ISBN 9781594488931. **M** **J**

> This young reader's edition starts with the November 4, 2008, election of the forty-fourth president of the United States in a chapter entitled "Winds of Change." An amply illustrated volume, it gives readers an introduction to Obama's background, including his family and his campaign for the presidency, while noting that he "did make mistakes." The book concludes with pictures and quotations from the inaugural ceremonies on January 9, 2009, including a double-page spread of the close to two million people who packed into the National Mall to celebrate.
>
> **Keywords:** Obama, Barack • Presidents

McClafferty, Carla Killough.

The Many Faces of George Washington. Minneapolis, MN: Carolrhoda Books, 2011. 120p. ISBN 9780761356080. **M** **J**

> Most people equate George Washington with the Athenaeum portrait, painted by Gilbert Stuart in 1796 and used on the dollar bill since 1869. Unfortunately, although there were hundreds of portraits painted of Washington, his contemporaries claimed that none of them presented a realistic picture of how he actually looked. In 2005 historians, scientists, and artisans at Mount Vernon combined a great deal of research with scientific and artistic processes to determine what George Washington really looked like at several stages of his life to create three fully realistic, life-sized representations of the first president. This book describes these processes, alternating with historical information about George Washington and what his life was like as a teenager, a general, and the president.
>
> **Keywords:** Presidents • Washington, George

Sandler, Martin.

Kennedy Through the Lens: How Photography and Television Revealed and Shaped an Extraordinary Leader. New York: Walker & Company, 2011. 96p. ISBN 9780802721600. **M** **J**

> John Fitzgerald Kennedy, the first American president born in the twentieth century, was a tremendous speaker, as well as the scion of a very photogenic family. The photo-essay here serves a dual purpose, allowing Martin Sandler to provide an overview of Kennedy's life up to his assassination and also showing how the president employed his oratorical skills to best advantage to use the media in a way that had not been done before. The darker aspects of Kennedy's story are not overlooked, and readers will find some wonderful photographs of the entire Kennedy family.
>
> **Keywords:** Kennedy, John Fitzgerald • Presidents

Shecter, Vicky Alvear.

Cleopatra Rules. Honesdale, PA: Boyds Mills Press, 2010. 128p. ISBN 9781590787182. **M** **J**

> This balanced portrayal of the last queen of Egypt shows her as more than the siren she is generally depicted as on stage and screen. Shecter uses a funny, readable, highly illustrated text to show that Cleopatra was actually an able, politically astute leader, as well as a writer and many other things. Readers are also given sidebars that provide information about Cleopatra's lifestyle, including Egyptian cosmetics, hairstyles, and the mythology surrounding her death.
>
> **Keywords:** Cleopatra • Egypt

Outstanding in Their Fields: Professional Biographies

This section includes biographies of people (other than presidents and social activists) who are thought of in conjunction with their chosen professions. Covered in either single or group biographies, the subjects of these books are leaders, exemplars, and innovators in their fields. The books usually offer information pertinent to the subjects' work that will give interested teens a glimpse of possibilities for their own futures.

Abrams, Dennis.

Rachael Ray: Food Entrepreneur. <u>Women of Achievement</u>. New York: Chelsea House Publishers, 2009. 128p. ISBN 9781604130782. **M** **J**

> Readers who aren't familiar with Ray or her contributions to American pop culture may be surprised, impressed, and intrigued by this very hardworking woman. Rachael Ray had no formal culinary training, and this fun, eminently readable biography follows her path as she worked her way up to become one of TV's most recognizable on-air personalities, an author of many best-selling cookbooks, and the driving force behind her own magazine. Abrams doesn't shy away from showing how unpredictable Ray's career has been; readers are shown both the comments of her detractors and how relatable she is. It is a very good thing that Ray can laugh at herself, and the many examples of her sayings and techniques offer readers a great role model.
>
> **Keywords:** Biography • Cooking • Food • Ray, Rachael

Aronson, Marc.

Bill Gates: A Twentieth-century Life. <u>Up Close</u>. New York: Viking, 2009. 192p. ISBN 9780670063482. **M** **J**

> Like other books in this series, this biography of the well-known software entrepreneur presents a balanced portrayal of its subject. Readers will see how Gates achieved his current position, enabling them to learn from his successes

and see how even his negative character traits have helped propel him to the top of the business world.

Keywords: Gates, Bill • Microsoft

Fleming, Candace.

🎗 *The Great and Only Barnum: The Tremendous, Stupendous Life of Showman P.T. Barnum.* Illustrated by Ray Fenwick. New York: Schwartz & Wade Books, 2009. 151p. ISBN 9780375945977. **M** **J** **H**

P. T. Barnum can legitimately be credited with creating the concept of celebrity as we know it today. In this circus ride of a book, laid out as though readers are being taken through Barnum's museum, in Candy Fleming's inimitable style with wonderful pictures, readers are introduced to the good and the bad of the ultimate showman, born dirt poor in 1810 but with the ideas, grit, and determination to create and re-create Barnum's American Museum. Anyone who wouldn't think of paying to see a "161-year-old" slave or meet Tom Thumb will still marvel at the exhibits he created, which were a natural forerunner to reality television. **AENYA Honor, ALA, BBYA**

Keywords: Barnum, P. T. • Barnum's American Museum • Circus owners

Now Try: P. T. Barnum is also featured prominently in George Sullivan's *Tom Thumb: The Remarkable True Story of a Man in Miniature*. Sullivan introduces readers to the greatest celebrity of his day, popular with heads of state around the world in the 1800s. Tom's desire to become known for more than his size led him to become a working actor on stage and in film as well as part of several of Barnum's exhibitions.

Heiligman, Deborah.

🎗 *Charles and Emma: The Darwins' Leap of Faith.* New York: Henry Holt & Co., 2008. 268p. ISBN 9780805087215. **J** **H**

After weighing the pros and cons of wedded life, Charles Darwin came down on the side of marriage and started to look for a wife, even though he was afraid marriage would distract him from his research. His cousin, Emma Wedgwood, a deeply religious woman who would become his wife, was just as doubtful at the outset of their marriage: if Charles was proven to be right in his theories, it would mean that all of her religious beliefs were false. How the two managed to have a long, successful, and collaborative relationship, with Emma being an important sounding board and editor for *The Origin of Species*, as well as a strong support in general, makes for a wonderful and novel account of Darwin's life and work. This finalist for the National Book Award was also a finalist for the Los Angeles Times Book Prize for Young Adult Literature. **AENYA, Printz Honor**

Keywords: Darwin, Charles • Evolution • Marriage • Married life • Religion • Wedgwood, Emma

Now Try: A very thorough look at Darwin, his life, and how he developed his theories of natural selection after returning from five years of travelling is presented in a graphic format that incorporates excerpts from his letters and imagined dialogue in Michael Keller's *Charles Darwin's "On the Origin of Species": A Graphic Adaptation.* Nicolle Rager Fuller's lovely illustrations allow the author not only to include the plants and animals being discussed but also to add an afterword that examines developments in science from Mendel and his study of pea plants right up to DNA and genetic diversity.

Krull, Kathleen.

Jim Henson: The Guy Who Played with Puppets. Paintings by Steve Johnson and Lou Fancher. New York: Random House, 2011. 37p. ISBN 9780375857218. **M**

Jim Henson was the lone man in home economics classes of six hundred women, which, along with the art classes he pursued, allowed him to create his puppets. Puppetry was an interest developed and sustained over his lifetime. It took him down paths that hadn't been followed before and that delighted all ages. Jim Henson's Muppets starred in the world's longest-running children's television show, hosted *Saturday Night Live,* and were the stars of the family-friendly television and feature films bearing their names. This is a tribute to Henson's work and legacy, work in which he believed and to which he devoted himself from an early age.

Keywords: Henson, Jim • Muppets • Puppetry • Puppets

Mitchell, Don.

Driven: A Photobiography of Henry Ford. Washington, DC: National Geographic, 2010. 64p. ISBN 9781426301551. **M J**

Henry Ford was deeply affected by seeing a steam-powered vehicle at a young age and determined to create one himself. Although he didn't invent the automobile, he is the one who made cars affordable for the average American, with his Model T. This well-balanced portrayal of the man, picturing his pacifist views and giving readers a clear picture of how his inventions affected American society, also shows the reader his anti-Semitism and stance against labor unions. Readers will find a generous number of photographs and additional resources, making this a valuable source for reports in addition to being an interesting book on its own.

Keywords: Ford, Henry • Ford motor cars • Model T Ford

VanHecke, Susan.

Raggin', Jazzin', Rockin': A History of American Musical Instrument Makers. Honesdale, PA: Boyds Mills Press, 2011. 136p. ISBN 9781590785744. **M J**

Readers will find in this book the stories behind eight of the best known and most highly regarded musical instruments, from Steinway pianos to Ludwig drums and Fender guitars. Each chapter presents a biography of the artist as well as information about the development of the instrument, including the materials and technology used and the artists who have helped to make that brand a household name over the years. This well-illustrated and readable text would be a welcome addition to any school or public library, and profits will be donated to a music advocacy program that supports music funding. **ALA**

Keywords: Music • Musical instruments

Change-Makers and Activists

The people featured in these books are truly worthy of respect. They are memorable for not only the end result of their battles, but also the endurance they showed in pursuing causes in which they believed. Of course this makes for engrossing reading, providing food for thought far beyond the turn of the last page. Readers will find role models and books that describe incredible moments in history, as well as titles that can demonstrate what has changed in the institutions and causes for which these people were fighting.

Colman, Judith.

Elizabeth Cady Stanton and Susan B. Anthony: A Friendship That Changed the World. New York: Henry Holt & Company, 2011. 256p. ISBN 9780805082937. **J H**

The friendship and partnership between these two formidable women lasted more than half a century. Colman introduces readers to "Mrs. Stanton" and Susan well before they meet each other, to help readers understand the dismal situations in which women were living and which they wanted changed. The text illuminates the incredible roles that these two played in ending slavery as well as the ongoing struggle for women's right to vote, a fight that took so many years that what was initially hoped to have been the Sixteenth Amendment was included in the Constitution as the Nineteenth Amendment.

Keywords: Anthony, Susan B. • Stanton, Elizabeth Cady • Suffrage • Women's rights

Hoose, Phillip.

🎗 *Claudette Colvin: Twice Toward Justice.* New York: Farrar, Straus and Giroux/Melanie Kroupa Books, 2009. 133p. ISBN 9780374313227. **M J H**

In March 1955, nine months before Rosa Parks triggered the bus boycott in Montgomery, Alabama, by refusing to surrender her seat to a white passenger, a fifteen-year-old Montgomery girl, Claudette Colvin, was arrested and dragged off the bus for the same reason. Colvin, found guilty of "segregation violation," had not been deemed "suitable" to be placed at the center of the bus boycott because of her age and the NAACP leaders' doubts about their ability to win an appeal of her case. By the time Rosa Parks became the focus of their efforts, Colvin was disgraced: pregnant, but not married. But she stepped up and became one of the central figures in the landmark case *Browder v. Gayle* in 1956, in which Montgomery's segregated bus system was declared unconstitutional. Readers will be introduced to a brave teenager who did the right thing, in a beautifully written book presented with impeccable design and lots of accompanying primary source materials. Among this book's honors are the National Book Award, a Newbery Honor, a Sibert Honor, being named a finalist for the Award for Excellence, and being chosen for the Amelia Bloomer list. **AENYA Honor, SIBERT Honor**

Keywords: *Browder v. Gayle* • Civil rights • Colvin, Claudette • Montgomery bus boycott

Lang, Glenna, and Marjory Wunsch.

Genius of Common Sense: Jane Jacobs and the Story of "The Death and Life of Great American Cities." Boston: David R. Godine, Publisher, 2009. 127p. ISBN 9781567923841. **M J H**

Readers will find in the story of Jane Jacobs an example of not only a great environmentalist but also an activist who believed in her cause. Jacobs, who moved to New York and fell in love with the city, fought battles large and small on the way to publishing her landmark book. She believed that urban renewal, which replaced deteriorating buildings and uprooted communities, destroyed the character of a city, rather than enriching it. Her articles and the projects she took on, such as preventing a highway from being built through Washington Square Park, pointed out how such structures would have substantially increased traffic while detracting from people's ability to use the green space, affecting the public's safety, culture, and lifestyle. Jacobs, who moved with her family to Toronto, remains a worthwhile role model for today's teens.

Keywords: Cities • Jacobs, Jane • Urban renewal

Now Try: Hadley Dyer's *Watch This Space: Designing, Defending and Sharing Public Spaces* provides an explanation and a history of public spaces, while also looking at how the concept of public spaces has changed in the information age. Marc Ngui's illustrations are colorful and teen-friendly and help show public spaces around the world and what makes them appealing. The book finishes with suggestions readers can incorporate in their own battles for improvements to local public spaces.

Historical Biography

Although the authors of the books in this subgenre use historical details to enrich their books, treating the setting almost as another character, the person, not the place and time, is the main focus of these books. That is the difference between these books and those in the historical biography subgenre in chapter 5, where it is the history that is remembered more prominently than the subject of the biography.

Fleming, Ann Marie.

The Magical Life of Long Tack Sam. New York: Riverhead Books, 2007. 170p. ISBN 9781594482649. **H** **GN**

Ann Marie Fleming, a Canadian filmmaker and animator, knew that her great-grandfather, Long Tack Sam, was born in northern China, and that he had been a magician. Actually, he performed on five continents, avoided capture during the world wars, faced the rampant racism of the times, and is still recognized as one of the most famous magicians of the twentieth century. So why don't more people know about him, including the members of his own family? Fleming's journey around the world to try to trace Sam's life presents not only his story but also insights into what it was like living in a mixed race relationship and as a member of a minority during the first half of the twentieth century.

Keywords: Graphic nonfiction • Long Tack Sam • Magic • Magicians

Fleming, Candace.

Amelia Lost: The Disappearance of Amelia Earhart. New York: Schwartz and Wade Books, 2011. 128p. ISBN 9780375841989. **M** **J**

Although the story of the world's most famous female pilot and her dramatic disappearance while attempting to circumnavigate the globe is not a new one, this presentation manages to be both gripping and enlightening. This highly involving story draws readers in by balancing biographical information about Amelia, her growing fame, and her desire to accomplish larger feats with accounts of the search for her plane and the effects that her disappearance had on her family, friends, and the public. Historical photographs, documents, and sidebars expand on information in the text, such as people, or Amelia's equipment or flights, giving readers a sense of the evolution of the aeronautic industry and Earhart's place in it. **ALA, OP Honor**

Keywords: Earhart, Amelia • Pilots • Transatlantic crossing

Now Try: Readers are introduced to Amelia Earhart through Grace, a young girl from Trespassey, Newfoundland, a town that was often the starting point for attempts at Atlantic crossings because of its proximity to England, in Sarah Taylor Stewart's *Amelia Earhart: This Broad Ocean*. This graphic version of Amelia's story presents the interactions between Grace, the writer and publisher of the *Trespassey Herald*, and Amelia, whose love for flying and determination to be the first woman to successfully cross the Atlantic inspired generations of women, to clearly illustrate to readers not only the difficulties faced by Earhart as a woman in a man's world but also Newfoundland in the 1930s. This title was chosen for the 2011 Great Graphic Novels for Teens list.

Freedman, Russell.

 Lafayette and the American Revolution. New York: Holiday House, 2010. 88p. ISBN 99780823421824. **M** **J**

While an account of a young man determined to follow his true calling may not be all that unusual, it is so when that young man is a marquis, one of the richest men in France, and he decides to prove his mettle by fighting in the American Revolution against his king's wishes. This Sibert Honor–winning book tells readers the singular story of a soldier who rose through the ranks and arranged financial help for America during the revolution, becoming a well-respected officer in both countries and taking ideas he garnered about liberty back to his own country after the war. **ALA, IRA, Sibert Honor**

Keywords Lafayette, Marie Joseph Paul Yves Roch Gilbert Du Motier, marquis de, 1757–1834 • United States Revolution

Geary, Rick.

 Trotsky: A Graphic Biography. New York: Hill and Wang/Serious Comics, 2009. 103p. ISBN 9780809095087. **H** **A/YA** **GN**

Geary presents a moderate and objective portrayal of one of the key figures behind the Russian Revolution, including Trotsky's relationships with both Lenin and Stalin, allowing readers to learn not only about the Russian Revolution but also about Trotsky's part in it. Trotsky's many exiles and imprisonments are explained, from the first imprisonment, during which he was introduced to Marxism, to his final, Mexican exile, which led not only to his relationship with Frida Kahlo but also to his murder. This title was chosen for the Great Graphic Novels for Teens list.

Keywords: Graphic nonfiction • Lenin, Vladimir Ilyich • Marxism • Russian Revolution • Stalin, Joseph • Trotsky, Leon • U.S.S.R

Giblin, James Cross.

 The Rise and Fall of Senator Joe McCarthy. Boston: Clarion Books, 2009. 294p. ISBN 9780618610587. **J** **H**

This thorough portrait of Joe McCarthy presents a detailed and comprehensive picture of his service on the bench, in the Marines during World War II, and as a senator. While many readers may have come across blacklisting and the McCarthy era as a concept in movies or on TV, the senator's drive, determination, and eventual downfall are a fascinating subject. His willingness to fabricate evidence and stretch the truth to promote himself and his desired ends make this a book worthy of inclusion in classrooms as well as general interest collections. This title was a finalist for the Los Angeles Times Book Prize for Young Adult Literature.

Keywords: Anticommunist movements • McCarthy, Senator Joseph

Rubin, Susan Goldman.

Irena Sendler and the Children of the Warsaw Ghetto. Illustrated by Bill Farnsworth. New York: Holiday House, 2011. 40p. ISBN 9780823422517. **M J**

> Irena Sendler, a diminutive woman who stood only 4'11", spent World War II working for an organization called the Council for Aid to Jews, code named Zegota, providing fake names and passports to Jewish children and smuggling them out of the Warsaw ghetto. She also managed to write down and save a list of the German and matching Polish names used by these children, allowing some of them to be reunited with their families after the war. The dangers she faced and the difficulties endured by the children and their families make for a gripping read and a book that will add to collections about World War II and the Holocaust.
>
> **Keywords:** Holocaust • Poland • Warsaw ghetto • World War II

Stone, Tanya Lee.

Almost Astronauts: 13 Women Who Dared to Dream. Somerville, MA: Candlewick Press. 2009. 133p. ISBN 9780763636111. **M J H**

> In the early 1960s, William Randolph Lovelace II, the NASA doctor who administered the rigorous physical and psychological tests to the men who would become the first U.S. astronauts, wondered if it might be possible for women to become astronauts as well. A period of extraordinary testing began for nineteen women with the extensive flight experience and drive to undergo the scrutiny from the public that these tests, which would be both physical and mental, would require of them. The tests, which were longer and harder than those the men had faced, winnowed down the original nineteen to thirteen successful candidates, including an exceptionally qualified Jerrie Cobb. Despite very public efforts by the group to get NASA to accept women, they were rejected, and in fact, NASA didn't accept women or people of color until 1978. The ultimately unsuccessful effort to get women into NASA's Mercury astronaut training program is presented here with historical photographs and without any sugarcoating. Readers will be given a clear sense of the personal and physical risks faced by the women in pursuit of their dreams as well as a better understanding of the political climate of the day, which helps us all celebrate just how far female astronauts have come. This title was chosen for the Amelia Bloomer list, as well as being awarded many other honors. **AENYA Honor, BG-HB, OP Honor, Sibert**
>
> **Keywords:** Astronauts • Cobb, Jerrie • Lovelace, William Randolph, II • Women pilots

Young, Beryl.

Charlie: A Home Child's Life in Canada. Toronto: Key Porter Books, 2009. 111p.
ISBN 9781554702008. **M** **J**

> Charlie Harvey was just thirteen when his father died in 1910. Shortly afterward,
> his mother sent Charlie and his younger brother, Arthur, to orphanages because
> she was unable to take care of all of her children. Charlie was sent to one of the
> Barnardo's Homes in London, where Dr. Barnardo's motto was "No Destitute
> Child Ever Refused Admission." Dr. Barnardo's 110 homes were just some of the
> homes that eventually sent 100,000 Home Children, including Charlie, overseas
> to Canada. Charlie's journey demonstrates the sacrifice made by parents to give
> their children a better future and shows the struggle these children had, as well
> as the different lives they had in Canada and the contributions they made in their
> new country, experiencing hardship and difficulties as well as kindness, a new
> home, and a satisfying career.
>
> **Keywords:** Home Children • Immigration

Partner and Group Biographies

Sometimes it is impossible to relate a life story without talking about that person's
relationships with other people. The interactions of these subjects make for involving
reading. The challenge an author faces when describing the accomplishments of more
than one life can result in a book that gives a reader extra insights, such as Andrew
Chaikin's *Mission Control, This Is Apollo: The Story of the First Voyages to the Moon*, which
benefits from many of the former Apollo astronauts' insights.

Chaikin, Andrew, with Victoria Kohl.

Mission Control, This Is Apollo: The Story of the First Voyages to the Moon.
Illustrated by Alan Bean. New York: Penguin Group/Viking, 2009. 114p. ISBN
9780670011568. **M** **J**

> The Apollo 11 moon landing is just one piece of a much larger and amazing
> story. It is presented here with pictures and behind-the-scenes information
> from a nonfiction writer and an actual Apollo astronaut. The book spotlights
> twelve significant missions, from the fatal cockpit fire of the Apollo 1 mission
> to the bittersweet success of the final, successful Apollo 17 mission that wound
> up the program. Andrew Chaikin's extensive research, including twenty-eight
> interviews with former Apollo astronauts, allows him to include a number of
> sidebars that will appeal to readers. Topics here vary widely and include the
> work of the Mission Control teams, the early fear of "moon germs," and how
> the astronauts dealt with evacuating in space. The design of the book is also
> complemented by NASA photos, which provide excellent color illustrations of
> the Apollo missions. An unusual choice that brings the reader closer to the text is
> the use of paintings by Apollo astronaut Alan Bean, rather than stock photographs
> from the NASA archives. Supplementary titles and Web sites are included.
>
> **Keywords:** Apollo missions • Astronauts • Space exploration

Now Try: Readers interested in finding more information about space exploration will get a good overview in Carole Stott's *Space Exploration*. This updated volume of Dorling Kindersley's Eyewitness Books provides readers with numerous pictures; an overview of the space race, with the back and forth between the United States and the Soviet Union; and many examples that may surprise readers, such as the advances in space exploration and a page of "fascinating facts." A timeline and suggested Web sites are included. Readers who wonder whether there is life on other planets, or who might believe that we have already been visited by extraterrestrials, will find both possibilities discussed in Kelly Milner Halls's *Alien Investigation: Searching for the Truth About UFOs and Aliens*. This evenhanded, well-illustrated presentation includes interviews with experts on both sides of the argument as well as many firsthand accounts and will be appealing to reluctant readers.

St. George, Judith.

The Duel: The Parallel Lives of Alexander Hamilton & Aaron Burr. New York: Penguin Group/Viking, 2009. 97p. ISBN 9780670011247. **M J**

This story starts as two men set out for the dueling grounds of Weehawken, New Jersey, on July 11, 1804. The events that brought these two prominent men to this confrontation, which will leave one dead and the other a fugitive, make for a fascinating account, particularly because their lives had so many common features. The successive chapters look at significant events in their lives, how Hamilton and Burr were affected by these events, and in turn the effects Hamilton and Burr had on the nation. Examples of the parallels between them include growing up as orphans; being excellent students; becoming lawyers; their involvement in the American Revolution, including taking positions on George Washington's staff; and their rivalry in politics, which ultimately led to the vice president's shooting the first U.S. Secretary of the Treasury.

Keywords: Burr, Aaron • Duel • Hamilton, Alexander • Revolutionary period

The Creative Life: Entertainers

A life devoted to one's creative passion is not easy. The phrase "suffering for one's art" is familiar to most people and is demonstrated in the pages of many of these books. These are not reverential or unbiased pictures; instead, they show the subjects of the biographies for what they are. The result is not only a picture of a subject's life and an examination of the times in which he or she lived, but also an understanding of some truly remarkable achievements, providing a picture of Alicia Alonso's difficult decision to stay in Cuba and a balanced portrayal of Charlie Chaplin. Books about artists are included in chapter 11. There are titles about individual authors in the "Books and Authors" subgenre of chapter 10. Readers will also find a collection about women writers in the section "Biography Collections" in this chapter.

Bernier-Grand, Carmen T.

Alicia Alonso: Prima Ballerina. Illustrated by Raul Colon. New York: Marshall Cavendish, 2011. 64p. ISBN 9780761455622. **M** **J**

> Ballerina and choreographer Alicia Alonso made stunning contributions to dance in both the United States and her native Cuba. Alonso moved to the United States at the age of fifteen and became a principal dancer in the Ballet Theatre, then later founded the Ballet Nacional de Cuba. Colon's pictures illustrate Alonso's effortless movements and love of ballet. This moving, free verse portrait of the renowned dancer, who raised the ire of her countrymen by choosing to leave Cuba under Batista but to stay during Castro's rule, and whose Giselle was an international sensation despite her own visual disability, will thrill readers interested in dance.
>
> **Keywords:** Alonso, Alicia • Ballet • Dancers

Carlson, Laurie.

Harry Houdini for Kids: His Life and Adventures. Chicago: Chicago Review Press, 2009. 136p. ISBN 9781556527821. **M**

> Ehrich Weisz started off as an $18 per week circus performer and ended up as an $1,800 per week, death-defying escape artist known as Harry Houdini, whose most famous tricks still confound magicians and audiences alike. Laurie Carlson recounts the rags-to-riches story of how Houdini's talent, hard work, and perseverance made him the ultimate "rock star" of his day, with sidebars that explain how to do several magic tricks and also introduce important historical figures such as the Wright brothers and Teddy Roosevelt, giving readers a feel for the times in a fun package.
>
> **Keywords:** Houdini, Harry • Magic • Magicians

Fleischman, Sid.

Sir Charlie Chaplin, the Funniest Man in the World. New York: Greenwillow Books, 2010. 268p. ISBN 9780061896408. **J** **H**

> Charlie Chaplin is widely recognized as one of the funniest actors and best filmmakers of the silent screen. His films are still shown around the world. This balanced, beautifully written portrayal of Chaplin shows his good and bad sides. Readers will understand how a young Cockney lad from a troubled home became one of the founders of United Artists and have a reason to seek out the Little Tramp for themselves.
> **Keywords:** Chaplin, Charlie • Comics • Filmmaking • Films

Biography Collections

Biography collections serve several purposes. By thematically linking biographies, they provide a great starting point for students looking for a research project. They also provide a great way to introduce readers to important people in a particular area or to biography as a genre, in the same way that a short story collection gives readers a chance to sample an author's writing. Readers who enjoy Michael Burgan's *Spies and Traitors: Stories of Masters of Deception* will find further choices in either the section on war stories in chapter 1 or the espionage section of chapter 2. Padma Venkatraman's book provides great examples of women who were ahead of their times and may lead readers back to "Change-Makers and Activists" in this chapter. Teresa Toten's *Piece by Piece* is a novel collection of original stories by authors about their experiences fitting into Canada after immigrating to that country.

Bausum, Ann.

Our Country's Presidents: All You Need to Know about the Presidents, from George Washington to Barack Obama. Washington, DC: National Geographic Society, 2009. 216p. ISBN 9781426303753. **M** **J**

> The latest edition of this book has been brought up to date to include the forty-fourth president of the United States, who not only is featured on the cover but also contributed the foreword. Other updates include coverage of George Bush's presidency and four new essays from the previous editions. Overall this is a well-written and thorough resource that is worthwhile not only for reports but also for readers interested in the position and the men who have held it.

> **Keywords:** Presidents • United States Presidents

> **Now Try:** Readers looking for a lighter look at the presidents may be interested in Don Steinberg's *America Bowl: 44 U.S. Presidents vs. 44 Super Bowls*. Steinberg, who was given a collection of presidential dolls as a child, memorized them in numerical order and had them "fight" each other. As an adult, he was struck by the once-in-a-lifetime opportunity afforded by the alignment of Super Bowl 44 being played in the same year as the forty-fourth president being inaugurated, and this book was born. Each chapter pits a president against a Super Bowl, with a sidebar presenting pertinent information about the president, including his home state, political party, electoral votes, dates of his presidency, and the reason he left office. The text is written in a tone meant to mimic a sportscast and summarizes the key event or events of both the particular Super Bowl and the president's years in office before awarding a victory.

Bryant, Jill.

Dazzling Women Designers. The Women's Hall of Fame Series. Toronto: Second Story Press, 2010. 123p. ISBN 9781897187821. **M** **J**

> Design affects everything, from clothing and furniture to landscapes and cities. In this volume Jill Bryant profiles ten famous designers from around the world, including former chief designer of General Motors Suzanne Vanderbilt and architects Zaha Hadid and Jane Jacobs, who have shaped and influenced their fields. These portraits show the pinnacles that very

talented women have achieved in fields that are generally dominated by men. Readers will find a long list of further resources for each of the women and a reminder that the women's success has been a result of talent and staying true to themselves.

Keywords: Architecture • Design • Designers • Landscape architecture

Burgan, Michael.

Spies and Traitors: Stories of Masters of Deception. Velocity: Bad Guys. Mankato, MN: Capstone Press, 2010. 48p. ISBN 9781429634243. **M**

This book presents some of the most famous and notorious traitors in history, from Judas Iscariot and Benedict Arnold to John Walker Lindh, who was found guilty of spying for al-Qaeda. Readers are given explanations of the various spies' misdeeds and what happened to them. The facthound Web site offers further resources.

Keywords: Espionage • Traitors

Dublin, Anne.

Dynamic Women Dancers. The Women's Hall of Fame Series. Toronto: Second Story Press, 2009. 129p. ISBN 9781897187562. **M** **J**

The ten dancers profiled in this book are masters of their art. They come from countries around the world and are known for styles that vary from ballet to flamenco to Indian Bharatanatyam. While the women are stars in the world of dance, they are also known for teaching, choreography, becoming involved in their communities, and working on behalf of social organizations. Readers will be introduced to impressive women such as Alicia Alonso, whose near blindness did not stop her from becoming a world famous ballerina or establishing her own company. Supplementary resources in this very readable volume include a glossary and a list of sources and additional resources.

Keywords: Dancers • Women dancers

Ellis, Deborah.

Children of War: Voices of Iraqi Refugees. Toronto: Groundwood Books, 2009. 128p. ISBN 9780888999078. **J** **H**

Ellis interviewed children whose lives were profoundly affected by the war in Iraq. A short introduction gives readers information about the children and their backgrounds, as well as other pertinent political and sociological information particular to their stories. Many of the children now live in Jordan, some have emigrated to Canada, and in either case they find themselves living in countries where they may or may not feel welcome. All have vivid memories of the violence visited on them and their families in Iraq.

Keywords: Children and war • Iraq War

Jocelyn, Marthe.

"Scribbling Women": True Tales from Astonishing Lives. Toronto; Plattsburgh, NY: Tundra Books, 2011. 198p. ISBN 9780887769528. **J H**

1

Marthe Jocelyn shares stories about the lives of eleven exceptional women. Each woman left behind a legacy in letters, journals, or another form of writing that helps provide a picture of both her life and the time in which she lived; in some cases these are the only existing historical documents of those times. The women, who include a convict, a doctor, and a reporter, lived through wars, arduous journeys, and terrible hardships and suffered terrible injustices, leaving behind first-person records of their feelings and experiences. Readers will find over 1,000 years of "scribbling" and may well be inspired to start their own journals.

2

3

Keywords: Authors • Journals • Women writers • Writers

Toten, Teresa, ed.

4

Piece by Piece: Stories about Fitting into Canada. Toronto: Puffin Canada, 2010. 183p. ISBN 9780670068494; 9780143169147pbk. **M J H**

Fourteen authors present stories of their journeys to Canada. Some arrived speaking perfect English, yet found that they could not fit into a French-speaking part of the country or that their accents marked them as different. They came at different ages and from different parts of the world and had vastly different reasons for coming to the country. Their receptions varied greatly, from Linda Granfield's anti-American treatment in the 1970s to Rachna Gilmore's disappointment when she determined that Prince Edward Island was not exactly as it is portrayed in her beloved L. M. Montgomery books. The one consistent and universal theme is that even when a new country becomes home, there is always a love and longing for the place that is left behind. This book provides unique views of immigration and Canada.

5

6

7

Keywords: Authors • Canada • Immigrants

Venkatraman, Padma.

8

🎗 *Women Mathematicians.* Profiles in Mathematics. Greensboro, NC: Morgan Reynolds, 2009. 160p. ISBN 9781599350912. **M**

The field of mathematics affects our lives daily, underpinning many of the sciences and contributing much to today's technology. Its advancement has taken centuries and has been credited to many of history's greatest minds, from Archimedes to Isaac Newton. This volume presents readers with the biographies of six notable women who helped develop new concepts and improved our understanding of mathematics. The women accomplished this against remarkable odds, given the conventions of their times: in order for Sonya Kovalevsky to obtain her doctorate in calculus, she had to write three dissertations, two more than were required of men, and presented

9

10

11

them at an alternate university, as hers would not allow a woman to try to obtain a doctorate. This title was chosen for the 2009 Amelia Bloomer list.

Keywords: Math • Mathematicians • Women in mathematics

Consider Starting with . . .

These are some recommended titles that are both accessible and captivating for readers new to the genre.

Bernier-Grand, Carmen T. *Alicia Alonso: Prima Ballerina.*

Chaikin, Andrew, with Victoria Kohl. *Mission Control, This Is Apollo: The Story of the First Voyages to the Moon.*

Ellis, Deborah. *Children of War: Voices of Iraqi Refugees.*

Fleischman, Sid. *Sir Charlie Chaplin, the Funniest Man in the World.*

Fleming, Candace. *The Great and Only Barnum: The Tremendous, Stupendous Life of Showman P.T. Barnum.*

Heiligman, Deborah. *Charles and Emma: The Darwins' Leap of Faith.*

Hoose, Phillip. *Claudette Colvin: Twice Toward Justice.*

Stone, Tanya Lee. *Almost Astronauts: 13 Women Who Dared to Dream.*

Fiction Read-Alikes

- **Brooks, Martha**. *Queen of Hearts.* Marie-Claire Côté is prepared to pitch in on the farm in the summer of 1940. Her family is thrilled to have a visit from madcap Oncle Gerard and is grief-stricken when he is diagnosed with TB and sent to the local sanatorium, where he soon dies and shortly thereafter Marie-Claire and her younger siblings are diagnosed with TB themselves. Marie-Claire documents her long recovery from long-term illness, along with the other denizens of the Pembina Hills San.

- **Eagland, Jane**. *Wildthorn.* Louisa Cosgrove had always been unusual by the standards of her day: she enjoyed learning from her father and would much rather have gone to medical school than get married and settle down with a husband, which was not at all proper for a Victorian young lady. Upon finding herself admitted to an insane asylum and being addressed as Lucy Childs, she was initially sure that it was an honest mistake. Only slowly did she find out the truth that would set her free not only from the asylum but also to live the life that would make her happy.

- **Miller, Sarah**. *Miss Spitfire: Reaching Helen Keller.* Annie Sullivan needs a change desperately, but she has no idea what she is in for when she agrees to become the teacher of a deaf and blind, almost feral six-year-old named Helen

Keller, who cannot be controlled by her family. This title was named to the Best Books for Young Adults list.

- **Preus, Margi.** *Heart of a Samurai.* When fourteen-year-old Manjiro survived a shipwreck while fishing with three of his friends in 1841, he had no idea what the scope of his future adventures would be. Once they had left Japan, they were considered deserters: beyond Japan, they knew, was nothing but barbarians. This fictionalized version of the true story of the first Japanese person to set foot in America shows how Manjiro left himself open to discovering that the world is a very large place and it would be up to him to find his place in it. This title was named a Newbery Honor book in 2011.

Reference

Aronson, Marc. 2003. "Biography and Its Perils." In *Beyond the Pale: New Essays for a New Era*. Lanham, MD: Scarecrow Press.

1

2

3

4

5

6

7

8

9

10

11

Part 3

Nonfiction Subject Interests

Chapter **5**

History

Definition

Nonfiction history books provide information about events from the past relating to people, places, things, time, or countries. This continues to be a very prolific area for publishing; there is no way that every historical book or series published could be considered in this guide. The books selected for this chapter are simply meant to introduce the subgenres of history. All meet the criteria for choosing nonfiction used in this guide, including accuracy, style, design, and documentation.

Appeal

Though it remains a mainstay in school and public libraries for informational reading, nonfiction history has much more to offer than its obvious connections to school curricula. There are the additional benefits of offering new points of view, introducing new evidence, and showing readers what actually happened during desperate times. A recent trend in this genre has been books published to celebrate anniversaries of historical events. The first middle-grade-appropriate book in this chapter points out the poignancy of teachers and librarians introducing children to events that happened before their lifetimes. Don Brown's *America Is Under Attack: September 11, 2001: The Day the Towers Fell* will remain relevant as these kids become teenagers in the next few years.

A continuing trend can be found in authors showing how historians work. An example of this is Eric Cline's *Digging for Troy: From Homer to Hisarlik*, which not only shows how archaeology has changed, but offers readers a balanced viewpoint of several subjects. Only through the literature of history does a reader experience another time from the point of view of someone who was there, as in Ruth Thomson's *Terezin: Voices from the Holocaust*, which incorporates stories and artwork from the camp's inmates.

There are several options for appealing to readers who believe history is boring. Choices for reluctant readers include graphic nonfiction and the Eyewitness Books series, which contain numerous illustrations and a format that breaks up the text so it doesn't overwhelm the reader.

Chapter Organization

Most readers are accustomed to thinking about history in terms of dates. This makes the section "Defining Times" a natural starting point for the chapter.

The section "History's Darkest Hours" follows, containing both man-made and natural tales of disaster. Next readers will find what has continued to be a popular area of publishing in the section "Micro-histories," in which authors provide detailed examinations of much more narrow subjects, such as Marc Aronson and Marina Budhos's *Sugar Changed the World*.

The entries in the next section, "Historical Biography: Ordinary People in Extraordinary Times," differ from those in the parallel section in chapter 4 in that they emphasize the time and place rather than the people; for example, most of the men who perished in Andersonville are a part of history because of their presence in the prison, rather than being famous in their own right.

The section "Ideas of History" follows the development of one issue through time. Subjects examined here are wide-ranging and include slavery and prohibition. The subjects explored in the section "New Perspectives" deal with changing times. They demonstrate how historical viewpoints change in response to new information, revisions in law, and changing attitudes.

Defining Times

Dates are needed to understand history. Of all the ways of looking at history, the chronological is the most common approach. People interested in history often look for materials relating to particular time periods and apply questions specifically to that time. Students are taught to start with a particular time period and then look at those dates and settings, asking what happened and how the events of that time changed the course of history.

Each book in this section provides a thorough examination of a period in history, covering the settings, people, and culture of that time, although readers will find different formats and writing styles. C. M. Butzer's *Gettysburg: The Graphic Novel* introduces the battle of Gettysburg, including a particularly moving presentation of Lincoln's Gettysburg Address, in a format appealing to reluctant readers.

Allen, Thomas B., and Roger MacBride Allen.

Mr. Lincoln's High-tech War: How the North Used the Telegraph, Railroads, Surveillance Balloons, Ironclads, High-Powered Weapons and More to Win the Civil War. Washington, DC: National Geographic, c2009. 144p. ISBN 9781426303807. **M** **J**

The Civil War was the first war in which technology played a definite role in the outcome, due to technological innovations that President Abraham Lincoln was able to apply during the war, including hot-air balloons; interchangeable parts for guns and repeating rifles; the telegraph; and a greater use of logistics, communication, and resources. Lincoln was the only president to be issued a patent, which reflects his interest in technology and how it could be used in the service of his country. This interest, presented with the help of photographs, magazine reproductions, political cartoons, and maps, is used to explain how the telegraph, railroads, surveillance balloons, and other inventions helped the North win the war and rebuild America's economy after the war.

Keywords: Civil War • Inventions • Lincoln, Abraham • Telegraph • Transportation • Weaponry

Butzer, C. M.

Gettysburg: The Graphic Novel. New York: HarperCollins/Bowen Press, 2009. 80p. ISBN 9780061561764. **M J GN RR**

After an introduction to the important Union figures, this graphic novel on the battle of Gettysburg really shines in its the depiction of the battle's aftermath and in the twenty pages devoted to one of the most important documents in American history, Abraham Lincoln's Gettysburg Address, which is depicted over a timeline of civil rights issues. It reminds readers not only that all people are created equal, but also to ask themselves what they owe to those who sacrificed themselves for their liberty. This title was chosen as a 2010 Great Graphic Novel for Teens.

Keywords: Civil War • Gettysburg • Graphic nonfiction • Lincoln, Abraham

Kaufman, Michael T.

1968. New York: Roaring Brook Press/Flash Point, 2009. 160p. ISBN 9781596434288. **J H**

Events in 1968 had profound effects not only in the United States but also in the rest of the world. A reporter with a four-decade career is the perfect person to impress upon readers the importance of journalism. Michael Kaufman introduces readers to this fascinating time by looking at important events that spanned the globe in that watershed year. Starting with the Tet offensive early in the year, moving on to uprisings in New York, then the assassinations of Martin Luther King Jr. and Robert Kennedy, and finishing with the first glimpse of the earth from the Apollo 8 spacecraft, the photographs, stories, and reflections bring the year 1968 to life.

Keywords: Apollo • Assassination • Kennedy, Robert • King, Dr. Martin Luther, Jr. • Vietnam

Now Try: Readers interested in the 1960s will be fascinated with Laban Carrick Hill's look at the decade. *America Dreaming: How Youth Changed America in the 1960s* provides a thorough examination of popular culture, while looking at the changes in civil, social, ethnic, and gender rights during the decade.

Osborne, Linda Barrett.

Traveling the Freedom Road: From Slavery and the Civil War Through Reconstruction. New York: Abrams Books for Young Readers, 2009. 128p. ISBN 9780810983380. **M J**

> Osborne, a senior writer and editor at the Library of Congress, presents a history of African American life in the United States between 1800 and 1877. She poses questions about the nature of slavery and conditions up to and during the Civil War as well as during Reconstruction. The plethora of illustrations added to the text includes photographs, prints, maps, and magazine reproductions, supplemented by numerous first-person recollections. These combine to give readers a very strong sense of place.
>
> **Keywords:** African Americans • History • Reconstruction • Slavery

History's Darkest Hours

Often a particular time or event captures a reader's attention. This subgenre represents the unfortunate, catastrophic stories that are a part of our past, whether naturally occurring or visited upon people by other people. We can learn important lessons from humanity's past intentional inhumanity. Readers have the opportunity to learn from the past through suspenseful, detailed books with high subject access and numerous fiction read-alikes. Readers will also find books about the victims of tragedies and desperate times. The stories here are not just about suffering; they also depict endurance and triumph. Those drawn to these titles will find personal accounts in "Overcoming Adversity" in chapter 3, as well as accounts of war and survival in chapter 1 and of crimes and how they are investigated in chapter 2.

Human Cruelties

These are stories of dark times, tragedies, and unfortunate events, visited upon people by other people. They include accounts of battles as well as stories of individuals or groups of people dealing with oppression, attacks, or unimaginable events. These books run the gamut from an account of Solomon Northrop's 1808 kidnapping into slavery to a detailed explanation of the 1999 Columbine school shooting and Don Brown's *America Is Under Attack: September 11, 2001: The Day the Towers Fell.*

Batten, Jack.

The War to End All Wars: The Story of World War I. Toronto: Tundra Books, 2009. 154p. ISBN 9780887768798. **M J H**

> *The War to End All Wars* is a very readable history of World War I. Batten does a great job of drawing readers into the events as they unfolded, starting from the perspective of one participant in a situation and then working outward. It would have been preferable to have the map somewhere other than on the inside of the

front cover, but being a well-written history written specifically for young adults makes up for the small flaw.

Keywords: Allies • Axis • World War I

Bausum, Ann.

Denied, Detained, Deported: Stories from the Dark Side of American Immigration. Washington, DC: National Geographic, 2009. 111p. ISBN 9781426303326. **M** **J** **H**

> Ann Bausum presents readers with historical cases in which people, because of their race, ethnic origin, or political beliefs, were either not allowed to enter the United States, not allowed to become full citizens, or deported from the country. Students are then given a timeline and a picture of the immigration situation that exists today.

> **Keywords:** Deportation • Immigration • Race relations

Brown, Don.

🎗 *America Is Under Attack: September 11, 2001: The Day the Towers Fell.* New York: Roaring Brook Press, 2011. Unpaged. ISBN 9781596436947. **M**

> This picture book recounts the terrorist events of 9/11 and was produced by Don Brown in time for the tenth anniversary as an introduction for readers who were too young to remember or were not yet born on the day that the planes crashed into the two towers of the World Trade Center, the Pentagon, and the Pennsylvania field. It also serves as a reminder of the rescue efforts on that day. An author's note includes a bibliography and source notes. **ALA**

> **Keywords:** Al-Qaeda • September 11 terrorist attacks, 2001 • World Trade Center

Cullen, Dave.

Columbine. New York: Twelve, 2009. 417p. ISBN 9780446546935. **H** **A/YA**

> There is no arguing that Eric Harris and Dylan Klebold's rampage at Columbine High School on April 20, 1999, in which thirteen students including the shooters were killed and countless others were injured, was a tragedy of epic proportions. What is harder to understand even today is why it took place at all. Cullen, perhaps the greatest expert on the event, examines not only the killers but also the media coverage and the ensuing investigations, debunking many of the myths surrounding the events and giving a clear picture of not only the shooting but also the aftermath of the event and the survivors.

> **Keywords:** Columbine • Shootings • Violence

1
2
3
4
5
6
7
8
9
10
11

Fradin, Judith Bloom, and Dennis Fradin.

Stolen into Slavery: The True Story of Solomon Northrop, Free Black Man. Washington, DC: National Geographic, 2011. 128p. ISBN 9781426309373. **M** **J**

Solomon Northrop was born a free man in the state of New York in 1808, by virtue of his mother having been a free black woman and his father having been liberated. Readers are told the story of his kidnapping and subsequent transportation to Louisiana, where he was sold several times and spent almost a dozen years in a succession of plantations under the name Platt. This book will supplement reports and debates while informing readers about a horrifying practice that was deemed acceptable in its time. Solomon was eventually returned to his family and went on to publish a successful account of his travails, which led to the arrest of his kidnappers, but they were acquitted on the grounds that he had been a party to the scheme to sell himself into slavery and had wanted to become a slave.

Keywords: Kidnapping • Northrop, Solomon • Slavery

Freedman, Russell.

The War to End All Wars: World War I. Boston: Clarion Books, 2010. 192p. ISBN 9780547026862. **M** **J** **H**

Freedman's introduction to World War I not only helps readers understand the complex relationships between the countries before the war but also how the "Great War" differed from the wars that had preceded it in numbers of casualties and methods of warfare. Freedman lucidly presents the difficult resolution of the war and how the Treaty of Versailles may have contributed to World War II. Readers will appreciate the quantity and quality of photographs that add to the text.

Keywords: Allies • Axis • World War I

Gourley, Catherine.

The Horrors of Andersonville: Life and Death Inside a Civil War Prison. Minneapolis, MN: Twenty-First Century Books, 2010. 192p. ISBN 9780761342120. **J** **H**

Catherine Gourley balances the stories of the prisoners and Captain Henry Wirz, the camp commandant, in the increasing squalor and overcrowded conditions of Camp Sumter, the prisoner-of-war camp in Andersonville, Georgia. Using a variety of primary sources, the author gives readers a detailed sense of the hopeless conditions that the prisoners faced and of the lack of support their jailors received. This makes for an interesting discussion point when Gourly describes Henry Wirz's postwar trial, which resulted in his being the only Confederate officer hanged for war crimes.

Keywords: Andersonville • Camp Sumter • Civil War • Wirz, Henry

Metselaar, Menno, and Ruud van der Rol.

🎗 *Anne Frank: Her Life in Words and Pictures (from the Archives of the Anne Frank House).* New York: Roaring Brook Press/Flash Point, 2009. 215p. ISBN 9781596435476. **M J H**

This scrapbook, originally published in the Netherlands in cooperation with the Anne Frank House, is a fascinating look at Anne's life, both before and during World War II. Excerpts from the diary, combined with pictures of Anne, her family, and the annex, are given added poignancy by Otto Frank's thoughts about his daughter's desire to publish her diary. Readers are shown exactly how the Franks lived, with pictures of their dining, living, and sleeping spaces. Although the annex is now a museum stripped of all furnishings, pictures show that the marks on the walls of Anne's and Margot's growth can still be seen. This book would pair wonderfully with Anne Frank's diary. **ALA, BG-HB**

Keywords: Frank, Anne • Frank, Otto • Holocaust • Scrapbook • World War II

Thomson, Ruth.

Terezín: Voices from the Holocaust. Somerville, MA: Candlewick Press, 2011. 64p. ISBN 9780763649630. **M J**

In 1941 the Nazis decided that the town of Terezín would make an ideal ghetto for the thousands of Jewish people in Czechoslovakia. While to the outside world the camp that was renamed Theresienstadt was a well-run "show" camp, where the denizens received adequate food and care, it was intended as a transport camp for the concentration camps, and fewer than 100 of the 15,000 children who passed through the camp survived. Many artists were among the inmates, and Thompson includes some of their artwork as well as stories from the inmates to show readers not only what life was like in the camp but also how the Nazis were able to deceive the outside world about what was going on there.

Keywords: Holocaust • Terezín • Theresienstadt • World War II

Natural Disasters and Disease Epidemics

These are the records of naturally occurring incidents and traumas, either plagues, weather, or some other unforeseen and uncontrollable event. Readers interested in disasters and the people who survived them may also be interested in the survival and disaster stories in chapter 1 and the section on survival skills in chapter 9.

Guiberson, Brenda Z.

Disasters: Natural and Man-Made Catastrophes Through the Centuries. New York: Henry Holt & Company, 2010. 228p. ISBN 9780805081701. **M** **J** **H**

Ten of the worst disasters that have befallen humanity take center stage in this book. These include both natural and man-made calamities, from the sinking of the *Titanic* to the 1918 worldwide flu pandemic to the 2004 tsunami, which affected twelve countries. What makes each of the discussions particularly interesting, whether for a reader interested in history or for one looking for material for a report, are materials added to each chapter that make the discussion more of a debate. The chapter on smallpox ponders the ramifications of biological warfare; the section on the Dust Bowl adds material about migrants, child labor, and soil conservation.

Keywords: Disasters • Natural disasters

Jurmain, Suzanne.

The Secret of the Yellow Death: A True Story of Medical Sleuthing. Boston: Houghton Mifflin, 2009. 104p. ISBN 9780618965816. **M** **J** **H**

At the turn of the century, doctors in both North and South America knew all too well how deadly yellow fever was, but they were at a loss to identify its cause. Jurmain follows four heroic American doctors, one Cuban doctor, and numerous volunteers as they put themselves in grave danger to find the source of a disease that affected millions. The resulting book is a beautifully designed, gripping page-turner, written in stylish language, about a disease that "killed the humble and humbled the important," which adds lots of photographs highlighted in yellow, reinforces the danger at every turn of the page, and adds every possible kind of supplementary detail.

Keywords: Cuba • Finlay, Carlos • Reed, Walter • Yellow fever

Marrin, Albert.

🎗 *Flesh and Blood So Cheap: The Triangle Fire and Its Legacy.* New York: Alfred A. Knopf, 2011. 182p. 9780375868894. **J** **H**

The deaths of the 146 people who perished in the fire at the Triangle Shirtwaist Factory on March 25, 1911, remained one of the worst workplace tragedies in American history until 9/11. Albert Marrin interweaves the stories behind the immigrants who ended up in the factories with the causes of the poor conditions, which were partly due to economics, and the resulting economic changes for workers, although such changes have yet to be implemented in other parts of the world. The information provided in this book, which is supplemented by abundant photographs and sidebars with helpful supplementary facts, as well as a list of further resources, will provide readers with an understanding of conditions that exist today in Third World countries, exemplified by a 2010 fire in Bangladesh that mimicked the Triangle tragedy. **NBA**

Keywords: Industrial safety • Shirtwaist Factory fire • Tragedies

🎗 *Years of Dust: The Story of the Dust Bowl.* New York: Dutton Children's Books, 2009. 128p. ISBN 9780525420774. **M** **J**

In his examination of the Dust Bowl, Marrin illuminates the roles of ranching, hunting, and farming practices in the changing ecology of the Great Plains. Buffalo, hunted nearly to extinction, were replaced on the plains by cattle. This in turn negatively affected the growth of native grasses, which had always protected the soil, just in time for the droughts of the 1930s. Large photographs of the storms accompany the text. By choosing to present the history with an ecological focus, Marrin shows how some of the damage could have been prevented and can yet be prevented in areas around the world such as China, where there are some ecological disasters in the making. **ALA**

Keywords: Depression • Dust bowls • Ecology

Now Try: Readers interested in the lives of the people affected by the tragedy of the Dust Bowl as much or more than the ecology will be attracted to Martin W. Sandler's *The Dust Bowl Through the Lens: How Photography Revealed and Helped Remedy a National Disaster*. This portrait of the Dust Bowl disaster, which includes pictures of the photographers who were sent to record it for the government, gives readers a complete idea of the extent of the disaster. The well-annotated photographs put a face to the calamity and prove Ansel Adams' assertion that these were not just photographers, but in fact "sociologists with cameras."

McPherson, Stephanie Sammartino.

Iceberg Right Ahead! The Tragedy of the **Titanic.** Minneapolis, MN: Twenty-First Century Books, 2012. 112p. ISBN 9780761367567. **M** **J**

This thorough account of the *Titanic* introduces readers to the great ship, its passengers and crew, and the people who searched for the ship and those who have kept its memory alive for the past century. The volume includes interesting sidebars and historical photographs that supplement the text and will draw readers into the story, both correcting and supplementing information about the famous and tragic voyage.

Keywords: Shipwrecks • *Titanic*

Now Try: Readers interested in the story of the *Titanic* will enjoy Allan Wolf's novel take on the doomed liner, *The Watch That Ends the Night: Voices from the* Titanic. The voyage of the great ship is narrated from multiple points of view. Readers will enjoy the poems, letters, and varying voices, which range from the iceberg eagerly waiting for the ship to many levels of passengers and crew, from the captain and a junior officer, to the richest man in the world, to a refugee, to the Halifax undertaker. An author's note includes a considerable amount of supplemental information, which combines to give a fascinating, insightful, and delicious view of the voyage.

Neufeld, Josh.

 A.D.: New Orleans after the Deluge. New York: Pantheon Books, 2009. 193p. ISBN 9780307378149. **J** **H** **GN**

> The physical, financial, and emotional devastation of Hurricane Katrina is told from the perspective of seven survivors. From a counselor and a doctor to two friends, a high school student, and a young couple, all of the protagonists start off assuming that the storm might be fun to watch and end up not only making choices to ensure their survival during the storm but also about how best to resume their lives after the water has receded. This title was chosen as a 2010 Great Graphic Novel for Teens.
>
> **Keywords:** Graphic nonfiction • Hurricane Katrina • Hurricane survivors • New Orleans

Micro-histories

Comprising a large subgenre for young adults, these books allow authors to narrow their focus to a single person, event, action, or object that fascinates them, starting when and where they like and adding as much detail as they choose. A study of one thing may then draw attention to its context and consequences. A good example of this is Marina Budhos and Marc Aronson's discussion of how sugar revolutionized farming to satisfy the worldwide need and desire for that commodity, which in turn led to changes in human rights. Karen Blumenthal's examination of the Prohibition years notes that this period began an era of lawlessness that it was originally intended to eradicate.

Aronson, Marc, and Marina Budhos.

Sugar Changed the World: A Story of Magic, Spice, Slavery and Freedom. New York: Clarion Books, 2010. 176p. ISBN 978061874926. **J** **H**

> There can be no doubt that humans have a taste for sweet things, although a long time before the invention of high-fructose corn syrup, the only way to sweeten things was with honey, until the discovery of cane sugar by the Greeks. Aronson and Budhos trace the changes made in the world as the magic of this sweet powder swept around the globe, affecting and being affected by farming practices, culture, slavery, and trade. Readers are presented with the development of plantations worked by increasing numbers of slaves, who in turn questioned their status as property, years before the American Civil War, while creating a ubiquitous substance that changed how and what people eat and drink. This title was a finalist for the Los Angeles Times Book Prize for Young Adult Literature.
>
> **Keywords:** Slavery • Sugar • Trade

Barnard, Bryn.

The Genius of Islam: How Muslims Made the Modern World. New York: Alfred A. Knopf, 2011. 37p. ISBN 9780375840722. **J** **H**

Bryn Barnard presents an overview of the many things that the Western world owes to Muslim civilization. Often learning from and developing upon earlier knowledge, Muslim scholars then furthered and disseminated their ideas and information in areas including mathematics, architecture, medicine, astronomy, art, and agriculture. The text is supplemented by Barnard's artwork and a list of resources.

Keywords: Islam • Islamic history

Behnke, Alison Marie.

The Little Black Dress and Zoot Suits: Depression and Wartime Fashions from the 1930s to the 1950s. Dressing a Nation: The History of U.S. Fashion. Minneapolis, MN: Twenty-First Century Books, 2011. 64p. ISBN 9780761358923. **J**

This era in fashion was not only a reflection of the economic times, allowing women to either escape from or help shoulder the hardships of the 1930s, it was also a time in which the United States, through innovations such as the zipper, the Sears and Roebuck catalogue, and the increasing fame of Hollywood's movie stars, moved to fashion's forefront. Looking back on prominent styles is always entertaining, and this well-illustrated and thoughtful guide is no exception. Readers will find information about recognizable designer names such as Dior and Chanel and men's styles along with a timeline and a list of further resources.

Keywords: Fashion • Men's fashions • Twentieth-century fashions

Now Try: Readers who wonder what they might have worn during another age, or those who are just interested in finding out more about the history of fashion in the United States, may look for other titles in the Dressing a Nation: The History of U.S. Fashion Series. Cynthia Overbeck Bix takes on the 1770s to the 1860s in *Petticoats and Frock Coats*, dividing her book into five chapters to introduce the clothing and the times.

Countries of the World.

This interesting series provides readers with introductions to individual nations. All of the titles are divided into five main sections: geography, nature, history, people and culture, and government and economy. What makes these books stand out are the "Special Feature" highlights in each section, which help illustrate points of interest, important moments in history, and things that make each country unique. Students working on a country report are offered suggestions to make their reports "more fun," which would in turn intrigue readers interested in the country.

Croy, Anita.

Guatemala. Washington, DC: National Geographic, 2009. 64p. ISBN 978 1426304712. **M J**

Keywords: Guatemala • History

Spain. Washington, DC: National Geographic, 2009. 64p. ISBN 978 1426306334. **M J**

> **Keywords:** History • Spain

Croy, Elden.

United States. Washington, DC: National Geographic, 2010. 64p. ISBN 97814 26306327. **M J**

> **Keywords:** History • United States

Dalal, A. Kamala.

Laos. Washington, DC: National Geographic, 2009. 64p. ISBN 9781426 303883. **M J**

> **Keywords:** History • Laos

Dekker, Zilah.

Poland. Washington, DC: National Geographic, 2008. 64p. ISBN 9781426 302015. **M J**

> **Keywords:** History • Poland

Portugal. Washington, DC: National Geographic, 2009. 64p. ISBN 9781426 303906. **M J**

> **Keywords:** History • Portugal

Gray, Leon.

Iran. Washington, DC: National Geographic, 2008. 64p. ISBN 97814263 02008. **M J**

> **Keywords:** History • Iran

Green, Jen.

Greece. Washington, DC: National Geographic, 2009. 64p. ISBN 9781426 304705. **M J**

> **Keywords:** Greece • History

Vietnam. Washington, DC: National Geographic, 2008. 64p. ISBN 9781426 302022. **M J**

> **Keywords:** History • Vietnam

Mace, Virginia.

South Africa. Washington, DC: National Geographic, 2008. 64p. ISBN 9781426302039. **M** **J**

> **Keywords:** History • South Africa

Phillips, Charles.

Sweden. Washington, DC: National Geographic, 2009. 64p. ISBN 9781 426303890. **M** **J**

> **Keywords:** History • Sweden

Shields, Sarah.

Turkey. Washington, DC: National Geographic, 2009. 64p. ISBN 9781426 303876. **M** **J**

> **Keywords:** History • Turkey

The National Children's Book and Literacy Alliance.

 Our White House: Looking In, Looking Out. Cambridge, MA: Candlewick Press, 2008. 241p. ISBN 9780763620677. **M** **J**

This unique and memorable volume introduces readers to one of the best-known landmarks in the United States using essays, memoirs, illustrations, poetry, and stories from more than 100 notable authors and illustrators. Arranged chronologically, this is an eminently browsable collection about the people who have made the White House their home as well as its visitors and the major events that have had an impact on it, from the War of 1812 to the Four Freedoms from Franklin D. Roosevelt's January 6, 1941, address to Congress, ably illustrated by Calef Brown, Peter Sis, Ed Young, and Stephen Alcorn. **ALA, IRA**

Keywords: United States history • White House

Sandler, Martin.

Secret Subway: The Fascinating Tale of an Amazing Feat of Engineering. Washington, DC: National Geographic, 2009. 96p. ISBN 97814263042620. **M** **J**

Even in the nineteenth century, long before cars and buses, the streets of New York were severely overcrowded. A publisher and inventor named Alfred Ely Beach turned his considerable brainpower to solving this problem by building a subway more than twenty feet under the city's biggest buildings, powered by blasting air. But a corrupt city boss named Alfred Tweed was as devoted to stopping Beach as he was to finishing the project. How Beach and his workers toiled in secret at night to finish the project and prove that a "subway" could become a reality is a fascinating story, especially as Beach died long before the completion of New York's subway, in 1904.

Keywords: Beach, Alfred Ely • Inventions • Inventors • New York • Transportation

Stone, Tanya Lee.

The Good, the Bad, and the Barbie: A Doll's History and Her Impact on Us. New York: Penguin Young Readers Group, 2010. 130p. ISBN 9789670011872. **J H**

One of the reasons for Barbie's enduring popularity is the strong emotions that she evokes. Readers will find a complete history of Ruth Handler, the businesswoman who formed Mattel with her husband and came up with the original idea for the doll, as well as discussions of potential positive and negative sociological implications. Photographs complement a text that shows how Barbie has evolved over the years while remaining one of the most ubiquitous toys in the world. There is a surprising and affecting additional discussion of Handler's further career, in which she used her knowledge of plastics to create an improved form of prosthetic breast after developing breast cancer.

Keywords: Barbie • Handler, Ruth • Toys

Walker, Sally M.

Frozen Secrets: Antarctica Revealed. Minneapolis, MN: Carolrhoda Books, 2010. 104p. ISBN 9781580136075. **M J**

Antarctica has long fascinated explorers. Because of the overwhelmingly difficult conditions found there, it required years, technological advances, and a phenomenal amount of international cooperation to first explore and then maintain a base on Earth's southernmost continent. The hardships endured in the past and by today's scientists are detailed in the text and well illustrated in both period and current photographs. Readers will find copious supplementary material, including a list of further resources.

Keywords: Antarctic explorations • Antarctica

Historical Biography: Ordinary People in Extraordinary Times

This subgenre provides a place for books about people caught up in extraordinary times. Their names may be recognizable for their own works and lives, or they might have become known primarily because of their presence at a place or event. In either case, these books provide a forum to highlight a historical event, time period, or subject, through research and detailed writing, rather than through the life story of a particular person. This differentiates these books from those in the section "Historical Biography" in chapter 4.

Bartoletti, Susan Campbell.

🎗 *They Called Themselves the K.K.K.: The Birth of an American Terrorist Organization.* Boston: Houghton Mifflin Books for Children, 2010. 172p. ISBN 9780618440337. **J H**

Here is a clear, compelling history of the origin and evolution of the Ku Klux Klan, which started at the end of the Civil War. A chapter on the ending of the war and the Reconstruction period and its immediate aftermath helps to set the stage for the initial meeting of the six men from Pulaski who, disillusioned by the turmoil and social changes inherent in freeing slaves, came up with the idea for the KKK. The text neatly balances the reforms instituted by the government and the actions of the Klan. The copious illustrations and use of period speech add to the authenticity. An epilogue discusses hate crimes and notes current activities, reflecting that although there are a considerable number of hate groups in the United States today, they do not have "the power or the prestige" that the KKK did. **ALA**

Keywords: KKK • Ku Klux Klan • Reconstruction

Bausum, Ann.

Marching to the Mountaintop: How Poverty, Labor Fights, and Civil Rights Set the Stage for Martin Luther King, Jr.'s Final Hours. Washington, DC: National Geographic, 2012. 112p. ISBN 9781426309397. **M J**

Martin Luther King Jr.'s final speech, delivered in Memphis on April 3, 1968, is still remembered for the passion with which he delivered it. What is not nearly as well known is that the group to whom he was speaking was composed of the city's striking sanitation workers, girding themselves for a peaceful march intended to advocate a settlement of their eight-week strike. Less than a day later, James Earl Ray assassinated Dr. King. Readers will find a thoughtful, well-laid out and illustrated presentation of the conditions and mitigating factors that led the garbage men to strike as well as the major incidents that occurred during the walkout. This includes marches involving some of the first uses of mace by law enforcement officials against U.S. citizens. Supplementary information in this gripping narrative includes a thorough timeline of the strike, information about eight of Dr. King's campaigns, and numerous photographs. Bausum's portrait of the times and strike in Memphis introduce Dr. Martin Luther King Jr. and his influence to readers unfamiliar with the man, his work, and his words.

Keywords: King, Dr. Martin Luther Jr. • Labor movement • Memphis • Ray, James Earl

Magoon, Kekla.

Today the World Is Watching You: The Little Rock Nine and the Fight for School Integration, 1957. Civil Rights Struggles Around the World. Minneapolis, MN: Twenty-First Century Books, 2011. 160p. ISBN 9780761357674. **J H**

Kekla Magoon presents not only an account of the difficulties undergone by the nine teenagers while the NAACP, politicians, and segregationists in the community around them fought over their right to attend Central High in Little Rock, but also an overview of slavery up to the time that the laws were changed and the standoff between the segregationists and the civil rights activists took place. The violence resulting from a mob determined to keep the black students out of the school on September 23, 1957, required presidential intervention and an escort by members of the 101st Airborne for the Little Rock Nine to safely integrate the school, although the students continued to suffer indignities from their fellow students.

Keywords: Civil rights • Little Rock • School integration • Segregation

Murphy, Jim.

Truce: The Day the Soldiers Stopped Fighting. New York: Scholastic, 2009. 116p. ISBN 978054513049. **M J**

Jim Murphy starts his story with an introduction to the causes of World War I as well as an explanation of trench warfare, to help readers understand what both Allied and Axis soldiers were facing at Christmastime in 1914, when a very unusual event took place. After readers have that background, he uses photographs, diaries, and soldiers' recollections to portray the Christmas armistice of 1914, in which lower-ranking soldiers on both sides of the Western Front trenches laid down their arms. In some places the two sides mixed, occasionally even exchanging gifts. Though the truce did not last, Murphy uses the last portion of the book to examine the idea that war need not be inevitable. **ALA, BBYA**

Keywords: Armistices • World War I

O'Brien, Anne Sibley, and Perry Edmond O'Brien.

After Gandhi: One Hundred Years of Nonviolent Resistance. Illustrated by Anne Sibley O'Brien. Watertown, MA: Charlesbridge, 2009. 181p. ISBN 9781580891295. **M J**

In the 100 years since Mohandas Gandhi first led the people of India in nonviolent protests, many others have followed. The mother and son team of Anne Sibley O'Brien and Perry Edmond O'Brien, both proponents of nonviolent resistance, present here a chronological succession of sixteen examples, starting in 1908 with Gandhi and spanning the globe. The examples chosen are meant to show his legacy and demonstrate the courage behind the choices of the resistors, whether it was a smaller action in a large struggle, such as Rosa Parks's refusal to give up her seat on the bus, or Nelson Mandela's refusal to run when ordered to do so by the guards on the way into the jail where he would spend the next twenty-seven years, or a much larger action, such as those undertaken by Cesar Chavez in organizing larger and larger groups of workers to strike, march, and boycott, finally undertaking a twenty-five-day hunger strike himself to convince the grape growers to sign a contract with the farm workers' union. **IRA**

Keywords: Gandhi, Mohandas • Labor movement • Nonviolence • Passive resistance

Partridge, Elizabeth.

🎗 *Marching for Freedom: Walk Together, Children, and Don't You Grow Weary.* New York: Viking, 2009. 72p. ISBN 9780670011896. **M** **J**

Books about civil rights are not uncommon; what makes this book stand out is its focus on the children and teens who were among the protestors and marchers on Bloody Sunday and the march from Selma to Montgomery in 1965. Partridge both catches readers' attention and alerts them to the danger of the times with the first sentence: "The first time Joanne Blackmon was arrested she was just ten years old." This well-written and illustrated volume reinforces to teens that they can make a difference by emphasizing the power these youths exerted in the struggle. This title was awarded the Boston Globe Horn Book Award for nonfiction and the Los Angeles Times Book Prize for Young Adult Literature. **ALA, BBYA**

Keywords: African Americans • Civil rights • Race relations • Selma to Montgomery Rights March

Walker, Sally M.

🎗 *Blizzard of Glass: The Halifax Explosion of 1917.* New York: Henry Holt & Company Books for Young Readers, 2011. 160p. ISBN 9780805089455. **M** **J**

The man-made explosion in Halifax Harbour on the morning of December 6, 1917, caused when a medical supply ship collided with a munitions ship carrying several different kinds of explosives, was the largest of its kind until Hiroshima. The resulting devastation flattened Halifax and Dartmouth. Walker puts a human face on the disaster, which was compounded by a blizzard that blew in almost immediately after the blast. Readers are introduced to many of the denizens of the area and follow the grisly and protracted efforts that were necessary to identify the dead and provide succor to the living. An accounting of the relief provided by other governments and cities continues to link the area to Boston and imparts a welcome reminder of the warmth of human generosity, even in the midst of war. **ALA**

Keywords: Explosion • Halifax Harbour

Warren, Andrea.

Under Siege! Three Children at the Civil War Battle for Vicksburg. New York: Farrar, Straus and Giroux/Melanie Kroupa Books, 2009. 166p. ISBN 9780374312558. **M** **J**

The Battle of Vicksburg was important in the Civil War because of the city's position on the banks of the Mississippi River. If the Union Army managed to take Vicksburg, it would have control over the Mississippi and be able to split the Confederacy in half. The story of how the Union Army laid siege to the city—a siege that lasted for forty-seven days and drove the 5,000 townspeople underground—is told through the eyes of three children:

Lucy McRae, the ten-year-old daughter of an affluent Vicksburg merchant; Willie Lord, the eleven-year-old son of an Episcopal minister; and twelve-year-old Frederick Grant, son of the famous Union General Ulysses S. Grant. Readers are also shown photographs and other primary source materials and are updated about the lives of many of the people they have read about.

Keywords: Children in war • Civil War • Vicksburg

Ideas of History

This section examines books in which the main subject is an idea important to history that at the same time cannot be defined as belonging to one specific period. Technology in Ancient Cultures draws parallels between modern and ancient technologies in areas including medicine and construction.

Albee, Sarah.

Poop Happened! A History of the World from the Bottom Up. Illustrated by Robert Leighton. New York: Walker, 2010. 170p. ISBN 9780802798251. **M J RR**

While students have been given pictures of historical events in books and videos, they have been given a sanitized version of the situations in which people lived. This entertaining account of the history of plumbing from prehistoric times to the modern day not only introduces readers to what it would have been like to live in a time and place without indoor toilets, but also provides a wide-ranging discussion of social distinctions, the evolution of waste disposal, and disease. The book's many illustrations and sidebars will keep reluctant readers interested.

Keywords: Plumbing • Toilets

Bausum, Ann.

Unraveling Freedom: The Battle for Democracy on the Home Front During World War I. Washington, DC: National Geographic, 2010. 88p. ISBN 9781426307027. **M J**

The sinking of the *Lusitania* by a German U-boat in 1915 was an act of wartime aggression that was the start of an increasing level of anti-German sentiment in the United States, which served as a major impetus for the United States to enter World War I. Bausum recounts the erosion of personal freedoms for German citizens in the United States, as well as other changes that were made as Americans expressed their displeasure with all things German during the war years, even though nearly 25 percent of the country's population had an ethnic link to Germany or Austria. A graphic foreword provided by Ted Rall notes similarities to other wartime situations. Additional resources include a guide to wartime presidents, from the Quasi War to the Afghanistan and Iraq Wars, that records the dates of the wars and explains the particular "unraveling" situation each president faced. A timeline for the main body of the text is also included.

Keywords: German American • Personal freedoms • Race relations • World War I

Blumenthal, Karen.

🎗 *Bootleg: Murder, Moonshine, and the Lawless Years of Prohibition.* New York: Flash Point/Roaring Brook Press, 2011. 154p. ISBN 9781596434493. **J H**

In 1920, after years of concerted effort, legislators in the U.S. Congress passed the Eighteenth Amendment, prohibiting the sale and manufacture of alcohol in the United States. People certain that a "dry" future would bring with it a healthier, more prosperous country, along with a certain decrease in crime, were doomed to be disappointed. Blumenthal's text details the fight to implement Prohibition, along with the nine years that it was in place and the ways that people circumvented it. These ranged from home stills to prescriptions for alcohol. Biographical information on the gangster Al Capone is included. The culminating horror of the Valentine's Day massacre in 1929, which swayed public opinion toward repealing the amendment, frames the story and gives readers a chance to ponder what might have been done differently, which leads into a note on parts of the country that chose not to repeal the amendment until much later in the twentieth century. **ALA**

Keywords: Capone, Al • Eighteenth Amendment • Prohibition • Temperance

Gann, Marjorie, and Janet Willen.

Five Thousand Years of Slavery. Toronto: Tundra Books, 2011. 168p. ISBN 9781897187562. **J H**

This broad-ranging history examines slavery over thousands of years and several continents. The book starts by looking at practices in ancient Egypt, Greece, and Rome, moves into the classical era in Europe and the Middle East, and then covers South America and the Caribbean. The authors then segue to North America before looking at Asia and concluding with a chapter that will allow readers to contemplate current dilemmas. The authors have created a Web site for their lengthy list of source materials. The historical presentation that this book provides allows readers to come to their own conclusions about the material and would be useful for classroom discussions. It is an informative and interesting volume.

Keywords: Slavery • Slaves

Technology in Ancient Cultures.

This series shows that many of today's common forms of technology, a term that readers will learn is actually derived from the Greek words meaning "art" and "craft," have their roots in ancient times. Individual volumes exploring construction; medicine; transportation; and machine technologies such as the wedge, bow, and press, show how these have been used and adapted over time. In each volume readers will be able to see the technologies' modern-day counterparts, demonstrating that although wheeled vehicles have changed significantly from early wagons, building materials have remained relatively constant.

Woods, Michael, and Mary B. Woods.

Ancient Construction Technology: From Pyramids to Fortresses. Minneapolis, MN: Twentieth Century Books, 2011. 96p. ISBN 9780761365273. **M** **J**

> **Keywords:** Ancient Egypt • Antiquities • Building • Construction techniques

Ancient Machine Technology: From Wheels to Forges. Minneapolis, MN: Twentieth Century Books, 2011. 96p. ISBN 9780761365235. **M** **J**

> **Keywords:** Machines • Tools • Wedges • Wheels

Ancient Medical Technology: From Herbs to Scalpels. Minneapolis, MN: Twentieth Century Books, 2011. 96p. ISBN 9780761365228. **M** **J**

> **Keywords:** Archaeology • Medical innovations • Medicine

Ancient Transportation Technology: From Oars to Elephants. Minneapolis, MN: Twentieth Century Books, 2011. 96p. ISBN 9780761365273. **M** **J**

> **Keywords:** Hunter-gatherers • Transportation • Travel

New Perspectives

History is not set in stone. Over time, new discoveries make it necessary to revisit how we interpret the past. This can happen for any number of reasons, including changes in law and cultural mores, new evidence, and technological and scientific advancements. Readers will find discussions about personal freedoms and how society's views have changed over time in Linus Alsenas's *Gay America: Struggle for Equality,* and stunning new views of Stonehenge and its purpose in Marc Aronson's *If Stones Could Speak: Unlocking the Secrets of Stonehenge.* These books provide new and often enlightening takes on historical subjects.

Alsenas, Linas.

Gay America: Struggle for Equality. New York: Amulet Books, 2008. 160p. ISBN 9780810994874. **J** **H** **A/YA**

> *Gay America: Struggle for Equality* gives readers a historical overview of homosexuality in American society. It starts with the 1893 murder of Freda Ward by her teenaged lover, moves on to American Indian "berdaches," then progresses essentially by decade, including Alfred Kinsey, Walt Whitman, a discussion of the Freudians, AIDS, Matthew Shepherd, and the push for civil rights for gays, finishing with the legalization of gay marriage in Massachusetts.
>
> **Keywords:** AIDS • Homosexuality • Kinsey, Alfred C.

Aronson, Marc.

If Stones Could Speak: Unlocking the Secrets of Stonehenge. Washington, DC: National Geographic, 2010. 64p. ISBN 9781426306006. **M** **J**

People have been visiting Stonehenge for thousands of years to try to determine the purpose of the immense and incredibly fascinating circle of stones. New technologies developed in the past 100 years have allowed successive generations of archaeologists to come up with new theories. Marc Aronson shows readers how Mike Parker Pearson and the Riverside Project's ongoing work have made some stunning discoveries that are radically different from the previously accepted view of Stonehenge as a temple. This fascinating, highly illustrated book demonstrates that our knowledge of the past will continue to evolve.

Keywords: Archaeology • Stonehenge

Cline, Eric H., and Jill Rubalcaba.

Digging for Troy: From Homer to Hisarlik. Illustrations by Sarah S. Brannen. Watertown, MA: Charlesbridge, 2011. 78p. ISBN 9781580893268. **J H**

The siege of Troy, a battle between the Trojans and the Greeks, started over an apple and was first recounted in Homer's *Iliad*; the question has long been whether this was a legend or a recounting of a historical event. The authors here provide a retelling of the tale, followed by the true tales of several people who, determined to find the actual site where it took place, looked for it over 100 years. It starts with Heinrich Schliemann, whose motivation was more to establish his own place in history and who was hampered by lack of any background in archaeology, then covers the technological advancements that aided the scholars who succeeded him with increasing knowledge of history and process, and finishes with Manfred Korfmann, whose use of a magnetometer found a very "Homeric picture" at the site.

Keywords: Archaeology • Hisarlik • Homer • Korfmann, Manfred • Schliemann, Heinrich • Troy

Consider Starting with . . .

Aronson, Marc, and Marina Budhos. *Sugar Changed the World: A Story of Magic, Spice, Slavery and Freedom.*

Bartoletti, Susan Campbell. *They Called Themselves the K.K.K.: The Birth of an American Terrorist Organization.*

Bausum, Ann. *Denied, Detained, Deported: Stories from the Dark Side of American Immigration.*

Butzer, C. M. *Gettysburg: The Graphic Novel.*

Jurmain, Suzanne. *The Secret of the Yellow Death: A True Story of Medical Sleuthing.*

Metselaar, Menno, and Ruud van der Rol. *Anne Frank: Her Life in Words and Pictures (from the Archives of the Anne Frank House).*

Partridge, Elizabeth. *Marching for Freedom: Walk Together, Children, and Don't You Grow Weary.*

Thomson, Ruth. *Terezin: Voices from the Holocaust.*

Walker, Sally M. *Blizzard of Glass: The Halifax Explosion of 1917.*

Fiction Read-Alikes

- **Boyne, John.** *The Boy in the Striped Pajamas.* Bruno's loneliness after his family moves from their home in Berlin to a place called "Out-With" in 1942 due to his father's new job leads him to befriend a boy behind the wire fence in an area he knows is off limits. All Bruno knows is that his father is in charge of the soldiers, and that he is alone. In his ignorance, his feelings of isolation lead him to burrow under the fence.

- **Kent, Trilby.** *Stones for My Father.* Twelve-year-old Corlie Roux has never been loved by their mother the way that her brothers are, but since her father died fighting the British in the Boer War, she has become the focus for even more of her mother's anger. When the Roux family find themselves driven into the bush and in hiding with the *laager*, families hiding in the woods, Corlie receives help from an unexpected source, a Canadian soldier. Corlie's resourcefulness and determination may not be her only allies when the *laager* are captured. This Notable title provides a masterful portrait of life during the Boer War, before the country became South Africa.

- **Little, Melanie.** *The Apprentice's Masterpiece.* This verse novel revolves around fifteen-year-old Ramon, a *converso*, or converted Jew, and Amir, a Muslim slave forced to give up his religion who has been taken in by Ramon's family. It takes place during the Spanish Inquisition and is rife with historical detail. It shows how the boys, who start out jealous and unsure of each other, end up dependent on one another for their survival. This title was an honor book for the Canadian Library Association YA Book of the Year Award.

- **Peet, Mal.** *Tamar: A Novel of Espionage, Passion and Betrayal.* This Carnegie Medal–winning novel presents the three things named in its title. A young girl researches her family and discovers some stunning secrets along with the parallel story of her grandfather's history as an operative in the Dutch resistance in Nazi-occupied Holland.

- **Phelan, Matt.** *The Storm in the Barn.* Readers are shown a very bleak place indeed, as eleven-year-old Jack faces the Dust Bowl in Kansas in 1937, not having seen rain since he was seven. When Jack sees a shadowy figure in the barn, he chalks it up to "dust dementia," until a confrontation lets him figure out what happened to the rain. This title was the winner of the 2010 Scott O'Dell Award for Historical Fiction and an ALA Notable Book.

- **Pignat, Caroline.** *Greener Grass* and *Wild Geese.* Readers can follow Kathleen "Kit" O'Byrne as she and her family deal with the difficulties of the Irish potato famine, in this Governor General's award-winning novel and its sequel. Kit faces a plethora of problems, from evolving into the sole support for her family to finding herself needing to emigrate to Canada to avoid a murder charge and facing the losses brought about by the fever.

- **Turnbull, Ann**. *No Shame, No Fear* and *Forged in the Fire.* Follow two young Quakers during a period when it was treasonous for the Quakers to meet. Will and Susanna's love story plays out against the wishes of their families and the persecution faced by the Quakers. *Forged in the Fire* occurs during the Great Plague and the Great Fire of London.

- **Sheth, Kashmira**. *Keeping Corner.* Based on a family story, this title introduces readers to India in the early twentieth century. Leela is engaged at age two, married at nine, and preparing to move to her husband's house when she is widowed at the age of twelve. Her life will never be the same: by custom, she will have to keep corner and stay apart from everyone for the next year, and she will never be allowed to marry again. Her only hope of regaining any sort of normal life rests with her brother and a female tutor, who have begun to follow Mahatma Gandhi.

- **Skrypuch, Marsha Forchuk.** *Daughter of War.* In Turkey during World War I, Armenian teens Marta and Kevork survive the deportation and genocide of their people, meet and fall in love in a city orphanage, and, after being wrenched apart, overcome enormous odds to find each other.

Chapter 6

Science, Math, and the Environment

Definition

As mentioned in the first volume of *Reality Rules*, one definition of *science* has remained relatively constant since 1775, as found in the *Oxford English Dictionary*: "a branch of study concerned with demonstrated truths, backed up by classified observations, with the possibility for the gathering of new truths." Modern usage separates pure mathematics from the natural sciences, while maintaining several large subdivisions: physical sciences, earth sciences, medicine, engineering, biology, and social sciences. Science nonfiction, then, focuses on literature with scientific themes. Readers are given a wide range of materials from which to choose, including reflective explanations of the natural world, as well as fascinating works about endangered species and the scientists and researchers who struggle to gain new knowledge about those species.

Appeal

Science and math writing provides answers to Earth's many mysteries. It appeals to the reader's curiosity or "need to know." Readers interested in these unknowns, or who have questions about how we got here and what might be happening in the world around us, are in the right place to find books to satisfy their curiosity. Joy Hakim introduces readers to complex scientific discoveries as well as important scientists in *The Story of Science: Einstein Adds a New Dimension*. Books on archaeology and paleontology give readers a chance to learn from the past; environmental books help prepare us for the future. Readers interested in how things work can find out about everything from bicycles to rockets.

Chapter Organization

The chapter starts off with the section "Science Adventures," which includes fast-paced stories about the people, discoveries, and scientific research in progress around the planet. This is followed by longer, more detailed works in "History of Science." Scientists learn an immense amount about the planet and its denizens from studying remains. The section "Digging into the Past" includes the subsections "Archaeology" and "Paleontology." Titles in "How Things Work" investigate a variety of subjects in two subsections: "General," which covers introductory science, and "Transportation," which provides information for car lovers and future engineers.

Subject-specific sections follow. "Micro-science" provides a closer look at specific topics, such as food and the elements. "Environmental Writing" contains the subsections "Ecology and Conservation" and "Animals." The environment has remained a popular topic in the media and in publishing.

Science Adventures

These books focus on the exciting stories of people, discoveries, research, and technological achievements that herald advances in our scientific knowledge. They are descriptive and frequently fast-paced, providing information about efforts undertaken around the world to gain knowledge as well as following the work of scientists endeavoring to ensure the survival of the planet and its denizens, several examples of which may be found in the Scientists in the Field series. These books, which provide a close up look at a scientist's efforts working on behalf of a specific endangered species, also give readers a greater understanding of the scientific method and what scientists do in their daily lives. More titles in this vein, but with the focus on the animal instead of the scientist, may be found in the subsection "Animals." An increasing trend in publishing since *Marley and Me* has been books about an author's relationship with an animal or animals and reflections on how this relationship has changed the author's life. Readers who enjoy titles in this section may also be interested in the action stories and fast reads found in chapter 1.

Burns, Loree Griffin.

The Hive Detectives: Chronicle of a Honey Bee Catastrophe. Scientists in the Field. Illustrated by Ellen Harasimowicz. Boston: Houghton Mifflin Harcourt, 2010. 66p. ISBN 9780547152318. 🅜 🅙

This title in the Scientists in the Field series starts out by introducing readers to Mary Duane, a hobbyist beekeeper, as she inspects a beehive, giving readers an understanding of both the complex system that is a hive as well as the care necessary to maintain it. When the book then jumps to Dave Hackenburg, whose livelihood depends on the 3,000 hives he keeps, it is much easier to understand his dismay and the magnitude of the disaster for both him and the bees and the larger ecosystem when Dave discovers that 400 of his hives—containing twenty million bees—are empty. The bees had vanished. Solving the mystery of what has come to be called colony collapse disorder (CCD) was assigned to four scientists. Readers are introduced to the scientists in notebook-styled pages that name their specialties and follow them through research that includes bee collecting; autopsies; and much pondering over pests, viruses, pesticides, and bee nutrition. Ellen Harasimowicz's photographs show both the scientists and their subjects through all stages of the research. Unlike earlier volumes in the series, a definitive solution to the problem at hand is not provided; readers will enjoy finding out about the research and the progress that has been made and are given a number of references for finding more information.

Keywords: Bees • Colony collapse disorder • Environment • Hackenberg, Dave • Pesticides • Scientific research

Flaim, Denise.

Rescue Ink: How Ten Guys Saved Countless Dogs and Cats, Twelve Horses, Five Pigs, One Duck, and a Few Turtles. New York: Viking, 2009. 244p. ISBN 9780670021161. **H**

At first glance, the tattooed, brawny men on the cover of the book would seem to be the sort who scare small children, until you note the defenseless puppies and kittens being held tenderly in their arms. Indeed, the motto of Batso, Big Ant, Johnny O, G, and the others is "Abusers are losers." The members of the group work to educate abusive owners or convince them to release the animals to homes where the animals will receive better care: Animal lovers will find this book a compulsive read.

Keywords: Animal rescue • Animals

Halls, Kelly Milner, and Major William Sumner.

Saving the Baghdad Zoo: A True Story of Hope and Heroes. New York: Greenwillow Books, 2009. 63p. ISBN 9780061772023. **M J**

As an archaeologist, U.S. Army Captain William Sumner was expecting to work in Iraq on the restitution of the country's cultural heritage. While he did save some of Baghdad's most precious resources, none were anything like the treasures he had originally studied. In April 2003 the war had left the city of Baghdad, including a zoo housing many animals, in ruins. Captain Sumner and a team of dedicated volunteers worked to save a variety of animals, including bears, pelicans, Arabian horses, lions, and tigers.

Keywords: Animals • Arabians • Baghdad zoo • Bears • Conservation • Lions

Jackson, Donna.

Extreme Scientists: Exploring Nature's Mysteries from Perilous Places. Scientists in the Field. Boston: Houghton Mifflin Books for Children, 2009. 63p. ISBN 9780618777068. **M J**

This volume in the Scientists in the Field series stands out from the rest of the series in that, rather than looking at scientists who focus their work on an endangered animal or an animal facing a specific threat, it covers three scientists whose field work places them in particularly adventurous conditions. The first profiled is meteorologist Paul Flaherty, whose work as a hurricane hunter for the National Oceanic and Atmospheric Administration (NOAA) requires him to fly his plane straight into the eyes of hurricanes on a regular basis. The next chapter is about "Cave Woman" Hazel Barton, a microbiologist looking for "extremophile" microbes in glacial caves far under ground and under water all around the world. The last scientist profiled is "Skywalker" Stephen Sillett, an ecologist who studies the organisms that live at the in treetops – notably at the tops of the world's oldest trees – and who has uncovered a whole new ecosystem. This book will introduce readers to new discoveries in science, as well as showing them devoted scientists and the results of their work. Additional supplements include photographs, which show these scientists in their unusual milieus, as well as a glossary and source notes.

Keywords: Ecologists • Extremophiles • Meteorologists • Microbiologists • Scientific discoveries • Scientists

Lourie, Peter.

Whaling Season: A Year in the Life of an Arctic Whale Scientist. Scientists in the Field. Boston: Houghton Mifflin Harcourt, 2009. 80p. ISBN 9780618777099. **M** **J**

Travel to Barrow, Alaska, with biologist John Craighead George as he studies bowhead whales and local whaling practices. Craig, as he is known, has been a researcher for years, and he takes readers with him as he accompanies the Inupiaq. While being given an up-close view of both the whaling and scientific research, readers learn that their cultural practices have not adversely affected bowhead numbers.

Keywords: Bowhead whales • Inupiaq • Whaling

Now Try: Readers interested in whaling, whales, and the work being done on their behalf will want to check out an earlier entry in the Scientists in the Field series. Fran Hodgkins's *The Whale Scientists: Solving the Mystery of Whale Strandings* starts with a description of the whale's evolution from a land mammal to a sea one and then examines various reasons why whales do something that can cause their own destruction, looking at cases of whale strandings. The book also discusses the various damaging ways that humanity has affected whale populations.

Montgomery, Sy.

Kakapo Rescue: Saving the World's Strangest Parrot. Scientists in the Field. Photographs by Nic Bishop. Boston: Houghton Mifflin Books for Children, 2010. 74p. ISBN 9780618494170. **M** **J** **H**

This appealing volume provides an introduction to a phenomenally intriguing animal, the honey-scented, flightless kakapo parrot, whose numbers have dwindled to less than 100, through a series of consequences explained by Sy Montgomery in a volume guaranteed to have readers turning pages, if not turning into outright conservationists. The birds, which are now under the constant watchful eye of New Zealand's Kakapo Recovery Team, live on a remote island where the scientists can monitor them; provide and watch over their food; protect them from predators and germs; and do their best to keep track of every possible threat to them, their eggs, and their chicks. Because they are so rare, each sighting of these endangered birds is a gift to the volunteers who work to save them. The sharing of their work with the author and photographer, who waited five years to see the birds, is an extension of this worthy endeavor. **ALA, Sibert**

Keywords: Conservation • Endangered animals • Kakapo parrots • Kakapo Recovery Team • New Zealand

Saving the Ghost of the Mountain: An Expedition among Snow Leopards in Mongolia. Photographs by Nic Bishop. <u>Scientists in the Field</u>. Boston: Houghton Mifflin Books for Children, 2009. 74p. ISBN 9780618916450. **M J**

The intriguing aspect of this introduction to the snow leopard, an elusive and endangered animal found in extreme habitats largely in Asia, is that it was written without the scientists ever actually sighting one of the animals. Sy Montgomery and photographer Nic Bishop, who accompanied Tom McCarthy, the director of the Seattle-based Snow Leopard Trust, introduce readers to McCarthy, Mongolia, and the animals he has been working to save for most of his career. Sidebars provide cultural and historical information about Mongolia, supported in the text by information about the people, how they live, and the trust they have developed, which makes it possible for them to work together to revive and support the snow leopard population. A final chapter gives information about the Snow Leopard Trust and working in the field.

Keywords: Conservation • Snow leopards

Turner, Pamela S.

A Life in the Wild: George Schaller's Struggle to Save the Last Great Beasts. New York: Farrar, Straus and Giroux/Melanie Kroupa Books, 2008. 58p. ISBN 9780374345785. **M J**

Readers are introduced to George Schaller, a world-renowned biologist and conservationist, who has lived all over the world in order to better understand and learn about endangered animals. When the Schallers moved to the United States from Germany, the young George chose to bring his collection of bird eggs. Later, after studying biology, he traveled the world to count, observe, and photograph animals in the wild. His field research has taken him to some of the most beautiful and remote places in the world and is illustrated here with maps and photographs of Schaller studying gorillas, tigers, lions, snow leopards, pandas, and antelopes. This title was the 2009 winner of the Golden Kite Award for nonfiction.

Keywords: Animal conservation • Biologist • Endangered animals • Schaller, George

The Frog Scientist. Illustrated by Andy Comins. <u>Scientists in the Field</u>. Boston: Houghton Mifflin Books for Children, 2009. 58p. ISBN 9780618717163. **M** **J**

This award-winning volume in the <u>Scientists in the Field</u> series opens with biologist Tyrone Hayes and his team collecting frogs at a pond in Wyoming. Readers are then given information about Hayes's background, depicting a young man who has always loved science in general and frogs in particular. In looking at his research, readers follow along with the team as they try to see if by studying the effects of a pesticide called atrazine on leopard frogs from a particular pond they can tell if it will help them figure out why amphibian populations are declining worldwide. **ALA, OP**

Keywords: Atrazine • Frogs • Hayes, Tyrone • Scientists

Project Seahorse. Photographs by Scott Tuason. <u>Scientists in the Field</u>. Boston: Houghton Mifflin Books for Children, 2010. 58p. ISBN 9780547207131. **M** **J**

This book makes scientific enquiry approachable and environmentalism understandable and relatable, without being at all didactic. It shows the dangers faced by the various species of seahorses living in tropical waters due to factors including overfishing and then shows how scientists, working with local fishermen, were able to create a Marine Protected Area (MPA) and study its effectiveness in helping to revive the seahorse population. There are now thirty-three MPAs along the Philippines' Danajong Bank, an indication that there is a continuing commitment among the local population to protect and nurture these creatures. Readers will also find a list of further resources.

Keywords: Blast fishing • Marine Protected Area • Philippines • Seahorses

History of Science

These books provide a combination of narrative and a wealth of details that makes them appealing to fans of both history and pure science. The authors in this section are able to provide a leisurely, enjoyable reading experience that incorporates and explains complex theories with information about the scientists and their times.

Boese, Alex.

Elephants on Acid: And Other Bizarre Experiments. Orlando, FL: Harcourt, 2007. 207p. ISBN 9780156031356. **H**

A background with the weird and the absurd as the creator of www.museumofhoaxes.com, combined with his master's degree in the history of science, makes Alex Boase just the person to present this compendium of often outrageous, but at the same time completely serious, scientific experiments. Readers are given not only an explanation of the experiments but also the reasoning behind them, including what the scientist hoped to learn and reactions from the scientific community.

Keywords: Experiments • History of science • Science experiments

Bryson, Bill.

A Really Short History of Nearly Everything. New York: Delacorte Press, 2008. 169p. ISBN 978038573810. **M** **J**

> This abridged, adapted edition of Bryson's *Short History of Nearly Everything* takes readers on a tour through the important events in the history of science to illustrate how scientific discoveries were made, who made them, and how they are "amazing and interesting." Starting with the big bang and moving all the way to the potential for global warming, readers will find this an entertaining foray into, well, nearly everything.
>
> **Keywords:** Biology • Cosmology • Fossils • History of science

Hakim, Joy.

The Story of Science: Einstein Adds a New Dimension. Washington, DC; New York: Smithsonian Books, 2007. 468p. ISBN 9781588341624. **J** **H**

> In this well-illustrated book, Hakim introduces the real people who strove to understand and further scientific knowledge. Turning information about some of the greatest scientific minds and their discoveries into a readable, interesting text is no small task, yet readers will find this a comprehensible introduction to many complex and intriguing scientific mysteries, including probability and quantum mechanics.
>
> **Keywords:** Cosmology • Einstein, Alfred • History of science

Digging into the Past

In these books readers have the opportunity to explore the past through everything from remains to monuments. These books will also appeal to readers interested in history, scientific research, and forensics. The section is divided into two subsections, "Archaeology" and "Paleontology."

Archaeology

These titles address the recovery and study of human remains and artifacts. Readers will find titles that show the work done by archaeologists who have undertaken these recoveries and learned from discoveries, providing insight into humanity's development and what life was like in earlier times.

Deem, James M.

Bodies from the Ice: Melting Glaciers and the Recovery of the Past. Boston: Houghton Mifflin, 2008. 64p. ISBN 9780618800452. **M** **J**

> The discovery of a dead person by hikers in the Alps in 1991 may sound disconcerting, but it was not surprising to the locals, because several had already turned up that year. What differentiated this body, named Ötzi by scientists, was that radiocarbon dating showed he lived more than 5,300

years earlier and that his body was almost perfectly intact, which was extremely unusual for a body recovered from a glacier. Readers will learn about his mummification process as well as what scientists have learned from some other remarkable recoveries and what they are doing to preserve them as the glaciers melt. In addition to numerous photographs, there are lists of recommended reading, Web sites, and glaciers to visit.

Keywords: Glaciers • Ice mummies • Ötzi

Rubalcaba, Jill, and Peter Robertshaw.

Every Bone Tells a Story: Hominin Discoveries, Deductions, and Debates. Watertown, MA: Charlesbridge, 2010. 185p. ISBN 9781580891646. **J H**

This volume informs readers about the discovery, identification, and information gleaned from four hominins, ranging from the 1.6-million-year-old Turkana Boy to the 4,600-year-old Iceman. Each section includes a detailed account of the recovery and scientific breakthroughs made by the scientists. Readers will find out about the disagreements scientists have over evolutionary views and also learn how scientists' painstaking efforts in the field give them a picture of the existing vegetation, animal life, and evidence of human occupation. **AENYA Honor**

Keywords: Archaeology • Excavation • Fossil hominids • Ötzi • Prehistoric peoples

Now Try: Katherine Kirkpatrick presents a thorough, detailed examination of the legal battle over Kennewick Man, one of the earliest hominid discoveries made in North America, in *Mysterious Bones: The Story of the Kennewick Man*. A skull found along the Columbia River in 1996 was just the start of the mystery that is explained by Kirkpatrick, along with a discussion of the nine-year trial, examples of other migrations, and implications for future findings. Supplementary material includes a glossary and a timeline.

Sloan, Christopher.

Mummies. Washington, DC: National Geographic, 2010. 48p. ISBN 9781426306952. **M**

Mummies may actually be "the world's most valuable treasure," readers are told in Christopher Sloan's book. Studying mummies gives scientists a chance to learn stories about humans from thousands of years ago, whether they were dried, wrapped, frozen, tanned, or preserved in a number of other ways. The gory details about eleven different mummies and what they have taught scientists are recounted and illustrated here, along with notes about when and where they were discovered and which process was used in each mummification. Two supplemental items are a timeline for the mummies and a world map that notes where mummies have been found.

Keywords: Mummies • Mummification

Walker, Sally M.

Written in Bone: Buried Lives of Jamestown and Colonial Maryland. Minneapolis, MN: Carolrhoda Books, 2009. 144p. ISBN 9780822571353. **M J H**

This is the sort of book that is sure to inspire students to become archaeologists. Readers are shown archaeological investigations of human and material remains from seventeenth- and eighteenth-century Jamestown and colonial Maryland. The excavations encompass burial sites of colonists from various backgrounds, including a teenaged indentured servant hastily buried in a trash pit, a grouping of prominent colonists laid to rest in lead coffins, and a woman of African heritage who likely toiled as a slave. In one example anthropologists provided the anatomical details of a recovered skull to artists, who were then able to use the data to produce the first sculpture of an American colonist of African ancestry by determining the gender and age of the skeleton and making a determination about whether the skull was a person originating from Europe or Africa. Walker writes with assurance, knowledge, and passion, giving readers a detailed explanation of the various types of scientists and the immense amounts of work and care that are required to make this particularly complex form of research a success. **AENYA Honor, ALA, BBYA**

Keywords: Colonial Jamestown • Colonial Maryland • Forensic anthropology • Forensics

Paleontology

Books in this subgenre examine the recovery and identification of fossil evidence. Readers are given insight into what paleontologists do as well as information about dinosaurs and their time on Earth.

Judge, Lita.

Born to Be Giants: How Baby Dinosaurs Grew to Rule the World. New York: Flash Point/Roaring Brook Press, 2010. Unpaged. ISBN 9781596434431. **M**

This nonfiction picture book looks at dinosaurs in a novel way: every one of these ferocious creatures must have started as a tiny, defenceless creature! Lita Judge finds similar behaviors in dinosaurs and modern-day animals, such as nesting and hunting in packs like wolves. She also provides additional information about the eight kinds of dinosaurs mentioned in the book and shows a timeline from sinosauropteryx, the first feathered dinosaur, to early birds. Dinosaur fans will rejoice.

Keywords: Dinosaurs • Evolution • Picture-book nonfiction

Lambert, David.

Dinosaur. Eyewitness Books. New York: DK Publishing, 2010. 72p. ISBN 9780756658106. **M**

Readers interested in dinosaurs will find a lavishly illustrated introduction to their world, including the various geologic eras, as well as information about how they evolved, behaved, and looked, and how fossil hunters find and categorize them. Double-page spreads provide a brief amount of text and photographs that complement the text in a way that will appeal to reluctant readers and make this a useful resource for ESL students. In addition to a classification guide, this updated edition also includes a resources list of Web sites and suggested museums and dig sites.

Keywords: Dinosaurs • Fossils

National Geographic Kids Ultimate Dinopedia: Your Illustrated Reference to Every Dinosaur Ever Discovered. Illustrated by Franco Tempesta. Washington, DC: National Geographic, 2010. 272p. ISBN 9781426301643. **M**

This thorough look at dinosaurs starts with general information about them, their lives, and the process that turned them into fossils, proceeding to the mystery behind their extinction. Subsequent chapters feature double-page spreads for meat eaters and plant eaters and an extensive "dino dictionary" that tells readers how to pronounce many dinosaur names, along with entries that give readers a picture, the dinosaur's size, and notes about where and what kind of fossils have been found. Young readers interested in dinosaurs will find a plethora of information.

Keywords: Dinosaurs • Fossils

Thimmesh, Catherine.

Lucy Long Ago: Uncovering the Mystery of Where We Came From. Boston: Houghton Mifflin Harcourt, 2009. 63p. ISBN 9780547051994. **M J**

On the day in 1974 when Donald Johnson discovered some fossilized remains in Hadar, Ethiopia, he had no idea that they belonged to the earliest example yet found of a bipedal primate, which would eventually be dated at 3.2 million years old. The fact that the song "Lucy in the Sky with Diamonds" happened to be playing in the background explains the naming of the skeleton. Thimmesh looks at how the scientists asked and answered the questions raised by the skeleton, completely changing how science looks at the theory of evolution and providing a detailed look at the processes of paleoanthropology and a great reproduction of how Lucy would have looked.

Keywords: Ethiopia • Fossil hominids • Lucy (fossil hominid) • Paleoanthropology

How Things Work

The books in this section present information about the technology, experimentation, and hard work required to advance scientific knowledge. They serve as a reminder that attaining knowledge is time-consuming and part of a lengthy, rigorous process. Readers will also find books that can help them add to their own knowledge about science, math, and physics. This category is divided into two subsections, "General" and "Transportation."

General

The books here provide readers with explanations of topics in science, math, and physics. They cover scientific investigations, the inner workings of the human body, and various technologies. The section also contains books with a narrower scope for looking at research, inventions, and how the scientific method is being put to use than those works found in the section "History of Science."

Benson, Michael.

Beyond: A Solar System Voyage. New York: Abrams Books for Young Readers, 2009. 121p. ISBN 9780810983229. **M J**

Michael Benson takes readers on a journey through the solar system and shows them the information we have gleaned from space probes. It is a magnificent presentation, complete with double-page spreads of some great photographs from NASA, the European Space Agency, and the Japanese Aerospace Exploration Agency. The pictures include views of Saturn's North Pole and Mars. The book also provides insights into each planet and asteroids, as well as unique views of meteorites.

Keywords: Asteroids • Meteorites • Planets • Science

Now Try: Readers looking for a more informational overview of the various celestial bodies found in space without the accompanying photographs will be delighted with Dan Green's *Astronomy*. This small volume presents the planets, stars, comets, and other bodies in a chatty, first-person presentation. Simon Basher's cartoon-style illustrations add to the book's appeal for reluctant readers.

Green, Dan.

Human Body: A Book with Guts. Illustrations by Simon Basher. New York: Kingfisher, 2011. 128p. ISBN 9780753466285. **M**

This overview of the parts of the human body, from the "building blocks" of cells and DNA to the "team players" of white blood cells and glands, gives readers a short, basic, and understandable introduction to everything going on inside. Each entry includes some basic facts, such as how much blood is found in the average human, the lifespan of a platelet, and each part's function, as well as a cartoon-style illustration by Simon Basher.

Keywords: Bodily functions • Human body

Hosler, Jay.

Evolution: The Story of Life on Earth. Art by Kevin Cannon and Zander Cannon. New York: Hill and Wang, 2011. 152p. ISBN 9780809094769. **H GN**

The grand and fictional Glargalian Empire has been watching earth carefully for several reasons, most notably because King Floorsh and Bloort hope that a study of evolution could be applied to the disorder on their own planet. This fun and thorough graphic novel recap covers the history of life on Earth and serves as a thorough primer on the notable scientists who discovered its concepts, from Darwin to Mendel.

Keywords: Adaptation • Evolution • Graphic nonfiction • Natural selection

Now Try: Readers looking for a more standard explanation of the theory of evolution may enjoy Daniel Loxton and Jim W. W. Smith's *Evolution: How We and*

All Living Things Came to Be. This presentation, which is a useful supplemental discussion of evolution, focuses largely on human evolution by answering common questions, and was the winner of the 2010 Lane Anderson Award, a nominee for the Silver Birch award, and a finalist for the Norma Fleck award.

Murphy, Glenn.

Inventions. New York: Simon & Schuster Books for Young Readers, 2009. 64p. ISBN 9781416938651. **M**

Inventions differ from discoveries in that they are the fruit of hard labor and a completely new product, rather than the uncovering of something that existed previously. This volume presents the reader with twenty-four inventions that changed people's lives, from the wheel to the printing press to the Internet. Each page is illustrated with computer graphics and given a timeline.

Keywords: Inventions

Nitta, Hideo.

The Manga Guide to Physics. Illustrated by Keita Takatsu. San Francisco, CA: No Starch Press; Tokyo: Ohmsha, c2009. 248p. ISBN 9781593271961. **H** **GN**

High school student Megumi may be an all-star athlete, but when she starts thinking about the question she got wrong on the physics test, which had to do with tennis, she can't keep her head in the game and loses her tennis match. Luckily for her, she is able to ask Nonomura-Kun, a medalist in the International Physics Olympics, to become her tutor. With his tutoring, she is able to learn about the three laws of motion—vectors, momentum, and energy—all with practical examples that she can use in her own game. Readers will be able to use this guide as a review of their own studies.

Keywords: Graphic nonfiction • Momentum • Physics • Vectors

O'Meara, Stephen James.

Are You Afraid Yet? The Science Behind Scary Stuff. Toronto: Kids Can Press, 2009. 78p. ISBN 97815545329409. **M** **J** **RR**

Scientist Stephen James O'Meara looks at what makes our skin crawl, asking what exactly induces the fight or flight response in the amygdala, the "terror alarm of the brain." Readers are then given examples that they will find intriguing and creepy, such as examining consciousness following beheadings, alien abductions, and out-of-body experiences. **QP**

Keywords: Curiosities • Ghosts • Science • Werewolves

Swanson, Diane.

Nibbling on Einstein's Brain: The Good, the Bad & the Bogus in Science. Illustrated by Francis Blake. Toronto: Annick Press, 2009. 151p. ISBN 9781554511877. **M** **J**

Diane Swanson demonstrates to readers the importance of quality research with plentiful examples of outright bad science and frauds, misrepresentations in the media, and misunderstandings by the public. This shows readers how shadow science can be "worse than misleading: it can be outright harmful." This fascinating look at poor science is used to show students quality research methods and what they should be doing in terms of challenging, analyzing, and questioning science. As a part of this very colorful volume, readers are given twenty-one Baloney Busters that offer ways to challenge research and apply critical thinking.

Keywords: Critical thinking • Frauds in science • Research methodology • Scientific research

Takahashi, Shin.

The Manga Guide to Statistics. San Francisco, CA: No Starch Press, 2009. 215p. ISBN 9781593271893. **H** **GN**

This nonfiction title is framed within a fictional story. When Rui develops a crush on her father's business associate, she comes up with a clever plan to impress him: convince her father to have him tutor her in statistics. Unfortunately, the tutor her father hires is Mr. Yamamoto, a bespectacled ubergeek, who nevertheless manages to teach her how to calculate means, determine probabilities, and graph data using practical examples. This manga guide is supplemented by exercises to reinforce the textual lessons and will be appreciated not only by anyone having difficulty understanding statistics but also by readers who will enjoy Rui's initial consternation and eventual appreciation when Yamamoto finally loses his Clark Kent glasses and reveals a Superman-like appeal.

Keywords: Graphic nonfiction • Mathematics • Statistics

Walker, Richard.

Human Body Q&A. London; New York: DK, 2010. 61p. ISBN 9780756657529. **M** **J**

This is a book for either a student looking for an answer about a particular physiological question or a reader who is simply intrigued by the body and how it works. As in all of Dorling Kindersley's books, the layout features ample color illustrations, and the text is broken into small, informative chunks. The book is broken down into five sections: body parts, fueling the body, brainpower, pumping blood, and life story. Readers looking to find a particular body part should start with the index.

Keywords: Anatomy • Human body • Physiology

Now Try: Visual readers will be attracted to Richard Walker's *Ask Me Anything: Every Fact You Wanted to Know.* This is an ideal book for readers used to looking at information on a computer screen. The information is arranged in several large groups: space, earth, dinosaurs, plants, animals, human body, transportation, places, society and culture, and history. Within each of these larger groups Walker presents a colorful double-page spread that starts with a question and gives a wide range of possible answers, while varying the page design, making this a fun book for browsing. The complete table of contents and index allows readers to look for specific information. Information junkies may also enjoy Marg Meikle's *How Much Does Your Head Weigh? The Great Big Book of Lists*, which presents one- to three-page answers to 305 questions on all kinds of topics, including animals, the body, and science.

Transportation

A child's early interest in pictures of cars and toy trains evolves into a teen's desire to own a vehicle or to travel: These are the enthralling books that help explain the different modes of transportation, how they work, and why they continue to keep us enthralled. What is the continuing lure of train travel? How does an engine work, and when should a car be taken to a mechanic? Readers will be shown how the bicycle contributed to women's rights. Books in this category also help readers prepare to own, operate, and maintain their favorite modes of transport.

Apelqvist, Eva.

Getting Ready to Drive. Life—A How-to Guide. Berkeley Heights, NJ: Enslow Publishers, Inc., 2012. 128p. ISBN 9781552639900. **J**

Given that car crashes are, according to the U.S. Department of Transportation, the leading cause of death for American fifteen- to twenty-year-olds, it is not surprising that getting behind the wheel of a car is one of the most exciting but potentially dangerous milestones in any teenager's life. This practical and readable guide looks at preparations for becoming a safe driver, with added sidebars, suggestions for further reading, and Web sites. Chapters discuss rules of the road, safety issues, obtaining a license, buying a car, maintenance, money and insurance, and environmental issues.

Keywords: Car maintenance • Driving

Christensen, Lisa.

Clueless About Cars: An Easy Guide to Car Maintenance and Repair. Toronto: Key Porter Books, 2007. 174p. ISBN 9781552639900. **H**

This solid guide to a car's systems introduces young drivers to the various noises a car makes and what they might mean, including tips on how and what can be fixed and how to fix things themselves. The section on diagnosing problems shows readers when to take their cars to a mechanic, followed by step-by-step directions for finding and dealing with the garage. The final chapter includes information on buying and selling a car. Lisa Christensen has updated her earlier guide with information about car owners and the environment.

Keywords: Car maintenance • Car repairs

Coiley, John.

Train. Eyewitness Books. New York: DK Publishing, 2009. 72p. ISBN 9780756650322. **M**

The lure of an Eyewitness book is that it combines an introduction to the topic, in this case the history of the train from the steam engine to the newest trains, with great visuals on every page and dynamic text that doesn't overwhelm the visuals. Readers looking for specific information for a report or who are just looking for fun information about the most famous train trips in the world can narrow their search using either the table of contents or the index. There is also a supplementary train timeline and a great list of resources.

Keywords: Train travel • Trains

Macy, Sue.

Wheels of Change: How Women Rode the Bicycle to Freedom (With a Few Flat Tires Along the Way). Washington, DC: National Geographic, 2011. 96p. ISBN 9781426307614. **M** **J**

This entertaining introduction to the history of the bicycle focuses on how it changed the world, particularly as women adapted their fashions and lifestyles to it and gained greater freedom by cycling. Readers may be greatly amused by the dangers that were seen in the clothing and exercise and will enjoy the photographs and period elements that show that cycling has been a liberating form of exercise for well over a century. **AENYA Honor**

Keywords: Bicycles • Bicycling • Women's rights

McMahon, Peter.

Ultimate Trains. Illustrated by Andy Mora. Machines of the Future. Toronto: Kids Can Press, 2010. 40p. ISBN 9781554533664. **M**

This volume is intended as a brief introduction to the evolution of train travel, from a nostalgic look at steam engines to the potential uses by NASA of magnetic levitation trains, known as maglevs, in space. Readers are given projects that demonstrate the technological advantages, including making a steam engine in a bowl and making an electromagnet. This title was a finalist for the Lane Anderson Award.

Keywords: Maglevs • Steam engines • Trains

Now Try: Readers interested in trains and train travel might enjoy Paul Yee's *Blood and Iron: Building the Railway.* This volume in Scholastic Canada's I Am Canada series is written from the point of view of Heen, a young Chinese worker who keeps a diary recording a year he spent traveling to British Columbia and then working clearing trees, digging tunnels, and the other jobs he undertook to help clear his father's and grandfather's debts. Paul Yee gives readers a very clear picture of the dangerous work done on the railroad by the many Chinese immigrants, along with the other trials and tribulations they faced.

Stalder, Erica.

In the Driver's Seat: A Girl's Guide to Her First Car. San Francisco, CA: Zest Books, 2009. 127p. ISBN 9780980073249. **J** **H**

This readable guide presents practical and no-nonsense advice for one of the most important purchases in a girl's life: her vehicle. Not only does this book cover the things a prospective owner should know; it also gives a solid overview of the parts under the hood, which leads into chapters that cover maintenance, tricky driving situations, a chart of possible problems and how to fix them, and suggestions for how to deal with mechanics when things come up that are beyond the scope of this book. The final chapter, "Styling Your Ride," offers some fun possibilities for the girl hoping to personalize her car.

Keywords: Car maintenance • Car repairs • Defensive driving • Driving

Micro-science

To be consistent with its usage in *Reality Rules*, although *micro-science* is still not an accepted term, it is being included here based on the popularity of the "microhistory" category and the continuing prevalence of publishing in this area. The authors in this category focus on a narrowly defined subject. Authors on these subjects—which include the elements, food, and fears—have a wide range of styles and themes.

Gray, Theodore W.

🏅 *The Elements: A Visual Exploration of Every Known Atom in the Universe.* New York: Black Dog & Leventhal, 2009. 240p. ISBN 9781579128142. **H**

This unique coffee table introduction to the elements is organized by the elements' appearance on the periodic table and supplemented by a narrative explaining the use of each element, as well as information about its discovery and use. Readers are treated to full-color photographs that show things in which each element may be found as well as all of the properties of the element, from its atomic weight, density, and radius to its crystal structure and boiling or melting point. **BBYA**

Keywords: Chemistry • Elements • Periodic table • Science

Hillman, Ben.

How Weird Is It? A Freaky Book All About Strangeness. New York: Scholastic, 2009. 47p. ISBN 9780439918688. **M** **J** **RR**

This book introduces scientific mysteries, making them immediately relevant and fascinating by means of oversized photographs and comprehensible explanations in sidebars. Readers are given a number of enticing topics, from space to bacteria to the world's most unattractive fish, the anglerfish. The pictures for this topic demonstrate the species' reproductive habits, which involve the male fusing to and becoming part of the female. The accompanying photograph shows a human female with a set of male legs attached. This delightfully gory picture helps to illustrate the anglerfish's love life and will fascinate reluctant readers.

Keywords: Curiosities • Science

Jackson, Donna M.

What's So Funny? Making Sense of Humor. Illustrated by Ted Stearn. New York: Viking, 2011. 64p. ISBN 9780670012442. **M J**

Humor is a complex subject; not everyone finds the same things funny. Doctors have studied the effects of laughter on the brain's pathways and know that laughing can be an effective workout. This book provides a history of humor, from the medieval *humors*, assumed to make up the body, to modern texting shortcuts and practical suggestions for telling jokes. Supplementary information includes further reading and suggested Web sites.

Keywords: Humor • Humors

Menzel, Peter, and Faith D'Aluisio.

What the World Eats. Berkeley, CA: Tricycle Press, 2008. 160p. ISBN 9781582462462. **J H**

Anyone who has ever looked in the refrigerator or cupboards without finding anything worthwhile to eat should pick up this book, which examines the eating habits, including shopping and food preparation over a week, of twenty-six families from different parts of the world. Pictures demonstrate the amounts and varieties of food available to families in the United States, China, Greenland, and Chad, and a large number of supplementary tables add pertinent health information about everything from available water to the number of McDonalds and life expectancy.

Keywords: Diet • Food • Food consumption • Nutrition

Murphy, Glenn.

Stuff That Scares Your Pants Off! The Science Scoop on More Than 30 Terrifying Phenomena! Illustrated by Mike Phillips. New York: Roaring Brook Press, 2011. 192p. 9781596436336. **M J RR**

Phobias, readers are told in this informative and amusing book, are terrors that may have their roots in a completely rational survival instinct and are generally a learned behavior. Whether a fear of the dentist, a shark, or alektorophobia, the lesser known but just as true and "devastating fear of chickens," Murphy includes explanations of fears, along with information about the chances of coming in contact with the cause of the fear and what to do should that happen, resulting in a book that will please readers of both humor and survival stories, as well as those interested in the science behind fear.

Keywords: Fear • Fears • Phobias

Pollan, Michael.

The Omnivore's Dilemma: The Secrets Behind What You Eat. Adapted by Richie Chevat. New York: Dial Books, 2009. 298p. ISBN 9780803734159. **J** **H**

> It's all about corn! In this young reader's edition Richie Chevat points out clearly that if we are what we eat then we really would all be mostly corn. This is a little more readable than the adult edition, with pictures and charts, including one that demonstrates everything made from corn (whether whole corn products or fractioned products, a group further subdivided into wet-milled corn, dry-milled corn, germ, starch, and sweeteners). Chevat introduces readers to food production today in terms of four kinds of meals and how exactly they would arrive at the table, from the farms and production to delivery, production, and cooking: a fast-food meal, an industrial organic meal, a sustainable meal, and one he hunts and gathers himself.
>
> **Keywords:** Food chains • Food supply • Organic food

Seven Wonders.

> The titles in this series take their name and their inspiration from the Seven Wonders of the Ancient World. Each volume then seeks to create a list of the most awe-inspiring examples in its subject area, from the crab nebula to a double planet and some of the technology used to explore outer space. Well-illustrated and thorough descriptions with timelines and further reading lists will encourage interested readers to find an eighth wonder.

Bortz, Fred.

> *Seven Wonders of Space Technology.* Minneapolis, MN: Twenty-First Century Books, 2011. 80p. ISBN 9780761354536. **M** **J**
>
> > **Keywords:** Astronautics • Outer space • Outer space exploration • Space vehicles

Miller, Ron.

> *Seven Wonders Beyond the Solar System.* Minneapolis, MN: Twenty-First Century Books, 2011. 80p. ISBN 9780761354543. **M** **J**
>
> > **Keywords:** Extrasolar planets • Nebulae • Solar system
>
> *Seven Wonders of the Gas Giants and Their Moons.* Minneapolis, MN: Twenty-First Century Books, 2011. 80p. ISBN 9780761354499. **M** **J**
>
> > **Keywords:** Extrasolar planets • Nebulae • Solar system
>
> *Seven Wonders of the Rocky Planets and Their Moons.* Minneapolis, MN: Twenty-First Century Books, 2011. 80p. ISBN 9780761354482. **M** **J**
>
> > **Keywords:** Earth • Inner planets • Life on Earth

Environmental Writing

Climate change and global warming continue to be prominent topics in nonfiction for young adults. Titles routinely balance introductions to the science behind the subject with information about what readers can do to make a positive change in the world. This section is divided into two subsections, "Ecology and Conservation" and "Animals."

Books about the scientists who study endangered animals are in the section "Adventures in Science." Books that look at what young adults can do to go safeguard the planet and adjust their environmental footprint are included in chapter 11 in the section "Social Concerns."

Ecology and Conservation

The books in this section focus on ongoing changes in the earth's ecosystems and among the world's wildlife. They usually contain suggestions for changes that people can initiate in their own lives to protect the environment.

Earth Matters. New York: Dorling Kindersley Limited, 2008. 253p. ISBN 9780756634353. **M J**

This book breaks down environmental topics into eight subsections about the planet's biomes. Within each of these sections are two-page illustrated introductions that include information about the ecosystems, wildlife, and threats, and "make a difference" sections that suggest potential ways that scientists, organizations, and ordinary citizens can help to protect the environment. An abundance of photographs and facts laid out in an appealing way make this a volume useful for reports as well as attractive to a reader interested in science. In addition, readers will find a very useful and practical introduction with an overview about the formation of the universe, the planet, the carbon cycle, and global warming.

Keywords: Ecology • Environmental conservation • Environmental protection • Environmental science

Delano, Marfé Ferguson.

Earth in the Hot Seat: Bulletins from a Warming World. Washington, DC: National Geographic, 2009. 63p. ISBN 9781426304347. **M J**

This introduction to global warming looks at the facts and the scientific evidence about global warming. Readers are shown the potential for long-term consequences to the planet, but what makes this book stand out from others on the subject is a "hot tip" section that offers suggestions for what readers can do to slow the problem. An additional resource guide at the end includes books, videos, Web sites, and reports.

Keywords: Environmental conservation • Global warming

Is It Hot Enough for You? Global Warming Heats Up. 24/7: Behind the Headlines: Special Edition. New York: Franklin Watts, 2009. 64p. ISBN 9780531218051. **M** **J**

> This introduction to global warming starts with some key facts, including information and statistics about greenhouse gases. This is followed by stories pulled from Scholastic's magazines that cover some of the warmest years the planet has known, listed chronologically from 2000 through 2009. Over the course of these years scientists measure ice melting in record amounts from Antarctica, monitor shrinking rain forests, and watch the shrinking polar bear numbers. The book concludes with suggestions about what readers can do for the environment on an individual basis.
>
> **Keywords:** Environment • Global warming

Animals

Books that focus on animals are especially popular with reluctant readers; they are usually highly illustrated and provide information about high-interest subjects. Readers will also find titles about research into endangered animals in which the focus is on the animal.

Bishop, Nic.

🎖 *Spiders.* New York: Scholastic Nonfiction, 2007. 48p. ISBN 9780439877565. **M** **RR**

> Even the squeamish will be awed by Bishop's oversized, dramatic, and vibrant full-color photographs of more than a dozen types of spiders in this compelling, conversational, and knowledgeable photo-essay. The photograph layouts, shown in close-up, double-page spreads, illustrate several species and will act as a magnet to any middle school reader interested in the subject. **OP Honor**
>
> **Keywords:** Arachnids • Spiders

Frogs. New York: Scholastic, 2008. 48p. ISBN 9780439877558. **M** **RR**

> The cover alone will attract an audience: Nic Bishop is one of the best photographers around, and the pages of this book depict colorful, entrancing specimens that will either enthrall or horrify. Each page is full of interesting facts, all illustrated in large, full-color pictures that will have reluctant readers returning to them again and again.
>
> **Keywords:** Frogs

Carson, Mary Kay.

The Bat Scientists. Photographs by Tom Uhlman. Scientists in the Field. Boston; New York: Houghton Mifflin Harcourt, 2010. 80p. ISBN 9780547199566. **M** **J**

> Bats are a fascinating, albeit frequently misunderstood animal. This volume in the Scientists in the Field series sets out to correct many of the myths and misapprehensions that have caused people to fear and in turn lash out at the least studied of all mammals. There are approximately 5,000 species of bats in the world, many of which are endangered, spread out over every continent except

Antarctica. Bats can be as small as a hummingbird or as large as an owl. In this fascinating, well-illustrated book, readers are given a thorough introduction to bats, their modes of communication, the threats they face, and the scientists and groups that are working to protect both them and the ecosystems in which they live.

Keywords: Animal conservation • Animals • Bats • Mammals • Scientists

Houston, Dick.

Bulu: African Wonder Dog. New York: Random House, 2010. 323p. ISBN 9780375847233. **M J**

Two former police officers, Anna and Steve Tolan, find a home and a purpose when they follow their dream to Zambia. Adopting an unusual Jack Russell puppy, whom they name Bulu, "wild dog," provides an impetus for their lives along the Luangua River. They could never have guessed how apt his name would be as he charms the locals and is drawn to the indigenous wildlife, whether dangerous or not, leading him to form protective relationships with many animals as well as putting him in some situations that would have made Marley jealous. This charming book will be popular with any readers interested in animals or conservation.

Keywords: Animals • Dogs • Wildlife conservation

Komiya, Teruyuki.

Life-Size Aquarium: Dolphin, Orca, Clownfish, Sea Otter and More—an All-new Actual-size Animal Encyclopedia. New York: Seven Footer Press, 2010. 48p. ISBN 9781934734599. **M RR**

This unique, oversized book takes readers on a tour of an aquarium, presenting double-page spreads that feature close-up pictures of the denizens. Three of the thirty-five spreads overflow onto a magnificent four pages, allowing readers to appreciate, for example, not only the Humphead Wrasse's brilliant blue-green color and size but also the detail of its scales. Sidebars on each page tell readers what to look for in the picture as well as providing facts about the fish or animal; they make the book appropriate for reluctant and ESL learners.

Keywords: Aquatic animals • Fish • Photographs • Whales

Lourie, Peter.

The Manatee Scientists: Saving Vulnerable Species. Scientists in the Field. New York: Houghton Mifflin Harcourt, 2011. 80p. ISBN 9780547152547. **M J**

Manatees are aquatic herbivores. The three known species share several characteristics, such as their large size and their ability to blend into their surroundings, but they are found in vastly different areas of the planet, from Florida to Brazil and West Africa. In explaining the differences between the species of manatee, the author discusses the various conservation efforts and scientific research in different parts of the world. Supplemental information includes further resources and a double-page spread about each of the species. The book also contains an explanation of Red List categories from Extinct to Not Evaluated. This book will appeal to readers interested in animals and conservation.

Keywords: Brazil • Conservation • Manatees • West Africa

McAllister, Ian, and Nicholas Read.

🏅 *The Sea Wolves: Living Wild in the Great Bear Rainforest.* Photographs by Ian McAllister. Victoria, BC: Orca Book Publishers, 2010. 122p. ISBN 9781554692064. **M** **J**

Wolves, according to the nicely flowing text of this narrative nonfiction book, have been given an undeservedly bad reputation. The coastal wolves found in the Great Bear Rainforest (GBR) of British Columbia are smaller and more adaptable than any other wolves, able to fend for themselves and having adapted to supplying much of their diet by fishing for salmon and feeding on the heads, which in turn leaves food for other scavengers and nourishment for the rest of the ecosystem. The authors integrate a lesson about what could happen should anything threaten this keystone species with one about the fragility of an ecosystem. Readers will find sidebars called "Wolf Bites" that supplement the text and lovely photographs of both wolves and the GBR. This title was a finalist for the 2010 Lane Anderson Award.

Keywords: Ecosystems • Great Bear Rainforest • Sea wolves • Wolves

O'Connell, Caitlin, and Donna M. Jackson.

The Elephant Scientist. Photographs by Caitlin O'Connell and Tim Rodwell. Scientists in the Field. New York: Houghton Mifflin Harcourt, 2011. 72p. ISBN 9780547053448. **M** **J**

Her studies of insects known as planthoppers led scientist Caitlin O'Connell to her discovery that elephants can communicate by detecting seismic signals through the ground through their feet and trunks. This fascinating volume of the Scientists in the Field series looks at Caitlin's studies in Namibia's Etosha National Park, where the elephants' preference for eating the easy pickings in farmer's fields explains their unpopularity and combines with a sad history of poaching for ivory and other difficulties. Information about this complex mammal is fascinating; the elephant is a very intelligent animal. Caitlin's research into the elephants' communication methods is explained clearly as a part of the work that she is doing to "ensure their future as a species." The book includes information about the program set up by Caitlin and her husband, scientist Tim Rodwell, to reduce conflict between elephants and farmers, as well as further resources and information about elephants in peril.

Keywords: Conservation • Elephants • Endangered animals • Namibia • O'Connell, Caitlin

Now Try: Readers interested specifically in the science behind elephant communication will find more detailed information in Ann Downer's *Elephant Talk: The Surprising Science of Elephant Communication*. This book examines in detail how elephants "talk" to each other and how scientists study these fascinating animals, from examining scat to what infrasound is.

Walker, Richard.

Animal Life. <u>One Million Things</u>. New York: Dorling Kindersley, 2009. 128p. ISBN 9780756652340. **M** **J**

This wide-ranging introduction to living things on our planet is divided into three main sections: diversity, which looks at animal classifications and then breaks them down by the individual classes; life skills, which examines the ways and means animals have developed to thrive; and diversity, which considers the different natures of species and the variability of the lands in which widely different species may exist. All of the pages are accompanied by colorful illustrations. Readers looking for a particular animal will find an index at the back, making this a useful tool not only for reports but also for browsing.

Keywords: Animal life • Animals

Consider Starting with . . .

These are some recommended titles for readers new to the genre.

Bryson, Bill. *A Really Short History of Nearly Everything.*

Halls, Kelly Milner, and Major William Sumner. *Saving the Baghdad Zoo: A True Story of Hope and Heroes*.

Hosler, Jay. *Evolution: The Story of Life on Earth.*

Komiya, Teruyuki. *Life-Size Aquarium: Dolphin, Orca, Clownfish, Sea Otter and More—an All-new Actual-size Animal Encyclopedia.*

Menzel, Peter, and Faith D'Aluisio. *What the World Eats.*

Montgomery, Sy. *Kakapo Rescue: Saving the World's Strangest Parrot.*

O'Connell, Caitlin, and Donna M. Jackson. *The Elephant Scientist.*

Rubalcaba, Jill, and Peter Robertshaw. *Every Bone Tells a Story: Hominin Discoveries, Deductions, and Debates.*

Thimmesh, Catherine. *Lucy Long Ago: Uncovering the Mystery of Where We Came From.*

Walker, Sally M. *Written in Bone: Buried Lives of Jamestown and Colonial Maryland.*

1
2
3
4
5
6
7
8
9
10
11

Fiction Read-Alikes

- **Boyce, Frank Cottrell.** *Cosmic.* Liam Digby isn't like other twelve-year-olds. Because of his height he has always been mistaken for an older child, if not an adult, something he is quite happy to take advantage of if it will get him repeated trips on the scariest ride at the local amusement park, but which he never suspects will leave him stranded in space.

- **McDonald, Abby.** *Boys, Bears and a Serious Pair of Hiking Boots.* Green Teen Jenna gets a new perspective on her environmental activities when she spends the summer with her godmother in British Columbia. Although she had wanted to avoid going to her grandmother's retirement village, she finds that Stillwater opens up new possibilities for romance, as well as differing views of nature, tourism, and sustainability.

- **Oppel, Kenneth.** *Half Brother.* Ben is not happy when his family moves from Toronto to Victoria, although he understands that they are doing so because of an important opportunity and potential scientific advancement: his family is going to take in a chimpanzee, which will become his new "baby brother" to see if it can learn language in the same way a human would. Ben starts to love Zan, the chimp, and only slowly does he realize that to his father, Zan is just a test subject.

Chapter 7

Sports

Definition

Sports by nature are competitive, allowing people to compete against themselves as well as others. To succeed in a sport, a person must acquire the necessary skills to participate in the chosen activity and maintain it for the amount of time required to finish. To successfully partake in a competition, one must have a level of skills beyond those of the other participants.

Nonfiction titles in this area appeal to readers on several levels. Readers may find information about a sport that will help them improve their ability to prepare for, participate in, or be a more qualified spectator of an activity. On the other hand, they can also find stories about sports stars and role models. These books also feature heroes, high endurance, fighting against the odds, and lots of challenges.

Appeal

Sports and games are more popular than ever. Teams have devoted fans who know their standings and keep up on the statistics of their favorite players on a day-to-day basis. Many of the books in the section "Rules and Tips" use color photographs to show athletes breaking records, doing signature moves, and participating in popular sports that readers play. Yet readers do not need to be able to play a sport themselves to feel the pull of a well-written book; sports biographies offer stories about underdogs, heroes, races for a finish line, and breaking of records. These titles also appeal to readers who enjoy the sports adventures found in chapter 1.

Chapter Organization

The first section, "Sports Biographies," includes fast-paced, engaging stories of heroes and people committed to becoming the best and attaining their goals. These include biographies of players who broke records, played in several professional sports, and broke barriers for other players. To participate in a sport or game, one must understand how it works, so the section "Rules and Tips" lists books that explain particular sports as well as how to participate in and excel at them. This is followed by "The Greatest Games," which includes books that show how sports have changed, as well as titles about sports legends. The final section, "Sports in Action," contains books with great photographs and coffee table books.

Sports Biographies

Athletes are heroic icons to many people. The qualities necessary to become a top competitor in any sport are admirable: strength, determination, self-discipline, and courage. A story behind the struggle to get to the finish line, a podium, or the end of a season has many appealing elements for readers, including exciting competitions, teamwork, drive, and overcoming difficulties. A recent trend includes biographies about athletes who overcame the racial or religious biases of their times to compete in their sports. The sports-minded reader may often feel empathy with the subject and seek validation of his or her own struggles.

Brignall, Richard.

Big Train: The Legendary Ironman of Sport, Lionel Conacher. Toronto: James Lorimer & Co., 2009. 163p. ISBN 9781552774519. **M J**

Lionel Conacher is an anomaly for any time: a phenomenally talented athlete whose drive led him not only to excel at sports but to compete as an amateur and a professional in five different sports: football, hockey, lacrosse, boxing, and baseball. Readers will be amazed by Brignall's narrative about this ultimate Canadian athlete, who earned the nickname "Big Train" for his unstoppable runs on the football field. Conacher, who began a career in politics after retiring from sports, is the namesake for the award given annually to Canada's best male athlete.

Keywords: Conacher, Lionel • Football players • Hockey players • Professional athletes

Now Try: Readers interested in unstoppable athletes will find another one in George Chuvalo. Richard Brignall's *Fearless: The Story of George Chuvalo, Canada's Greatest Boxer* provides a nonfiction narrative of a young man whose bouts included fights with Sonny Liston and Muhammad Ali.

China Clipper: Pro Football's First Chinese-Canadian Player, Normie Kwong. Toronto: James Lorimer & Co., 2010. 152p. ISBN 9781552775271. **M J**

Norman Kwong was one of six children raised in Calgary at a time when Chinese people still faced discrimination. His father paid a head tax to come to Canada. One of the ways that Norman fit in was through his love of sports; he was voted the MVP of the Calgary junior football league in 1947. Scouted by the Calgary Stampeders at the age of eighteen, he was the first athlete of Chinese descent to play football professionally in Canada and set records with the Edmonton Eskimos for rushing, passing, and the most ball carries in one game. Life didn't end when Kwong retired from football, either; he went on to become a successful business and family man before being appointed Alberta's sixteenth Lieutenant Governor by the prime minister. Fans of football will particularly enjoy this title, because it includes some history of the Grey Cup, as well as information about the evolution of the game played by the Stampeders and the Eskimos during the time in which Kwong was on the team and recaps of several of his pertinent games, including several Grey Cup games.

Keywords: Calgary Stampeders • Canadian Football League • Edmonton Eskimos • Football • Kwong, Norman

Hampton, Wilborn.

Babe Ruth: A Twentieth Century Life. Up Close. 208p. Penguin/Viking, 2009. 203p. ISBN 9780670063055. **M J**

Babe Ruth was the "Sultan of Swat." Wilborn Hampton's frank look at the "greatest player ever to step on a baseball diamond" covers all of George Herman Ruth's fifty-four records, ten World Series, and twenty-two seasons and still presents a complete picture of the man, including his notorious bad temper and womanizing. Readers will find out that the man who would become famous for visiting children in hospitals and orphanages was himself a very bad boy, stealing by the age of seven, whose parents sent him to a reform school for orphans and delinquents. It was while at this school that the Babe began his lifelong love of baseball, which led him to eventually sign with the Orioles.

Keywords: Baseball • Baseball players • Ruth, Babe

Leonetti, Mike, and John Iaboni.

Football Now! Buffalo, NY; Richmond Hill, ON: Firefly Books, 2009. 176p. ISBN 9781554074495. **M J**

The second edition of *Football Now!* looks at eighty-nine of the NFL's best players, based on their play in the 2008 season, in chapters organized by their positions. The chapters start with quarterbacks, running backs, and receivers, then move on to front lines, special teams, linebackers, and defensive backs. Readers will find photographs of the players, along with their biographies, career highlights, and recountings of their 2008 seasons.

Keywords: Football • Football players • National Football League

Sommer, Shelley.

Hammerin' Hank Greenberg: Baseball Pioneer. Honesdale, PA: Calkins Creek, 2011. 135p. ISBN 9781590784525. **M J**

Hank Greenberg played thirteen years as a first baseman and left fielder in the major leagues, which also included four World Series, five selections to the All-Star team, and being a two-time American League MVP. Religious bigotry was as common during his era as racism was during

Jackie Robinson's; in fact, Sommer points out that Greenberg was "one of the few people who understood what Robinson was going through" during his first season, because his situation had been very similar. This is a readable, interesting biography of a great athlete who loved his game and did whatever he could to play it, from moving teams to changing positions and ignoring vicious and racial taunts from the crowds. Readers will also find photographs, source notes, Hank Greenberg's own all-star team, further reading, and a note about Greenberg's lasting legacy, which attests that he will be remembered "not only as a great ballplayer, but even more as a great Jewish ballplayer."

Keywords: Baseball • Greenberg, Hank

Sturm, James, and Rich Tommaso.

Satchel Paige: Striking out Jim Crow. New York: Hyperion/Jump at the Sun, 2007. 89p. ISBN 9780786839001. **J H**

Satchel Paige was arguably one of the greatest baseball players ever, a man who walked two men on purpose, before striking out the next three, in the 1942 Negro World Series. He went on to pitch for another thirty years after this amazing feat, before finally being inducted into the Baseball Hall of Fame in 1971. This involving and unique graphic novel by James Sturm, the head of the Center for Cartoon Studies, uses Paige's story as a device to introduce readers to what life was like under the Jim Crow laws in the 1940s in the South.

Keywords: Baseball • Paige, Satchel

Rules and Tips

Readers interested in becoming competent participants in or observers of a sport need look no further than these titles. They feature histories, equipment, rules, and setup and are generally written by people with a close association with and love of that particular activity. Many of these books are colorful and highly illustrated, which often appeals to boys and reluctant readers. Features generally include important competitors, which may lead interested readers to the sports biographies above. Books about specific toys and games, gaming information, and technology are covered in chapter 9.

Buckley, James.

Baseball. <u>Eyewitness Books</u>. New York: DK, 2010. 72p. ISBN 9780756659349. **M J**

This introduction to the game of baseball fits well into the <u>Eyewitness</u> series. Its author, a veteran of baseball writing, has produced a book that manages to touch on everything from the history of the game to its mechanics, important players, equipment, and leagues in the United States and internationally, and it has a supplemental page with additional facts. All of this is presented in the expected highly illustrated style that allows an astonishing amount of information to be presented in a remarkably slim and readable volume.

Keywords: Baseball

Goldblatt, David, and Johnny Acton.

The Soccer Book: The Sport, the Teams, the Tactics, the Cups. New York: DK, 2009. 400p. ISBN 9780756650988. **J H**

This comprehensive volume provides a complete history of the world's most popular sport, as well as how it is played, soccer skills, and major competitions. There is a comprehensive page for each country that provides a wide range of information, including statistical information on the country's population and numbers of players, domestic clubs and international honors, information about World Cup appearances, and biographical information and statistics for great players. Further sections cover the numerous competitions held around the world and international record holders. **QP**

Keywords: Soccer • Soccer skills

Goldner, John.

Hockey Talk: The Language of Hockey from A–Z. Illustrated by Ted Heeley. Markham, ON: Fitzhenry & Whiteside, 2010. 103p. ISBN 9781554550920. **M J**

Readers interested in learning about hockey from a novel point of view will find this A–Z dictionary of hockey terms provides them with an insider's view of the sport. Terms are defined using natural language and dialogue, with cross-reference in boldface type. Supplements include colorful illustrations and biographies of several well-known sports figures and broadcasters, sprinkled throughout the text.

Keywords: Hockey • Hockey terminology

Hon, Shek.

BMX Riding Skills: The Guide to Flatland Tricks. Richmond Hill, ON: Firefly Books, 2010. 128p. ISBN 9781554074006. **J H**

This is a guide intended specifically for riders interested in learning tricks. The author provides a short introduction to the various disciplines of BMX biking, the anatomy of a BMX bike, and recommended clothing, but most of the book is reserved for instructions and tips for the individual tricks. The instructions are divided by skill level into sections for beginner, intermediate, and advanced tricks. Every trick is presented in several steps, each of which is illustrated with a color photograph.

Keywords: BMX riding • Stunt cycling

Krasner, Steve.

Play Ball Like the Pros: Tips for Kids from 20 Big League Stars. Atlanta, GA: Peachtree Publishers, 2010. 193p. ISBN 9781561455355. **M**

Professional baseball players offer advice and tips in a question-and-answer format for every part of the game, from the pitcher's pregame stretching to running the bases, to playing each position, to the final pitch. The players also share some of their memories of the game, and readers are given sidebars describing relevant moments in baseball and a glossary of the baseball terms in the text. An additional supplement for each position poses a scenario and then explains what to do.

Keywords: Baseball • Sports

Stutt, Ryan.

🎖️ *The Skateboarding Field Manual.* Buffalo, NY; Richmond Hill, ON: Firefly Books, 2009. 143p. ISBN 9781554074679. **J** **H**

This introduction to skateboarding starts out with a primer on its equipment, culture, and history, then discusses the ins and outs of how to ride a skateboard. The fully illustrated guide starts with the basics of standing on a board and works through to grinds and slides. This Quick Pick for reluctant young adult readers will appeal to every level of reader, from the novice looking at etiquette and board art to more experienced riders interested in the "how-to" sections.**QP**

Keywords: Skateboarding • Sports

Thomas, Keltie.

How Figure Skating Works. Illustrated by Stephen MacEachern. Toronto: Owlkids Books, 2009. 64p. ISBN 9781897349588. **M**

Keltie Thomas provides readers with a quick, precise, and well-illustrated introduction to one of winter's most popular spectator sports in eight chapters. Find out what makes figure skating ice different from regular ice, the legends of the sport from Dick Button to the battle of the Brians, the science of the spin, and exactly how to tell those six jumps apart.

Keywords: Figure skating • Sports

The Greatest Games

This subgenre shows how sports have changed, from the ten sports that debuted at the first Olympics, to the twenty that were played at the 2010 Winter Olympic Games. In this section, the reader will find compelling sports histories, legends, and stories. There are also humorous looks at novel sporting events from people who have spent their lives immersed in the sporting world, such as Rick Reilly's *Sports from Hell: My Search for the World's Dumbest Competition.*

Nelson, Kadir.

🎖️ *We Are the Ship: The Story of Negro League Baseball.* New York: Hyperion Books for Children, 2008. 88p. ISBN 9780786808328. **M** **J**

This stunning volume introduces readers to the players and owners of the Negro League, which started in 1920. It is a story of baseball and barnstorming played for the love of the game in the face of racial discrimination, segregation, and no pay. Most of these great players will be unfamiliar to readers; they are introduced here for the first time in Kadir Nelson's text and oil paintings. Jackie Robinson broke the color barrier in 1947 when he crossed over to the major leagues, effectively ending the Negro League. He was followed by a number of other players. **ALA, CSK, OP, Sibert**

Keywords: Baseball • Negro League • Robinson, Jackie

Reilly, Rick.

Sports from Hell: My Search for the World's Dumbest Competition. New York: Random House, 2010. 204p. ISBN 9780385514385. **H**

After thirty-one years of covering professional sports, Rick Reilly set out to cover sports that only the competitors took seriously. He found himself circling the globe and not only writing about but also taking part in the tournaments. They varied from the strictly physical World Sauna Championships in Finland, to the mind game of the Rock Paper Scissors championship in Toronto, to the World Homeless Soccer tournament in Copenhagen, which ended up being a life-changing experience for almost all of the players.

Keywords: Sports • Sports humor

Wallechinsky, David, and Jaime Loucky.

The Complete Book of the Winter Olympics: The Vancouver Edition—Winter 2010. Vancouver, BC; Toronto: D & M Publishers/Greystone Books; London: Aurum Press, 2009. 322p. ISBN 9781553655022. **H**

Devotees of the winter games will appreciate the thoroughness of this compendium, which provides not only explanations about the sports but also historical information for each event at the games, with scores for the winners, right down to the ordinals that the judges gave the men in the 1908 figure skating competition and supplementary photographs. Appendices include medal totals up to the Vancouver games and winter Olympic records.

Keywords: Olympics • Sports • Winter Olympics

Zweig, Eric

Tough Guys: Hockey Rivals in Times of War and Disaster. <u>Recordbooks</u>. Toronto: James Lorimer, 2009. 138p. ISBN 9781552774281. **M J**

Eric Zweig presents a history of the early days of the Stanley Cup in Canada, long before the NHL as we know it today. Readers will find eleven short chapters of narrative with sidebars that highlight notable hockey players such as Georges Vezina, Newsy Lalonde, and Scotty Davidson and pertinent historical facts, such as the teams of the day and the length of the season. Readers are introduced to the difficulties that the league faced, including players being conscripted during World War I and the Spanish influenza epidemic. Zweig's background in journalism helps transport the casual reader right to the arena in his descriptions of the Cup games.

Keywords: Hockey • Influenza epidemic • Stanley Cup

Sports in Action

Given the number of photographers assigned to sporting events, it is surprising there aren't more coffee table books dedicated to them. This subgenre is composed of books devoted to a particular sport.

Grange, Michael.

Basketball's Greatest Stars. Buffalo, NY; Richmond Hill, ON: Firefly Books, 2010. 216p. ISBN 9781554076376. **H**

The fifty players profiled in this book have been chosen by sports columnist Michael Grange as the greatest basketball players of all time. The text for each athlete makes a compelling case for his inclusion, from expected choices such as Michael Jordan and Magic Johnson to long-retired greats like George Mikan and current players like Allen Iverson. Readers interested in basketball can find new information about their favorite players as well as sidebars with their career highlights, statistics, and large, full-color pictures of these stars demonstrating what they do best on the court.

Keywords: Basketball • Basketball players

Senft, Jean Riley.

Triumph on Ice: The New World of Figure Skating. Photographs by Gérard Châtaigneau. Vancouver, BC: Greystone Books/D&M Publishers Inc., 2011. 136p. ISBN 9781553656579. **H**

The International Skating Union (ISU) changed the judging system used in 2010, and this book explains both their old and new judging rules and shows the evolution to the judging system currently used by the ISU, with concrete examples in choreography, execution, and interpretation. It features 140 full-color photographs taken at international meets, including the 2010 Olympics and world championships, which will appeal to skating fans as well as newcomers to the sport. Even skating afficionados will appreciate the text, which shows what the stars in the field are doing to merit the high scores that they receive and how exactly they receive them. This is a clearly written text by an Olympic judge and referee that highlights both current and upcoming stars of figure skating.

Keywords: Figure skaters • Figure skating • Ice skating

Consider Starting with . . .

These are suggested titles for readers new to the genre.

> Brignall, Richard. *Big Train: The Legendary Ironman of Sport, Lionel Conacher.*
>
> Goldblatt, David, and Johnny Acton. *The Soccer Book: The Sport, the Teams, the Tactics, the Cups.*
>
> Nelson, Kadir. *We Are the Ship: The Story of Negro League Baseball.*
>
> Reilly, Rick. *Sports from Hell: My Search for the World's Dumbest Competition.*
>
> Senft, Jean Riley. *Triumph on Ice: The New World of Figure Skating.*
>
> Sommer, Shelley. *Hammerin' Hank Greenberg: Baseball Pioneer.*
>
> Sturm, James, and Rich Tommaso. *Satchel Paige: Striking out Jim Crow.*

Fiction Read-Alikes

- **Alexie, Sherman. *The Absolutely True Diary of a Part-Time Indian.*** Arnold Spirit Jr.'s teacher suggests that he go to school in Reardon in the nearby town, off the reservation. Arnold travels twenty miles each way, sometimes on foot, to get to a school in a place where the only other Indian is the school's mascot and everyone views him as a traitor for leaving the reservation. At first the kids just see a goofy-looking Indian boy. His only friend is a geeky kid who is also an outcast. When Arnold makes the basketball team, things change—initially, not for the better. Arnold's determination, talent on the court, and cartooning may just take him places, in this National Book Award–winning and Top 10 BBYA title.

- **Calame, Don. *Swim the Fly.*** In this very funny novel, swim team members and best friends Matt, Sean, and Coop set a summertime goal of seeing a live girl naked. While the chances of that happening seem very slim, Matt's personal goal to swim the one-hundred-yard butterfly to impress the new girl on the team seems even less likely to be achieved, especially as Matt is a string bean who hasn't ever managed to complete a whole length of the pool in a single lap, much less a race in competition.

- **Carbone, Elisa. *Jump.*** Two teens with unhappy home lives and a love of rock climbing find each other and work on avoiding their troubles, including the security force sent by their parents to retrieve them.

- **Van Draanen, Wendelin. *The Running Dream.*** Jessica dreams of running with her dog by her side. Unfortunately the car that plowed into her track team's bus, leaving her with a stump instead of a right leg, has taken away her ability and left her with only her dreams. She never imagined that she would be able to go back to school, or that her team would stand beside her and actually encourage her to try a prosthetic running leg or raise the money for her to get one of the legs when her family couldn't afford it. What seemed like too much a dream to even contemplate might just be within her reach after all.

- **Wyshynski, Sue.** *Poser.* When Tallulah Jones was asked whether she had ever surfed back home in Florida by one of the most popular girls in school, it didn't seem like a big deal to say yes; she had tried surfing once, even though she had ended up in the emergency room. When that one lie spins into a story about her being an extreme surfer who has even tried surfing in a hurricane, Tallulah winds up being exposed as a liar before the entire student body after an embarrassing and dangerous accident. Luckily, Tallulah is given an opportunity to learn how to surf from a decidedly unhip but very good surfer, giving her the chance to redeem herself at school and showing her a thing or two about friendship.

- **Yolen, Jane.** *Foiled.* The chapters in this graphic novel, like much of Aliera's life, are set out in the stages of a fencing match. That is an apt choice, as it is only when she is fencing that Aliera, who feels invisible in high school, is sure of what she is doing. Little does Aliera know that the new foil her mother picked up for her at a tag sale is much more than it seems. This title was chosen for the 2011 Great Graphic Novels for Teens list.

Chapter 8

All About You

Definition

Adolescence is defined in the *Encyclopaedia Britannica* (2007) as "the transitional phase of growth and development between childhood and adulthood," which roughly encompasses the period between the ages of twelve and twenty. The changes undergone during the "teenaged" years are concentrated in two primary areas. The first is the onset of puberty and questions that arise with it as the body matures physically and sexually; the second deals with psychological, social, and moral issues. This genre contains books that contend with physical changes and well-being, as well as the issues that teens deal with in their daily lives.

Appeal

The transition to adulthood is a time when teenagers become increasingly independent. Books that give teens the opportunity to learn what is happening in their lives and how to take control of their own situations are frequently in demand. When they have questions too personal or embarrassing to ask someone, about new and different things happening to their bodies and lives, it can be comforting to consult a book and learn that these changes are not only normal, but happen to other people as well. Publishing in this area responds to real life; this has been particularly notable in the past few years in regard to bullying and cyberbullying, with titles that look at the consequences from the point of view of both the bullied and the bully.

In our age of consumerism, supermodels, burgeoning anorexia, and unrealistic body images, there are solid examples available of what is normal, healthy, and realistic. Self-esteem, health, and nutrition are popular topics, and the books in this chapter provide realistic views about weight and body shapes. Books on relationships examine friendships and families. This is a complex time of life, and teens deal with serious concerns such as drugs, cutting, and depression. Books on these topics usually offer other resources for teens seeking help or who may have further questions.

Chapter Organization

The first section, "Personal Growth," contains books that help readers develop and maintain a healthy self-image and find their inner beauty. This is followed by the section "Health," containing informational books about how to stay healthy and various diseases and disorders; interested readers can find some crossover with "Cooking" in chapter 9. The next section is "Sexuality," containing titles dealing with both puberty and sexuality. "Relationships" covers romantic relationships as well as relationships with friends and family. Some of today's most difficult issues, including drugs, violence, and depression, are covered in the books listed in the section "Tough Stuff." "Career Directions" offers teens materials on finding jobs and adding to their resumes, and several inside looks at the fashion industry. The chapter concludes with the section "Fun Stuff," including Daniel Wilson's novel take on how to deal with one's siblings.

Personal Growth

Self-esteem involves a person's feelings of worth. While an adult's self-esteem includes feelings about one's abilities, behaviors, and characteristics, there is an overwhelming tendency among teens, especially girls, to measure self-worth solely by how they think they look. The APA's *Shared Risk Factors for Youth Obesity and Disordered Eating* pointed out in a 2002 survey that 46 percent of female adolescents and 26 percent of male adolescents had body image concerns. This is very important, because that body dissatisfaction "could lead to the development of obesity" and was a "risk factor in the development of eating disorders." The goal of the books in this category is to help provide teens with coping strategies and a way to find their own intrinsic beauty, rather than focusing on the unrealistic and unhealthy images shown in the media. Books about beauty and self-esteem are very popular and are usually directed at a female audience. Rather than providing strictly didactic books about how to improve one's self-esteem, in the past few years there has been a trend toward books that emphasize a teen's inner beauty, creating a realistic self-image, and becoming more comfortable in one's own skin.

Berkley, Elizabeth.

Ask Elizabeth: Real Answers to Everything You Secretly Wanted to Ask About Love, Friends, Your Body . . . and Life in General. New York: G.P. Putnam's Sons, 2010. 240p. ISBN 9780399254482. **J** **H**

> Berkley, a film and television actress, conducts workshops with teenagers around the United States that have provided a forum for teens to ask and answer the questions they can't pose anywhere else. Berkley has included here the most common questions from those workshops on topics such as self-esteem, bullying, relationships, and depression, providing a number of her own and the participants' responses, as well as expert opinions. Readers are also offered "Action Steps" throughout the book for overcoming negativity. The book has been designed to look like an admittedly messy journal, using red penned-in thoughts

added to journal pages and several different written and typewritten fonts, for pages meant to be e-mails. The directness in the author's communication to her readers is bolstered by a high level of intimacy in her own stories, such as her humiliation over the vindictiveness of the reviews of the movie *Showgirls* and her performance in particular.

Keywords: Confidence • Depression • Self-esteem • Social life

Katz, Anne.

Girl in the Know: Your Inside-and-Out Guide to Growing Up. Illustrated by Monika Melnychuk. Toronto: Kids Can Press, 2010. 111p. ISBN 9781554533039. **M** **J**

Knowing that developmental changes, including the onset of puberty and menstruation, can start any time between the ages of ten and fourteen, this colorfully illustrated guide to female adolescence discusses not only these changes and their associated topics but also mood swings, exercise and hygiene, relationships, and diet and nutrition. The chapter on nutrition also covers the dangers of dieting, including anorexia and bulimia.

Keywords: Health • Menstruation • Personal hygiene • Puberty

Redd, Nancy Amanda.

🎗 *Body Drama.* New York: Gotham, 2008. 271p. ISBN 9781592403264. **J** **H**

This book addresses the dramas and issues that come up for real girls with real bodies with the goal of delivering "real answers." It does so in a remarkably up-front way, presenting photographs that answer questions about different breast sizes and "down there," including a row of pictures of (over eighteen-year-old) female genitalia to reassure readers that not everyone looks alike. Other issues covered focus on skin, hair, nails, and shape. This title was chosen for the Amelia Bloomer list. **QP**

Keywords: Beauty • Confidence • Grooming • Health • Personal care • Self-esteem

Wallach, Marlene, and Grace Norwich.

My Self: A Guide to Me. New York: Aladdin Mix/Simon & Schuster Childrens Pub., 2009. 115p. ISBN 9781416979128. **M** **J**

This guide for girls, from the president of the Wilhelmina Kids & Teens Modeling Agency, is meant to help readers understand that nobody is perfect and that it is okay to ask for help, whether from friends, family, or any appropriate resource. Chapters look at self-esteem and how to boost confidence, external stressors and how to deal with them, and caring for oneself and others. Readers are offered a quiz and given a pointer to Just Ask Marlene, the author's Web site.

Keywords: Beauty • Confidence • Grooming • Self-esteem • Self-image

Health

A publication of the APA, entitled *Shared Risk Factors for Youth Obesity and Disordered Eating*, highlights several pertinent factors, including poor nutrition and activity, body dissatisfaction, and teasing. Aside from the associated health risks of being overweight or obese, teens are likely to be discriminated against, teased, or victimized. The books in this section offer advice about lifestyle changes, exercise, and fitness for those who are overweight as well as for those who are not. There are also books about other health concerns and disorders.

Reber, Deborah.

 Chill: Stress-reducing Techniques for a More Balanced, Peaceful You. Illustrated by Neryl Walker. New York: Simon Pulse, 2008. 195p. ISBN 9781416955269. **J H**

Stress is pretty much a fact of life for most teenagers today, although the root cause, side effects, and physiological effects that it can have may come as a nasty shock. Reber here presents an introduction to stress that covers all of these, but concentrates on managing stress, by practical methods such as time management and getting help from others by building and maintaining a support system. It also offers tips for self-help, from journaling to exercise and nutrition. The book is presented in a chatty tone with quizzes and tips. Reber also advises readers facing more serious issues to seek professional help, offering hotline numbers and Web sites. **QP**

Keywords: Stress • Stress reduction

Now Try: Readers interested in a more scientific examination of stress for reports will find it in Margaret Hyde and Elizabeth H. Forsyth's *Stress 101: An Overview for Teens*. This book presents a more thorough, clinical discussion of what stress is and how it affects the body. Readers will also find a discussion of potential causes and effects, including neonatal complications and separation anxiety, as well as treatments such as support groups and meditation.

Wallach, Marlene, and Grace Norwich.

My Life: A Guide to Health and Fitness. New York: Aladdin Mix/Simon & Schuster Childrens Pub., 2009. 117p. ISBN 9781416979111. **M J**

This quick and readable guide for girls looks at fitness and health in three chapters, broken down into keeping fit, good eating, and sleep matters. The information, which is presented in a quick, readable format accompanied by a number of pictures and sidebars, finishes up with the section "Just Ask Marlene," which points readers to the author's Web site and a Fitness and Nutrition Challenge.

Keywords: Fitness • Health • Nutrition

USA Today Health Reports: Diseases and Disorders.

The titles in this series are not only helpful for readers interested in finding out about the history, causes, and treatments of the various disorders covered, but would also be of interest to those readers looking for information about case studies or information from people, including children and teens, who have themselves been diagnosed. Each volume contains reproductions of newspaper articles from *USA Today*, a glossary, and resources, including further reading and a list of Web sites.

Keywords: Diseases • Disorders

Moragne, Wendy.

Depression. Minneapolis, MN: Twenty-First Century Books/Lerner Publishing Group, 2011. 128p. ISBN 9780761358824. **H**

> This book starts by introducing readers to five teenagers who suffered from and overcame depression. Readers are then given an explanation of different types of clinical depression, along with their symptoms, which helps to illustrate that depression requires professional treatment. The next section discusses diagnosis and treatment, using the five cases studies from the introduction, and is followed by information on suicide and its prevention. Web sites and further resources are included, and each chapter contains articles from *USA Today*.
>
> **Keywords:** Depression

Sonenklar, Carol.

AIDS. Minneapolis, MN: Twenty-First Century Books/Lerner Publishing Group, 2011. 128p. ISBN 9780822585817. **H**

> The introduction of this volume in the <u>USA Today Health Reports</u> series starts in 1981 with the emergence of Acquired Immune Deficiency Syndrome, which was identified through the deaths of 234 people from diseases that "doctors had previously considered absolutely harmless." Readers will find a scientific explanation of AIDS, as well as statistics on its exponential spread and information about how scientists track it, along with the stories of people who have it, treatments, prevention, and what is currently being done in research.
>
> **Keywords:** Acquired Immune Deficiency Syndrome • AIDS

Sexuality

During the teen years children develop secondary sexual characteristics (such as a deeper voice in boys and breasts in girls) as their hormonal balance shifts strongly toward the adult state. During this time hormonal fluctuations also affect emotions and relationships and cause expected physical changes. Books in this section talk about these changes in a frank, forthright manner that lets tweens and teenagers know they are not the only ones with questions about sex, relationships, and the complications that can arise.

Corinna, Heather.

S.E.X.: The All-You-Need-to-Know Progressive Sexuality Guide to Get You Through High School and College. New York: Marlowe, 2007. 332p. ISBN 9781600940101. **H**

> This comprehensive reference about sexuality, sex, and relationships starts with a discussion of both genders' bodies. It moves on to body image; arousal; sexual identity; relationships; and very candid discussions about sex, pregnancy, contraception, and the possible repercussions of sex and abstinence.
>
> **Keywords:** Adolescence • Contraception • Menstruation • Sex • Sex instruction • Sexuality • Social situations

Harris, Robie H.

It's Perfectly Normal: A Book About Changing Bodies, Growing Up, Sex and Sexual Health. Illustrated by Michael Emberley. Somerville, MA: Candlewick Press, 2009. 93p. ISBN 9780763644833. **M** **J**

> The third edition of Robie Harris's introduction to human sexuality has added information about the HPV vaccination, as well as updating the sections on HIV and sexually transmitted diseases and including the 2007 Supreme Court ruling on abortion in *Gonzales v. Carhart*. What hasn't changed are the book's friendly, approachable tone; reliable, detailed information; and colorful, engaging illustrations. Knowing that readers are likely to go to the Internet, Harris also gives them valid advice about how to seek reputable sources and verify the information. She also includes information about Internet safety and cyberbullying.
>
> **Keywords:** Adolescence • Birth control • HIV • Sexual health • Sexuality

Rapini, Mary Jo, and Janine Sherman.

Start Talking: A Girl's Guide for You and Your Mom about Health, Sex, or Whatever. Talk at the Table. Houston, TX: Bayou Pub., 2008. 198p. ISBN 9781886298316. **J** **H**

> Although presenting information about menstruation, health care, sexuality, sexually transmitted diseases, relationships, birth control, psychological health, and body image is not new, the format of this book is. The book's authors are an OB/GYN nurse practitioner and an intimacy and sex counselor, who each have two daughters and believe that providing education and guidance is the best way to arm them to make strong decisions. The chapters provide information about the main subject, followed by questions daughters and mothers might ask and then a "table talk" section to encourage mothers and daughters to discuss health-related matters together.
>
> **Keywords:** Birth control • Body image • Health • Menstruation • Relationships • Sexuality • Sexually transmitted diseases

St. Stephen's Community House.

The Little Black Book for Guys: Guys Talk About Sex. Toronto: Annick Press, 2008. 244p. ISBN 9781550379624. **H**

> This frank and open guide to everything about sex, sexuality, and relationships is written from and for the teenaged male perspective. The book is divided into five sections: it starts with a chapter on the penis before moving onto relationships, sex, sexually transmitted diseases, and birth control. Each chapter includes factual information as well as cartoons, poetry, and stories contributed by teenagers. There is a glossary and a list of resources at the end of the book, which includes both American and Canadian Web sites.
>
> **Keywords:** Birth control • Sex • Sexually transmitted diseases

Relationships

The teen years are a time for self-discovery, shifting boundaries, exploring identity, and beginning to establish one's independence. It is only natural that the relationships teens have with friends and family will change a great deal during these years, not to mention that they will form new romantic relationships. This is a subgenre in which readers can find books that look at the psychology behind why teenagers behave the way they do toward other people as well as books with more general advice about dealing with family; information about sex can be found in the section "Sexuality." Books on more difficult relationship issues, such as abuse and violence, can be found in "Tough Stuff."

Burton, Bonnie.

Girls Against Girls: Why We Are Mean to Each Other and How We Can Change. San Francisco, CA: Zest Books, 2009. 126p. ISBN 9780979017360. **M J H**

> It is more than likely that almost every teen girl will be faced with one of the six common methods of girl-on-girl cruelty that Bonnie Burton discusses as a means to alienate, punish, bond, or hide a torturer's own jealousy or insecurity. Understanding why girls are mean can go a long way to providing tools for stopping the harassment, finding the solution, gathering reinforcement in the form of friends, and ending what becomes a cycle of cruelty. This book promotes working together, as it will take a united front to stop gossip and reinforce positive communication.
>
> **Keywords:** Bullying • Communication • Gossip

Buscemi, Karen.

Split in Two: Keeping It Together When Your Parents Live Apart. Illustrated by Corrine Mucha. San Francisco, CA: Zest Books, 2009. 120p. ISBN 9780980073218. **M J**

This book is intended to impart the skills needed to deal with a two-household family, including scheduling, packing, organizing, and negotiating. These are all things that the author and the many teens whose comments are included in the book believe make things easier in the long run when dealing with the separation or divorce that has disrupted the reader's life. This is a chatty book, broken up by teen comments and stories in speech bubbles, and Corinne Mucha's cartoons, used to illustrate the author's points, are scattered liberally through the text. While overall many of the points here may seem obvious, they serve as a good reminder of the things teens can do to take and keep control over their own situations.

Keywords: Divorce • Self-esteem • Self-reliance

Dear Bully: Seventy Authors Tell Their Stories. Edited by Carrie Jones and Megan Kelley Hall. New York: HarperTeen, 2011. 369p. ISBN 9780062060983. **J** **H**

This collection of shared recollections is of interest to readers who have found themselves the subject of bullying and is of use to teachers, counselors, librarians, and parents who are looking for a resource that will speak directly to teenagers. The stories in this book include examples of different kinds of abuse endured by the authors, times they witnessed bullying, and examples of their own past behavior. Given the number of authors included, the stories also contain a variety of formats; Cecil Castellucci and Mo Willems employ a graphic format, and several authors use poetry. All of the authors add detail to their stories that show the consequences of their own behavior, providing an opportunity for discussion. Supplementary material includes information about the contributors as well as resources for readers, educators, and parents.

Keywords: Bullying

Fox, Annie.

Middle School Confidential. **M** **J**

This series revolves around six middle school friends dealing with common adolescent issues such as peer pressure, self-esteem, and family problems, presented in a graphic novel format. Integrated into their ongoing story are quizzes, resources, and quotes from real teens.

Be Confident in Who You Are. **Book 1.** Minneapolis, MN: Free Spirit Pub., 2008. 92p. ISBN 9781575423029. **M** **J** **GN**

In the first volume of the graphic <u>Middle School Confidential</u> series, Annie Fox introduces readers to six very different characters who nevertheless have a lot in common. By discussing their problems, they realize that they are more alike than they realize: none is perfectly happy with the way he or she looks, they could all use ways to handle stress, occasionally they all worry about what other people think of them, and they can have doubts about themselves. The book is supplemented by quizzes to help deal with these worries and comments from real teens to add assurances that these are, indeed, common thoughts.

Keywords: Graphic nonfiction • Self-confidence • Self-esteem

Real Friends vs. the Other Kind. **Book 2.** Minneapolis, MN: Free Spirit Pub., 2009. 96p. ISBN 9781575423197. **M** **J** **GN**

> Book 2 in the <u>Middle School Confidential</u> series asks teens to consider what makes a real friend. Different situations are examined; the goal is to look at how to deal with potential problems before they happen by using real-life examples from other teenagers, always with an eye to letting readers know that they are not alone, for a range of situations including dealing with pressure, worrying about a friend, dating, and broken promises. The book also offers suggestions, titles of books, and thoughts from teens who have found themselves in tricky situations either before or after breakups or have had their feelings hurt.
>
> **Keywords:** Dating • Friends • Friendships • Graphic nonfiction • Relationships

What's Up with My Family? **Book 3.** Minneapolis, MN: Free Spirit Pub., 2010. 90p. ISBN 9781575423333. **M** **J** **GN**

> Families provide plenty of opportunities for hurt feelings and redefining boundaries, particularly during adolescence. The third volume of this series offers scenarios from the six main characters, with numerous suggestions from real-life teens, to help readers deal with issues, rules that they're likely to find in all families, and other tough situations, such as divorce and getting along with a new stepfamily.
>
> **Keywords:** Adolescent psychology • Family • Family relationships • Teenagers

Hantman, Clea.

30 Days to Getting Over the Dork You Used to Call Your Boyfriend. New York: Delacorte Press, c2008. 161p. ISBN 9780385735490. **M** **J**

> It is a given that almost everyone will go through a breakup, if not several, and that it is unlikely to be a pleasant experience. To help teens facing this situation, Clea Hantman offers this practical, music- and activity-packed guide engineered to steer the broken-hearted through the five stages of grief—denial, anger, bargaining, depression, and finally acceptance—and back to "better than ever" in just a month.
>
> **Keywords:** Breakups • Relationships • Self-help

Tough Stuff

The books in this category address some of the difficult issues that teens deal with during adolescence, including gangs, violence, and depression. These are problems that have longstanding impact. Anrenee Englander presents an updated edition of her *Dear Diary: I'm Pregnant* that illustrates an ongoing issue with ten new stories. A series of public attacks on homosexual teenagers in 2010 drew bullying and homophobia into the public eye, which in turn made bullying and how to deal with it a much more common reference question in both school and public libraries. Bullying has remained a high-profile topic in the media internationally, with emotional and devastating accounts that have provoked teenagers into drastic action, including suicide. Several of the titles use first-person accounts and have real emotional resonance. Minor emotional upheavals that happen between friends and families are common themes in young adult nonfiction, just as they are in fiction, and are covered in "Relationships."

Ellis, Sarah.

We Want You to Know: Kids Talk About Bullying. Regina, SK: Coteau Books, 2010. 120p. ISBN 9781550504170. **M** **J**

> Bullying happens for a number of reasons, which can be divided into various types: Teens are perceived to be different, groups pick on outsiders, bullies have their own reasons that don't make sense, and relentless bullying can even lead its victims to commit suicide. Here kids between the ages of nine and sixteen share how they have been bullied and their reactions, including how the bullying made them feel and what they did. After each story readers will find questions that could be used for a reader's group and a comment from a child or teen in another country. Supplements include a list of resources in the United States and Canada for kids and parents and a chapter on redemption, which contains stories from bullies and bullied alike, with resolutions, intended to replace the negative messages of bullying with ones of "courage and joy."
>
> **Keywords:** Bullies • Bullying

Englander, Anrenee.

Dear Diary, I'm Pregnant: Ten Real Life Stories. Richmond Hill, ON: Annick Press, 2010. 159p. ISBN 9781554512362. **J** **H**

> This revised edition presents first-person accounts from interviews with ten girls. Their situations vary, as do the decisions the girls make upon finding out that they are pregnant.
>
> The girls' backgrounds and their stories vary widely, from a girl who gets pregnant during her first sexual experience to another who is raped by a stranger on her way home. The girls grapple with whether or not to give up their babies for adoption, have an abortion, or keep their children, as well as the consequences of their decisions. Readers will find a list of resources at the back of the book that includes emergency resources and health clinics in the United States and Canada, as well as books with information about pregnancy.
>
> **Keywords:** Abortion • Adoption • Pregnancy • Unplanned pregnancy

Moon, Sarah, ed.

The Letter Q: Queer Writers' Notes to Their Younger Selves. New York: Arthur A. Levine/Scholastic Press, 2012. 282p. ISBN 9780545399326. **J** **H**

Sixty-four authors and illustrators send thoughtful letters back to the younger, frequently bullied, more naïve, or alone versions of their GLTBQ selves in this smart, engrossing, and empathetic collection. Containing both prose and illustrated formats, the advice is heartfelt, funny, sarcastic, and genuine as the authors, including Gregory Maguire, David Levithan, Jacqueline Woodson, and Brian Selznick, offer reassurance that readers' lives will indeed change for the better.

Keywords: Adolescence • Gays (Identity) • Self-acceptance • Sexual orientation

Scowen, Kate.

I.D.: Stuff That Happens to Define Us. Toronto: Annick Press, 2010. 160p. ISBN 9781554512256. **J** **H**

Twelve teenagers present events from their lives that helped shape them, in first-person, illustrated accounts. These vary from a boy who was kidnapped away from his custodial parent by his father, in *Drive*, to a boy who decides he is never going to hit his own children after his father hits him, in *Punched*. The other stories deal with a wide variety of subjects, including divorce, sexuality, parental expectations, and self-confidence. A Q&A following each story allows its writer to reflect on how he or she was affected by the event. Readers will find a list of Web sites for resources on sex and sexuality, violence, mental health, and kids' help lines.

Keywords: Adolescent experiences • Psychology • Violence

Shapiro, Ouisie.

Bullying and Me: Schoolyard Stories. Pictures by Steven Vote. Chicago: Albert Whitman & Company, 2010. 28p. ISBN 9780807509210. **M** **J**

Readers will find thirteen personal accounts of bullying in this spare, readable volume. The stories are accompanied by photos of the victims and comments from a well-known expert on the subject. They all reinforce that bullying is not the fault of the person being bullied, and that left unchecked, it is often cyclical: Katie's story notes that even though her clique turned on her in middle school, she became a "mean girl" at the age of sixteen; Jan's experience made her sensitive to bullies and allowed her to step in when her son was being bullied. A list of tips for dealing with bullies accompanies the text.

Keywords: Bullying

What's the Issue?

This is a series of books that look at real-life issues that teenagers deal with every day. Each book presents real-life examples to make them relevant to readers, changing the names to protect the privacy of the people involved. The language used in the books is realistic without becoming didactic. Readers are given a quiz and a list of organizations should they need professional help. The books are well illustrated and sourced, with additional resources available on the Facthound Web site, searchable by grade level.

Allman, Toney.

Mean Behind the Screen: What You Need to Know about Cyberbullying. Mankato, MN: Compass Point Books, 2009. 48p. ISBN 9780756541453. **M** **J**

> Cyberbullying, also known as cyber abuse and Internet aggression, is a particularly vicious and dangerous form of abuse. It is hard to trace, can be perpetuated far beyond the original perpetrators, and is almost impossible for the victims to escape, given the pervasive nature of the Internet. Victims frequently suffer depression. In this collection readers will learn about several victims of "relentless cyberbullying." This well-rounded look at the issue considers why these crimes are committed and the effects the bullying can have on the victims, as well as the ways in which cyberbullies may be caught, potential punishments, and means of prevention.
>
> **Keywords:** Cyberbullying • Internet bullying

Brown, Anne K.

Virtual Danger: Staying Safe Online. Mankato, MN: Compass Point Books, c2010. 48p. ISBN 9780756542511. **M/J**

> Dangers online come in many forms. True-life examples in this volume of <u>What's the Issue</u>? include identity theft, cyberbullying, electronic theft, and predators. Internet pranks and crimes can have very serious and long-lasting consequences for both the victims and the perpetrators. A chapter on staying safe online and a list of resources for where to get further help will be much appreciated.
>
> **Keywords:** Cyberbullying • Internet bullying • Internet crimes

Friedman, Lauri S.

Dangerous Dues: What You Need to Know About Gangs. Mankato, MN: Compass Point Books, 2010. 48p. ISBN 9780756542535. **M** **J**

> While children as young as the age of eight join gangs, the Violence Prevention Institute has found that the majority of those joining gangs do so between the ages of thirteen and twenty-one. This volume compares the perceptions and motivations about gangs with the realities and consequences of being in a gang, illustrated with real-life stories from gang members.
>
> **Keywords:** Gang initiations • Gang membership • Gangs

Hirschmann, Kris.

Reflections of Me: Girls and Body Image. Mankato, MN: Compass Point Books, 2009. 48p. ISBN 9780756541323. **M** **J**

> Many body features, including sex, height, body shape, and hair and eye color, are genetically predetermined. That means there will be things

about one's body that can't be changed, and expecting changes is completely unrealistic, despite magazine covers of airbrushed models. This volume of the <u>What's the Issue?</u> series discusses body image in adolescent girls, including the prevalence of eating disorders and impossible images presented in the media, and looking at how much money is spent on cosmetics and cosmetic procedures. Girls are presented with information about weight and dieting, positive influences, and where to get help.

Keywords: Body image • Eating disorders • Self-esteem

Mooney, Carla.

More Than the Blues. Mankato, MN: Compass Point Books, 2010. 48p. ISBN 9780756542658. **M** **J**

Depression is the most common mental health disorder in the United States: At any point in time, 5 percent of teens are struggling with major depression. This volume explains different kinds of depression, offers examples of the ways that depression can affect the life of a depressed person, and includes a chapter with information about obtaining treatment.

Keywords: Depression • Mental health

O'Neill, Terry.

Secret Scars: What You Need to Know about Cutting. Mankato, MN: Compass Point Books, c2009. 48p. ISBN 9780756541422. **M** **J**

Cutting is deliberately hurting oneself by poking or slashing at one's own skin. It can be done with almost any sharp object. Some 27 percent of cutters start before the age of fifteen; 5 percent start before the age of ten. There are many reasons why people cut themselves, including physical and emotional problems. Chapters here explore cutting and what people can do to get help for themselves or others who are cutting themselves.

Keywords: Cutting • Self-mutilation in adolescence

Rechner, Amy.

The In Crowd. Mankato, MN: Compass Point Books, 2009. 48p. ISBN 9780756518912. **M** **J**

While peer pressure is something that starts in the sandbox and continues through adulthood, it intensifies in adolescence. Social status can be affected by clothing and hairstyles and choices about whether or not to go along with a particular group. In this collection, readers are presented with real-life examples of teenagers who chose not to go along with negative peer pressure about smoking, borrowing homework, and indulging in various forms of risky behavior, as well as information on maintaining a good group of peer influences. A final chapter offers advice for becoming one's own "best self."

Keywords: Conformity • Peer pressure

Stewart, Gail B.

Drowning in a Bottle: Teens and Alcohol Abuse. Mankato, MN: Compass Point Books, 2009. 48p. ISBN 9780756541514. **M** **J**

What is the big deal with drinking? This short, smart book includes real-life examples to illustrate how alcohol affects the body, how quickly it can become addictive, and what the dangers of alcohol actually are. The book concludes with chapters on dealing with peer pressures and what to do when you think you have a problem.

Keywords: Alcohol • Alcohol use

Traugh, Susan.

Sex Smarts: You and Your Sexuality. Mankato, MN: Compass Point Books, 2009. 48p. ISBN 9780756418783. **M** **J**

Rather than just providing readers with an explanation of the human reproduction systems, this book explores a number of potential pitfalls teenagers encounter when exploring their sexuality, including Internet safety, dating, sex, pregnancy, and STDs. Real-life examples and statistics help show readers that they are not the only ones in any given situation. Quizzes give them a chance to judge for themselves how they compare to the case studies.

Keywords: Pregnancy • Sexuality • Sexually transmitted diseases

Woog, Adam.

Mirror Image: How Guys See Themselves. Mankato, MN: Compass Point Books, 2009. 48p. ISBN 9780756541361. **M** **J**

It's true: guys are just as concerned with their body image as their female counterparts. Adolescent males have as little control over their genes as girls do. They might like to be taller, more muscular, or fitter, and finding ways to stay happy and healthy are just as important for them. One-tenth of the eleven million Americans with an eating disorder are male. That means one million guys need information about developing a realistic body image. The chapter on diet and supplements provides basic information. A list of resources includes hotlines and associations that can provide further information.

Keywords: Male body image • Male self-esteem • Self-esteem

Career Directions

Planning a career path has become more complicated and starts earlier than ever before, now that today's teenagers are more than likely to work in several positions, or possibly several different fields, in the course of their careers. This section lists books about different kinds of jobs and the education they require as well as how known people in the field got their start, as well as offering a practical guide for writing resumes, geared to teens. A particular trend in the past few years has been publishing in the area of career guides in the fashion industry, likely spurred by the popularity of television shows about models, designers, and stylists.

Directories for colleges and test preparatory materials can best be found through specific, annually updated resources. Career materials need not be boring: novel examples here include suggestions for starting a business, including examples from some of the richest and youngest entrepreneurs in the United States.

Beker, Jeanne.

Passion for Fashion: Careers in Style. Illustrated by Nathalie Dion. Toronto; Plattsburgh, NY: Tundra Books, 2008. 80p. ISBN 9780887768002. **M** **J**

> Rather than providing information on breaking into the various fashion fields, this book by Fashion TV star Jeanne Beker breaks down the various careers individually, from designers and models to publicists, people behind the scenes, and retailers. She uses her intimate knowledge of the industry to bring a personal touch to this guide, not only contributing biographies of industry stars but also using her own story as an example for vocational guidance. Readers will find a casual writing style and practical suggestions about the demands of the business throughout the book.
>
> **Keywords:** Careers • Designers • Fashion • Models • Photographers • Publicists

Strutting It: The Grit Behind the Glamour. Toronto: Tundra Books, 2011. 88p. ISBN 9781770492240.

> With a short foreword from internationally known model Coca Rocha, this guide is intended to present a realistic view of what is actually a very demanding, difficult career. Models are more than just pretty faces; indeed, the most famous models throughout history have rarely been conventionally pretty, and Beker's experience with Fashion TV and *Canada's Next Top Model* has given her insights into what helps to make a model a star. Each chapter of the book integrates profiles of current and recognizable supermodels, along with information about what helped them become great. Beker's overall message includes suggestions about keeping up with education and maintaining realistic goals.
>
> **Keywords:** Modeling • Models

Faerm, Steven.

Fashion Design Course. Hauppauge, NY: Barrons Educational Series, Inc., 2010. 144p. ISBN 9780764144233. **H**

> This unique and thorough introduction to fashion design starts with a crash course that shows readers what it is that fashion designers actually do, and includes a well-rounded discussion of the important names in the history of fashion design, the various categories of fashion, and the kinds of

customers who might wear them. Faerm starts from the beginning, with "design foundations" such as color, fabrics, and creating a collection, before looking at building garments and then giving the reader assignments and advice, in a book that will attract and challenge teens interested in the fashion industry.

Keywords: Clothing design • Designers • Fashion • Fashion design

Funk, Joe, John Gaudiosi, and Dean Takahashi.

Hot Jobs in Video Games: Cool Careers in Interactive Entertainment. New York: Scholastic, Inc., 2010. 127p. ISBN 9780545218504. **J H**

This book introduces readers to the process of video game production and then to several prominent people in the industry. It allows readers to find out not only what kind of skills they would need to be an animator, creative director, or game designer but also, from professionals, what they do on a regular basis, how they prepared to enter the job market, and what their advice is for people interested in the industry.

Keywords: Careers • Game design • Games • Interactive games • Video games

Hansen, Mark Victor.

The Richest Kids in America: How They Earn It, How They Spend It, How You Can, Too. Newport Beach, CA: Hansen House Publishing, 2009. 153p. ISBN 9780981970905. **J H**

Meet models of entrepreneurship: citizens who were not only able to identify an opportunity but able to turn a hobby they enjoyed and were good at into an incredibly profitable business. That all of them happened to be minors when they did it is proof that the principles behind entrepreneurship may be applied at any age and that it pays to follow one's dreams.

Keywords: Business • Entrepreneurship

🎗 *The Teen Vogue Handbook: An Insider's Guide to Careers in Fashion.* New York: Razorbill, 2009. 276p. ISBN 9781595142610. **J H**

This book provides pertinent advice to budding stylists, photographers, models, designers, and editors from working professionals. The contributors, who include both stars in their fields and relative newcomers, offer realistic information about how to break into their fields, what it takes to make it, and reinforcement that in every career it will be necessary to start small and work hard. The glossy photographs and content make this a fun read for anyone with an interest in fashion. **QP**

Keywords: Careers • Designers • Fashion • Photographers • Stylists

Rankin, Kenrya.

Start It Up: The Complete Business Guide to Turning Your Passions into Pay. San Francisco, CA: Zest Books, 2011. 159p. ISBN 9780981973357. **H**

This guide is geared to helping encourage and develop a teenager's entrepreneurial spirit. It starts out slowly to help readers find the best possible business idea before coming up with a business plan and follows through to obtaining the resources, starting the business, hiring needed help, marketing, managing customer service, and dealing with upkeep and feedback to maintain the business. Each step in this very readable and practical guide contains tips and a list of resources to help a beginning businessperson get started and keep going.

Keywords: Business • Business plans • Entrepreneurs

Troutman, Kathryn Kraemer.

Creating Your High School Resume: A Step-by-Step Guide to Preparing an Effective Resume for College, Training and Jobs. Indianapolis, IN: JIST Works, 2009. 150p. ISBN 9781593576622. **H**

Filling out an application, whether for a job, college, scholarship, internship, or volunteer position, can be terribly daunting. This practical guide introduces readers to the different types of resumes that most teenagers need for their first foray into the job market. This is accompanied by tips and examples, providing a CD with templates of the possible resumes. Readers are then asked to consider both their skills and previous experience and are directed to think about the needs and wants of the organization to which they are applying. Further instructions are provided for college applications and essays, and case studies are included for different careers. A final chapter offers hints for job, college, and internship interviewing and searching.

Keywords: Internships • Job applications • Resumes

Fun Stuff

When dealing with rapidly changing bodies, hormones, and emotions, teens have a multitude of questions. These titles, which present a lighter side as well as insights into the human condition, are often popular with reluctant readers. These titles offer readers a more lighthearted version of the offerings that may be found in "Relationships," as well as titles that offer some relief from these issues. An example of this is Daniel Wilson's humorous theory for obtaining family domination, which will appeal to readers interested in relationships, martial arts, or family situations.

Almerico, Kendall, and Tess Hottenroth.

Whoogles: Can a Dog Make a Woman Pregnant? . . . and Hundreds of Other Searches That Make You Ask "Who Would Google That?" Avon, MA: F + W Media/Adams Media, 2010. 224p. ISBN 9781440510861. **J H**

Created as an inventory of strange and wondrous questions posed to the Google search engine, each page has a screenshot with an incomplete phrase and a list of the resulting searches that were posed in Google, leading the authors to wonder, "Who Googled . . . ?" One of the searches from each section is highlighted and answered, providing a range of thoughts from the practical to the outright silly and occasionally frightening, but never mundane, in this Top 10 Quick Pick title. **QP**

Keywords: Advice • Humor • Internet searches

Benson, Richard.

🎖 *F in Exams, the Very Best Totally Wrong Test Answers.* San Francisco: Chronicle Books, 2011. 128p. ISBN 9780811878319. **J** **H**

This collection of the very best real answers used by students on tests when they had no idea what the correct answer was is enough to make teachers, parents, and anyone who has ever studied for a test shudder. This would likely also include those children who are chosen to participate on *Are You Smarter Than a Fifth Grader?* One can hope, however, that it may encourage a greater amount of studying by anyone still in school. **QP**

Keywords: Humor • Incorrect test answers

Stalder, Erika.

The Date Book: A Teen Girl's Complete Guide to Going Out with Someone New. Illustrated by Helen Dardik. San Francisco, CA: Zest Books, 2010. 120p. ISBN 9780977266081. **M** **J**

Going out on a date can be exciting, fun, casual, awkward, or any combination of these. Deciding if, when, and how to approach that gorgeous guy; what to wear; where to go; and what to do on a date are just some of the questions tackled by Erika Stalder in this guide to approaching that first date. Girls will find a well-balanced approach to the topic that complements sensible considerations with an amusing, practical, and lighthearted look at dressing and dealing with possible parental objections before they come up.

Keywords: Dating • Relationships

Wilson, Daniel H.

Bro-Jitsu: The Martial Art of Sibling Smackdown. Illustrated by Les McClaine. New York: Bloomsbury, 2010. 151p. ISBN 9781599902791. **M** **J** **H**

There is no doubt that sibling relationships can be fraught with tension, angst, and fighting. Fighting moves are proposed by Daniel Wilson to give siblings, especially younger siblings, a chance to dominate their families, ensuring their survival in the difficult adolescent years and forging a lifetime of memories and a closer bond. The clever and funny bro-jitsu moves include both physical and psychological means of torture, which range from hiding the remote's batteries to the clever use of "throw" pillows and various means of grossing out one's siblings.

Keywords: Family relationships • Humor • Martial arts—humor • Sibling rivalries—humor

Consider Starting with . . .

Ellis, Sarah. *We Want You to Know: Kids Talk About Bullying.*

Englander, Anrenee. *Dear Diary, I'm Pregnant: Ten Real Life Stories.*

Reber, Deborah. *Chill: Stress-reducing Techniques for a More Balanced, Peaceful You.*

Redd, Nancy Amanda. *Body Drama.*

Scowen, Kate. *I.D.: Stuff That Happens to Define Us.*

Troutman, Kathryn Kraemer. *Creating Your High School Resume: A Step-by-Step Guide to Preparing an Effective Resume for College, Training and Jobs.*

Wilson, Daniel H. *Bro-Jitsu: The Martial Art of Sibling Smackdown.*

Fiction Read-Alikes

- **Calame, Don. *Beat the Band.*** Cooper Redmond faces an almost insurmountable obstacle on his path to "tagging all the bases" during his sophomore year: he has been paired with Helen Harriwick, known far and wide as "Hot Dog Helen," for a health class project, which has already caused him to start being known as "Corn Dog." Instead of resigning himself to a year at the bottom of the social totem pole, Cooper decides to hijack some tunes from an obscure Canadian band and enter himself and his best friends, albeit without their knowledge or permission, in the school's battle of the bands contest. Cooper's attempts at social redemption in Calame's irreverent and hilarious novel are full of the plots, machinations, and social commentary that readers who first became familiar with Cooper, Matt, and Sean in *Swim the Fly* will know and enjoy.

- **Day, Susie. *My Invisible Boyfriend.*** When everyone assumes Heidi must already have a boyfriend because she wouldn't make out with a guy at her boarding school's first party, she goes along with them and comes up with an imaginary and perfect guy named Ed. She doesn't expect him to become popular online with her friends, and never expects anyone to start e-mailing him, especially when her friends start e-mailing Ed about her. When she starts getting e-mails from "a real boy," things become very interesting.

- **Dessen, Sarah**. ***Along for the Ride.*** Dessen provides another solid example of a teen coming to terms with herself, her family, and a teen with baggage of his own. Auden has spent her life studying and consumed by academics. While she continues to blame herself for her parents' divorce two years before, the summer before college, which she spends at her father's house, gives her a chance to see them as individuals.

- **Emond, Stephen.** *Happyface.* In an effort to start fresh after a series of difficult events, the narrator of this funny, bittersweet tale re-creates himself in a new school. His new persona allows him to mask his pain over events of his past, the difficulties of high school, and his pathetic attempts to fit into its social scene in sarcastic journal entries and his artwork.

- **Howe, James.** *Addie on the Inside.* Addie's seventh-grade year is expressed in poems that are funny, poignant, and filled with ups and downs, as she debates her relationship with her boyfriend, DuShawn, and the cruelty of the girl who had been her BFF, in this involving, fast-moving verse novel.

- **Ignatow, Amy.** *The Popularity Papers: Research for the Social Improvement and General Betterment of Lydia Goldblatt & Julia Graham-Chang.* Readers will find an amusing, insightful look at girls, friendship, and the mysteries of popularity in Amy Ignatow's combination graphic novel and journal. When two best friends decide that their best route to popularity in middle school lies in observing the popular kids in school and performing social experiments that they will then record in a journal, little do they know that their future holds a bald patch, stick-fighting lessons, and potential humiliation in front of the whole school when a boy writes one of them a song declaring his feelings. They must decide if popularity is really worth losing a friend or find if friendship is truly more than skin deep, in a book that reads like a combination of Lynda Barry's artwork and the movie *Mean Girls.*

- **Tamaki, Mariko, and Jillian Tamaki.** *Skim.* Kimberly Cameron, known as Skim "because I'm not," endures many things in her Toronto High School, including dabbling in wicca, a tentative romance with a teacher, and her best friend's grief when her ex-boyfriend commits suicide. This was the first graphic novel to be chosen as a finalist for the Governor General's literary award, as well as being named a Top 10 Great Graphic Novel for Teens.

References

"Adolescence." 2007. *Encyclopædia Britannica.* Available at http://search.eb.com. elibrary.calgarypubliclibrary.com/eb/article-9003766 (accessed September 8, 2007).

American Psychological Association (APA). 2008. *Shared Risk Factors for Youth Obesity and Disordered Eating.* Available at http://www.apa.org/about/gr/pi/advocacy/2008/shared-risk.pdf (accessed October 29, 2011).

Chapter **9**

How To

Definition

"Do-it-yourself" (DIY) is defined in the *Oxford English Dictionary* as "the action or practice of doing work of any kind for oneself." The phrase, which came into popular usage in the 1950s in reference to household repairs, applies equally well to any number of activities—from crafts and beauty to technology, games, and even survival skills. The continuing popularity of DIY is reflected in the number of reality television programs that show houses being remodeled, cars being remade, and houses being readied for resale, as well as competitions for chefs, hairdressers, dancers, fashion designers, and models. New television channels, as well as new television stars, have been devoted to fixing up and maintaining houses, wardrobes, and lifestyles.

When Betty Carter first surveyed junior high school libraries in 1987, drawing books had high circulation numbers; readers interested in drawing can still find books to help with honing their drawing techniques. Readers can also find a plethora of craft books, as well as books for making clothes or jewelry and adapting and repurposing one's wardrobe. In addition, this category includes titles that help teens develop life skills, such as cooking and using technology, as well as books in a number of practical, artistic, and recreational subgenres.

Appeal

These books provide more than just a chance to learn something new. Finishing a project that has a tangible result can be very satisfying. Handcrafted items make great gifts and develop skills that last a lifetime. Some craft books provide historical details and are of interest to history buffs, while others give teens ideas that are just seriously cool or provide options to help fill time when they can't think of anything else to do. As teens test their abilities and interests and stretch their limits, many are particularly drawn to how-to books.

DIY books also have a great appeal to reluctant readers; each year several titles are named to the Quick Picks for Reluctant Readers list. These books are colorful and clearly written and usually contain projects that are worth spending considerable time and attention on. A number of new cookbooks have also been published in the last few years that provide readers with mouthwatering recipes, with helpful directions from chefs and teens.

Most crafts can be done in groups, with friends or family. Knitting, which has a long history as a social activity, has become a popular pastime and library program. Game books provide the same opportunity for competition as sports books, except that they generally allow people to interact with each other in a venue that often does not require a significant amount of physical activity.

Chapter Organization

This chapter is organized into activity-based sections. Readers not sure what kind of project they would like to try or looking for a wide variety of options will find titles that provide a number of choices in "General Crafts." The following sections include books that tackle specific topics. Readers can give themselves a makeover and find advice about looking their best with the books in the section "Beauty and Style." They can add to their closets and find out how to repurpose clothing into something more fashionable with the titles in the section "Clothing and Accessories." The next sections list books on artistic pursuits, including "Drawing" and "Comics and Graphic Novels." Three hands-on sections are next, titled "Cooking," "Technology," and "Games," which provide readers with instructional information that they can use in their daily pursuits. The final section is "Survival Skills."

General Crafts

Unlike the general craft books in the first volume of *Reality Rules*, many craft books published recently for teenagers have not been thematic in nature. Rather, authors have concentrated on providing a wider variety of projects with clear instructions meant to allow the reader to follow through any undertaking from beginning to end, with an eye to encouraging creativity.

Fagerstrom, Derek, and Smith, Lauren.

🎗 *Show Me How: 500 Things You Should Know - Instructions for Life from the Everyday to the Exotic.* New York: Collins Design, 2008. 320p. ISBN 9780061729621. **H**

The authors of *Show Me How* provide instructions, including graphics and step-by-step guides where necessary, for 500 things, from the simple to the downright obscure. This is an adult book: a note about adult supervision suggests that all of these activities are for entertainment value and that many "shouldn't really even be performed by adults if they can possibly help it." Nevertheless, readers will find many useful items, as well as a number of strictly entertaining ones, in the eleven groupings of "things," which show them new ways to make, style, love, eat, drink, nest, grow, thrive, go, survive, and "wow." **QP**

Keywords: Crafts • Design • How-to

Hines-Stephens, Sarah and Bethany Mann.

Show Off: How to Do Absolutely Everything One Step at a Time. Somerville, MA: Candlewick Press, 2009. 224p. ISBN 9780763645991. **M J**

This appealing book features ideas for 224 activities grouped into six sections: amaze, investigate, create, explore, cook, and move. Each activity is fully illustrated, giving instructions, ingredients where necessary, additional information that would be helpful or cross-references, and other pertinent information, such as how long a project will take, if it will be very messy, or if more information is available on the authors' Web site at www. showoffbook.com. **QP**

Keywords: Crafts • How-to

Now Try: John Woodward's *This Book Made Me Do It: Cool Things to Make, Do and Explore* is an instructional book that provides readers with a wide variety of activities. Readers will find puzzles and magic in "Amaze Your Friends"; recipes and nutritional information in "Food, Glorious Food"; suggestions for projects in "Get Creative"; ways to enjoy the outdoors in "Explore the World," followed by suggestions on how to survive in the wild; and ideas on how to be a sports hero in the final section, followed by trivia to impress others with their knowledge of world events.

Johnson, Arne, and Karen Macklin.

Indie Girl. Illustrated by Michael Wertz. San Francisco, CA: Orange Avenue Pub., 2008. 136p. ISBN 9780979017339. **J H**

The nine activities described in this book have two things in common: they are all artistic in nature and all are fairly complicated. For an artistically inclined teenager, this book offers a plethora of ideas, with the plans and organizational tips to help pull them off. There is a way for teens to use any art form, from starting a band, to making a zine; to putting on a play; to filming a TV show; to creating an art exhibit, forming a dance troupe, or creating a fashion company. Readers who enjoy this book will find more information about starting their own company in the career directions subgenre.

Keywords: Careers • Crafts • How-to

Peot, Margaret.

Inkblot: Drip, Splat and Squish Your Way to Creativity. Honesdale, PA: Boyds Mills Press, 2011. 56p. ISBN 9781590787205. **M J**

Margaret Peot offers readers a novel way to find inspiration and then expands on it. The book starts off with an explanation of why creativity is important and the basic supplies needed to make inkblots. Readers are then shown a number of ways to make inkblots, from simple to complex. Each is accompanied by examples, such as the famous Rorschach test and examples from literature. Succeeding chapters include "The Next Level of Creativity," which looks at how readers can use their inkblots to stimulate their creativity, and a chapter that encourages readers to create an inkblot journal, providing examples from the actual journals of "inkblot heroes," with comments on some of the inkblots. A final chapter includes examples from kids and adults and an invitation to find more examples on the author's Web site at www.theinkblotbook.com.

Keywords: Crafts • Creativity • Inkblots • Journaling

Beauty and Style

Advice from professionals should be taken seriously, as it provides the benefits of experience and education. In the areas of fashion and makeup guides, books can serve to help direct teenagers to find the right looks and products and, where warranted, avoid making faux pas. An additional valuable service provided by these DIY guides is to help people avoid spending money on unflattering styles and unnecessary makeup and tools by providing information about skin care and advice about style. They can also supplement the books found in the personal growth subgenre in chapter 8, by helping readers to emphasize their best features. Both subgenres are very popular with female readers.

Beauty

Books in this section are devoted to the process of beautification: helping to improve one's outward appearance and finding ways to emphasize one's best features. Readers will find books that discuss skin care and ailments, with information about skin cancer, as well as about finding and using the right colors, makeup, and tools. The recently published *Bobbi Brown Makeup Manual* is used to train her consultants. These books can help teenagers find the tools and makeup to create an appropriate, stylish, and attractive look, for any number of occasions.

Bergamotto, Lori.

Skin: The Bare Facts. San Francisco, CA: Zest Books, 2009. 98p. ISBN 9780980073256. **M J**

This guide to skin and how to care for it provides explanations for a number of common issues that teenagers will face, including how to determine one's skin type and what the best daily treatment is for each type, acne's cause and potential treatments, various skin ailments, hair removal methods, and skin cancer. Bergamotto does not overlook the positive side of skin treatments, including recipes for DIY spa treatments and instructions for using makeup.

Keywords: Makeup • Skin • Skin care

Brown, Bobbi, with Rebecca Paley.

Beauty Rules: Fabulous Looks, Beauty Essentials, and Life Lessons for Loving Your Teens and Twenties. Photographs by Ondrea Barbe and Ben Ritter. San Francisco, CA: Chronicle Books, 2010. 288p. ISBN 9780811874687. **J H**

This comprehensive book on looking one's best includes advice for teenagers on how to feel their best, as well as a multitude of tips from the makeup master about how to make the most of their best features. Brown includes many lessons gleaned from her own life, as well as those of friends and family. She emphasizes health, fitness, and beauty from the inside out. Readers will be reassured to know that there are ways to emphasize what they like best about their appearance, and she provides lots of examples that demonstrate this technique. It is also nice to be given an update on the people featured in Brown's original book about teen makeup. Readers who enjoy makeup, style, and learning new techniques from top stylists will gravitate to this book.

Keywords: Health • Makeup • Makeup techniques

Bobbi Brown Makeup Manual. New York: Springboard Press/Grand Central Publishing, 2008. 221p. ISBN 9780446581349. **H A/YA**

Bobbi Brown distills all of her expertise with makeup into a guide that breaks down makeup and makeup techniques into their parts. This is the textbook for Bobbi Brown consultants, offering photographs and explanations for anything and everything one will find, use, or buy from a makeup counter, with suggestions about what is appropriate for skin conditions, hair and eye colors, and travelling, as well as supplementary chapters on makeup for fashion shows and famous names in makeup.

Keywords: Makeup • Makeup techniques

CosmoGirl! Editors.

Ask CosmoGirl! About Beauty: [All the Answers to Your Questions about Hair, Makeup, Skin & More]. New York: Hearst Books/Sterling Publishers, 2008. 143p. ISBN 9781588166449. **M J**

Readers who have a question about acne, skin care, hair care, or makeup are more than likely not the first or the only ones to be seeking that answer. The editors of *CosmoGirl!* either answer or provide answers from reputable sources, including dermatologists, dentists, and makeup artists, for their readers' beauty dilemmas.

Keywords: Acne • Beauty • Hair care • Makeup • Skin care

Oldham, Kristen.

🎖 *Seventeen Presents . . . 500 Beauty Tips: Look Your Best for School, Weekend, Parties & More!* New York: Hearst Books, 2009. 528p. ISBN 9781588166425. **J H**

Readers looking for beauty tips will find a plethora of them in this pocket-sized guide. In six sections readers can find quick suggestions from beauty experts appropriate for school, weekend, party, date, work, and poolside. The tips offered have a wide range of applications, from skin and hair care to makeup, and where applicable they specify the coloring that would be appropriate. **QP**

Keywords: Hair care • Makeup • Skin care

Wallach, Marlene, and Grace Norwich.

My Beauty: A Guide to Looking & Feeling Great. New York: Aladdin Mix/Simon & Schuster Children's Pub., 2009. 115p. ISBN 9781416979098. **M J**

This practical, quick guide, from the president of the Wilhelmina KIDS and TEENS modeling agency, covers beautification from head to toe, including hair and skin care, makeup, and dental advice for getting and keeping a great smile. The chapter "The Rest of You" covers manicures and pedicures. This is a great overview that includes quizzes and advice from someone with real knowledge.

Keywords: Beauty • Hair care • Makeup • Skin care

Style

Books in this section concentrate on wardrobe and accessories. They show readers how to put clothes and accessories together for a great look and demonstrate how the right clothes can make the most of any body type. These titles are immensely popular with female readers. Those interested in pursuing a career in fashion, modeling, or fashion design can find titles to guide them toward a future in the industry in the "Career Directions" section in chapter 8.

Conrad, Lauren, with Elise Loehnen.

Lauren Conrad Style. New York: Harper, 2010. 230p. ISBN 9780061989148. **J H**

Television star turned designer Lauren Conrad presents a very complete guide to creating a wardrobe. Readers will find shopping, hairdressing, and makeup tips. She doesn't overlook accessories and shoes, and her chatty, lively text includes reassurances that everyone has something he or she would change about the way he or she looks. Additional inclusions that set this book apart are chapters devoted to travel, with suggestions for "strategic packing" and creating outfits suitable for the road for several different types of trips; special events; and work and school.

Keywords: Makeup • Packing • Shopping • Style • Wardrobe

Daman, Eric.

You Know You Want It: Style-Inspiration-Confidence. New York: Clarkson Potter, 2009. 207p. ISBN 9780307464583. **H**

After a foreword from Gossip Girl Leighton Meester, readers are given instructions and advice from costume designer Eric Daman to enable them to find their body type, clean out their closets, and start fresh in creating a fully accessorized signature style, bearing in mind that a well-dressed woman is a confident woman. After presenting different articles of clothing and their best uses and suitability for body types, Daman also looks at colors and overall styles and provides some information on wardrobe maintenance.

Keywords: Accessorizing • Body types • Fashion • Style

Now Try: A much more lighthearted guide to style is Clinton Kelly's *Oh No She Didn't: The Top 100 Style Mistakes and How to Avoid Them*. The star of TLC's *What Not to Wear* mixes irredeemable style faux pas, such as the Pacific Northwest's "Canadian tuxedo," dressing in denim from head-to-toe, with those that can be rectified, such as incorrect hem lengths. While Kelly pokes fun indiscriminately, it is usually at the over-thirty crowd and with a clever manner that stylish teenage readers will appreciate.

Shoket, Ann.

"Seventeen" Ultimate Guide to Style: How to Find Your Perfect Look. Philadelphia, PA: Running Press Book Publishers, 2011. 192p. ISBN 9780762441938. **J H**

This book aims to help teens find their perfect style, by providing a key to six different looks: girly, edgy, boho, classic, glam, and indie. Each chapter includes a definition, key wardrobe elements, and "must haves," which are shown on a teenager and a celebrity deemed to typify the look, as well as a list of shops that carry items suitable for the style. Readers will also find additional lists that have suggestions for accessories geared to each style and guides with lots of pictures for finding their "perfect fit" for articles of clothing that often require additional tips, such as jeans, swimsuits, and bras and undies.

Keywords: Clothes • Fashion • Style

Stalder, Erika.

The Look Book: 50 Iconic Beauties and How to Achieve Their Signature Styles. San Francisco, CA: Zest Books, 2011. 127p. ISBN 9780981973388. **M J H**

Erika Stalder presents fifty of the most iconic beauties, starting with Clara Bow, and uses each to illustrate a singular "look" that is frequently associated with that representative beauty, divided into five sections: lips, eyes, brows, skin and face, and hair. From Kate Winslet's "No-makeup makeup" to Bjork's face ornamentation, each section includes suggestions about the time and tools needed to re-create the style as well as instructions for re-creating the look, a photograph of the titular beauty, and a list of other stars known for that style.

Keywords: Hairstyles • Makeup styles • Styles

Wallach, Marlene, and Grace Norwich.

My Look: A Guide to Fashion & Style. New York: Aladdin Mix/Simon & Schuster Children's Pub., 2009. 117p. ISBN 9781416979104. **M J**

This guide to style by the president of the Wilhelmina KIDS and TEENS modeling agency sets out to help tweens and teens define their own personal style. She then offers clear advice about colors, shopping, accessorizing, and creating and maintaining a great wardrobe, followed up with a fashion quiz, in a colorful, fun package that girls will appreciate.

Keywords: Accessorizing • Fashion • Style

Clothing and Accessories

Books about knitting, as well as making and accessorizing clothing, remain popular, among teens as well as adults. The ability to produce something wearable, durable, and beautiful is a life skill that may be taken up at any age. Genevieve Miller has even taken advantage of the recent popularity of paranormal fantasies to produce a book of knitting patterns, *Vampire Knits*, specifically geared to readers of that genre. Guides may also be found to help crafters learn ways to remake their clothing, which can serve a dual purpose of using items languishing in the back of readers' closets to save money while also turning secondhand items into something new and fashionable.

Alvarado, Melissa, Hope Meng, and Melissa Rannels.

Subversive Seamster: Transform Thrift Store Threads into Street Couture. Newtown, CT: Taunton Press, 2007. 188p. ISBN 9781561589258. **J H**

This extremely adventurous, fun take on repurposing shows how to make the best use possible of thrift store finds. The authors start by giving readers advice for shopping in thrift stores and then a guide to help kick their "sewing skills up a notch," before offering a wide variety of projects, from pillows to clothing and accessories, that will allow crafters from novice to advanced sewers to transform items. Each project indicates what kind of fabric or item(s) is needed, as well as the techniques to be used and the amount of time the project will take.

Keywords: Crafts • Repurposing • Sewing

Blakeney, Faith, Justina Blakeney, and Ellen Schultz.

99 Ways to Cut, Sew, Tie & Rock Your Scarf. New York: Potter Craft, c2008. Unpaged. ISBN 9780307395672. **J H**

All of the projects include a picture, directions, an estimate of the length of time they will take to complete, and illustrations. The finished products vary widely, from a headscarf or bracelet to a top, skirt, or dress. The authors encourage readers to seek out the appropriate material for the desired result: The baby bib and barrel bag shown are decidedly more practical than the party gown and baby doll top.

Keywords: Repurposing • Scarves • Sewing

Miller, Genevieve.

Vampire Knits: Projects to Keep You Knitting from Twilight to Dawn. New York: Potter Craft, 2010. 144p. ISBN 9780307586605. **H**

A professed lover of the *Twilight* series provides twenty-eight patterns for projects inspired by vampires. The projects include a "Tourniquet Scarf" with a red center that drips into grey edges and a "Vampire Diary Protector" suitable for Elena or Stefan. Knowledge of knitting is assumed; although patterns are given, notes and instructions for stitches and finishing are minimal.

Keywords: Crafts • Knitting • Vampires

Nicolay, Megan.

Generation T: Beyond Fashion: 110 T-shirt Transformations for Pets, Babies, Friends, Your Home, Car, and You. New York: Workman Publishing Company, 2009. 310p. ISBN 9780761154105. **H**

The second *Generation T* book moves beyond simple fashions into looking at repurposing T-shirts as good for the environment. The directions are clear and straightforward, with levels of difficulty ranging from beginner projects that don't require any sewing, through level three projects, which start to need a needle and thread, to advanced level five projects, which require some time and effort. Most projects also offer a suggested list of "variations" along with the directions. The projects give readers the opportunity not only to add to their wardrobe but also to find the perfect gift for almost anyone, with chapters on children's clothes, pet accessories, projects for men, things for the car, and clothes and accessories perfect to take "out on the town."

Keywords: Repurposing • Sewing • T-shirts

Smith, Alison.

The Sewing Book. New York: Dorling Kindersley Limited, 2009. 400p. ISBN 9780756642808. **H** **A/YA**

This comprehensive guide provides crafters with an introduction to the tools and techniques for both hand and machine sewing. Large, full-color illustrations are coupled with step-by-step instructions to both help the novice and improve the skills of a competent sewer. Information about fabrics and patterns precedes the final section, which includes a large selection of projects to encourage sewers to practice their skills.

Keywords: Sewing • Sewing skills

Warwick, Ellen.

Everywear. Illustrated by Bernice Lum. <u>Planet Girl</u>. Toronto: Kids Can Press, Ltd., 2008. 80p. ISBN 9781553377993. **M** **J**

> This offering in the <u>Planet Girl</u> series covers accessories that help punch up a plain wardrobe. Following a quick DIY guide to explain the prepping instructions and sewing stitches used in the directions, readers will find sixteen crafts, laid out with step-by-step directions and enticing pictures of the finished products.
>
> **Keywords:** Accessories • Crafts • Sewing

Webber, Carmen, and Carmia Marshall.

Denim Mania: 25 Stylish Ways to Transform Your Jeans. New York: St. Martin's Griffin, 2008. 154p. ISBN 9780312359911. **H**

> Carmen and Carmia Marshall, the team behind the Sistahs of Harlem clothing label, have included a history of denim and information that takes this book well beyond a guide for repurposing the jeans languishing at the back of your closet. Starting with information about denim shades, styles, washes, types, and finishes, the Sistahs then provide readers with tips on caring for denim and how to choose the best style for their body types, before moving on to "adorning your denim." This segues into sewing supplies and equipment and tips for sewing denim, before providing a number of projects for tops, bottoms, and accessories to turn those unused and old jeans into stylish, like-new garments.
>
> **Keywords:** Jeans • Repurposing • Sewing

Drawing

Drawing was a popular subject with young adult readers when Betty Carter first did her circulation study, and it still is. What has changed since then is the subject matter. The overwhelming popularity of graphic novels is evident in the number of books that give teens instructions and advice about cartooning, manga, and anime. This section is divided into two categories, "Techniques" and "Manga," in which readers can find books specifically on those subjects. Teens interested in writing and creating graphic novels, as well as in information about genres of graphic novels, will find material in the section "Comics and Graphic Novels."

Techniques

In this section are guides that help readers refine their drawing and suggestions for budding artists. Most of these have useful, step-by-step illustrations. Supplemental information often includes interviews, suggestions for supplies, and tips. Readers looking for inspiration will appreciate Lynda Barry's *Picture This*, which discusses many different types of drawing.

Barry, Lynda.

Picture This. Montreal, QC: Drawn & Quarterly, 2010. 226p. ISBN 97818972996471. **J** **H**

> Lynda Barry's follow-up to *This is It* contemplates the art of doodling in the form of a graphic semi-memoir that gives an alter ego named Marlys and a new character named the Near-Sighted Monkey the opportunity to offer a mini drawing course. Other projects discuss collage, outline, tracery, color-work, paper dolls, and why creativity changes as children get older.
>
> **Keywords:** Creativity • Drawing

Hart, Christopher.

Cartoon Cute Animals: How to Draw the Most Irresistible Creatures on the Planet. New York: Watson-Guptill Publications, 2010. 160p. ISBN 9780823085569. **M** **J**

> Readers interested in cartooning will enjoy this comprehensive guide to creating darling, doe-eyed animals that pop off the page. The step-by-step sketches include Hart's trademark hints to define and highlight parts of the drawings. After an initial chapter on the essentials, readers will discover a wide assortment of animals, divided into sections, including dogs and cats, bears, woodland creatures, animals of the jungles and plains, for the birds, and a final group of sea life and reptiles.
>
> **Keywords:** Cartooning • Drawing

Drawing Vampires: Gothic Creatures of the Night. New York: Chris Hart Books, 2009. 143p. ISBN 9781933027814. **M** **J**

> This introduction to drawing vampires includes tips and tricks for vampire faces and poses as well as a number of chapters designed to add mystery and ambiance to these fanciful beings. Instructions for different kinds of vampires, vampire slayers, and other beings one might expect to find around creatures of the night are especially useful.
>
> **Keywords:** Drawing • Vampires • Werewolves

Manga

Manga is a Japanese genre of cartoons and animation, usually recognizable by the style of illustration. The books in this category help readers learn how to draw this distinctive style of illustration.

Hart, Christopher.

Manga for the Beginner: Everything You Need to Start Drawing Right Away. New York: Watson Guptill Publications, 2008. 192p. ISBN 9780823030835. **M** **J** **H**

> This comprehensive introduction provides guidelines that break down the manga drawing process into steps, which is especially useful for beginners.

Sections are provided for characters, the manga head, body, clothing and costumes, manga animals, and anthros and shonen characters. A final section discusses drawing techniques that will help animators develop their skills.

Keywords: Drawing • Manga

Now Try: Jason Yadao's *The Rough Guide to Manga* will be of interest to both manga fans and readers who have been unable to appreciate the form. The author starts by giving readers a historical overview, including an introduction to the influential names in Japanese comics. This is followed by a discussion of manga's increasing popularity overseas, a primer complete with examples, and then a detailed listing of fifty essential manga. This is followed by other anime, such as video games, information about publishers, and lists of further resources that include books, Web sites, and conventions.

Manga Mania Romance: Drawing Shojo Girls and Bishie Boys. New York: Chris Hart Books, 2008. 144p. ISBN 9781933027432. **M** **J** **H**

In this great introductory guide for a novice illustrator interested in learning or adding to a manga repertoire of drawing, Chris Hart concentrates his instructions on the two characters, starting with the basics for girls and bishies, pretty girl, and handsome boy characters. He then provides lots of options for clothing, setting the scene, and finishing touches.

Keywords: Bishie boys • Drawing • Manga • Shojo girls

Shonen: Drawing Action-style Japanese Comics. Manga Mania. New York: Chris Hart Books, 2008. 143p. ISBN 9781933027692. **M** **J**

Christopher Hart's first book in the Manga Mania series focuses specifically on the "action styles of Japanese comics." Readers are presented with a full-color drawing and several black-and-white sketches that illustrate the steps to get from start to finish, along with several hints about the various parts of the picture. Sidebars give further hints for techniques, background information about the various characters, and ways to personalize the illustrations.

Keywords: Drawing • Manga • Shonen

Comics and Graphic Novels

Graphic novels remain a very popular format with teenagers. Nowadays they are receiving more critical praise and recognition, including a literary award and an annual selection list with the Young Adult Services Association. The books in this section provide information about how to create comics and graphic novels. Books about cartooning, including drawing manga, can be found in the previous section.

Abel, Jessica, and Matt Madden.

Drawing Words & Writing Pictures: Making Comics: Manga, Graphic Novels, and Beyond. New York: First Second, 2008. 282p. ISBN 9781596431317. **H**

This complete guide to creating comics could be used by an individual or a class. Each of the fifteen chapters, which start with the building blocks of comics and progress to a 24-hour comic, includes suggestions for further reading and homework to improve upon a reader's own designs. Readers are given encouragement by the authors with a note that neither of them had professional training. The inclusion and discussions of noteworthy comics add an extra touch to this smart teaching tool.

Keywords: Cartooning • Graphic novels • Manga

Li, Yishan.

Shonen Art Studio: Everything You Need to Create Your Own Shonen Manga Comics. New York: Watson-Guptill Publications, 2010. 128p. ISBN 9780823033324. **J** **H**

This book provides a comprehensive introduction to the art of shonen manga, manga targeted to a male audience age ten and up. Instructions are also provided for the accompanying CD (which will work with either Windows or Mac OS X, along with Photoshop 7 or later), so that novice artists can learn from the ideas in the book and then use the templates provided to make their own comics. Should the CD disappear, there is enough information about the drawing process for this to be a useful tool about the process of drawing manga in its own right, but this is primarily a book that will be of interest for readers wanting to learn about using Photoshop to make comics.

Keywords: Comics • Shonen manga

Sturm, James, Andrew Arnold, and Alexis Frederick-Frost.

Adventures in Cartooning: How to Turn Your Doodles into Comics. New York: Roaring Brook/First Second. 2009. 109p. ISBN 9781596433694. **M**

The director of the Center for Cartoon Studies and two of his former students present this charming and fun combination graphic novel/how-to book. Readers are introduced to a questing knight searching for a captive princess. His voyage brings him into contact with a candy-eating dragon and a very merry elf. The clever and amusing layouts illustrate panels, gutters, movement, and other elements of cartooning in much the same way as Scott Macleod's *Understanding Comics*, but presented for a younger audience. **ALA**

Keywords: Cartooning • Cartoons • Graphic novel

Williams, Freddie E.

The DC Comics Guide to Digitally Drawing Comics. New York: Watson-Guptill Publications, 2009. 144p. ISBN 9780823099238. **H** **GN**

A professional artist for DC Comics provides not only solid reasons about why he chooses to use Adobe Photoshop for his illustrations, but also detailed instructions for everything from keeping backups to the individual tools he uses for making comics. Williams introduces readers to each step, from creating a library of images to the individual tool that makes the software a better choice for him than drawing by hand, as well as the various processes needed to create a comic and to market an artist.

Keywords: Comics • Digital illustrations • Graphic artists • Graphic nonfiction

Cooking

Cooking is an activity that many teens are interested in as they become more independent. Teen cookbooks are usually illustrated and often feature glossaries and supplementary information that is not found in adult cookbooks. Their authors are generally subject specialists. Male chefs like Sam Stern, author of *Sam Stern's Get Cooking* and *Sam Stern's Real Food Real Fast*, offer male readers a viable role model as a presence in the kitchen. The popularity of this subgenre is evidenced by the large number of titles produced in the last few years, authors writing several books, and the publication of updated editions of titles, such as the new edition of Evelyn Raab's *Clueless in the Kitchen*.

Carle, Megan, and Jill Carle.

College Cooking: Feed Yourself and Your Friends. Berkeley, CA: Ten Speed Press, 2007. 144p. ISBN 9781580088268. **J H**

Readers will find recipes for an incredibly small, usually empty (what's a baking sheet?) kitchen, from two girls who had written two cookbooks, but found upon moving into a dorm room with roommates who hadn't "progressed beyond ramen noodles and frozen dinners" that they needed to adapt their style of cooking. In addition to a great introductory section, chapters cover survival cooking, avoiding the freshman fifteen, cheap eats, eating greens, and feeding the masses.

Keywords: Cooking • Desserts • Recipes

College Vegetarian Cooking: Feed Yourself and Your Friends. Berkeley, CA: Ten Speed Press, 2009. 160p. ISBN 9781580089821. **H**

Aspiring chefs will find ninety recipes organized neatly into sections that group food into commonsense categories for a young adult or college student: just like mom makes, avoiding the freshman fifteen, survival cooking, party food, cheap eats, and impressing your date. Each recipe is accompanied by a helpful sidebar, such as a "cooking 101" tip. The introductory section covers vitals such as kitchen basics, stocking the pantry, and tools and equipment.

Keywords: Cooking • Recipes • Vegetarian cooking

Gerasole, Isabella, and Olivia Gerasole.

The Spatulatta Cookbook: Recipes for Kids, by Kids, from the James Beard Award-winning Web Site. New York: Scholastic Reference, 2007. 128p. ISBN 9780439022507. **M J**

As preteens, Isabella and Olivia Gerasole created a Web site that was awarded a prestigious James Beard culinary award. Here they have translated some delicious, enticing recipes into seasonal sections as well as additional sections for vegetarian dishes and snacks. Readers can find and prepare the freshest ingredients, whether it's making a sweet potato pie during the fall or capitalizing on local fare for an end-of-summer salad. The accompanying photographs and cooking tips will encourage aspiring chefs.

Keywords: Cooking • Recipes

Now Try: Readers looking to develop their cooking skills will be interested in food writer Amanda Grant's *The Silver Spoon for Children: Favorite Italian Recipes*. This is a young readers' version of *The Silver Spoon*, an international best seller also known as the Italian *Joy of Cooking*. Readers not only can learn how to cook Italian food, but also can find cooking techniques, along with step-by-step recipes that have been checked by a nutritionist and are all presented with a color picture of the finished product.

Gold, Rozanne.

Eat Fresh Food: *Awesome Recipes for Teen Chefs.* Photographs by Phil Mansfield. New York: Bloomsbury Children's Books, 2009. 160p. ISBN 9781599902821. **J H**

The food in this book was created in accordance with what has become a trend—buying and eating food while paying attention to its origins—and the recipes practice what Gold and her "all star team" preach. The introduction points out that "Fresh" stands for farmer-friendly, ripe-ready, easy-exciting, sustainable, and honest-healthy. The resulting recipes are enticing and are beautifully depicted in the photographs. The cast of sous-chefs range in age from nine to nineteen. This book will easily encourage readers to try something more challenging.

Keywords: Cooking • Fresh food • Recipes

Goodall, Tiffany.

The Ultimate Student Cookbook: From Chicken to Chili. Photography by Claire Peters. Richmond Hill, ON; Buffalo, NY: Firefly Books, 2010. 160p. ISBN 9781554076024. **H**

Aimed at novice chefs moving out to start college and beginning to cook for themselves, this cookbook starts with the basics and presents recipes broken down into steps, each of which is accompanied by a color photograph. All of the recipes include supplementary suggestions for leftovers, serving suggestions, and optional extras. The recipes cover a wide range of dishes, from single-serving risottos to a Thai green curry that feeds eight. From breakfasts to desserts to house parties, no occasion is overlooked, although a younger reader looking for a solid introductory guide to basic dishes would also be interested in the information about kitchen equipment and food hygiene.

Keywords: Cooking • Kitchen equipment • Recipes

Locricchio, Matthew.

Teen Cuisine. Photographs by James Peterson. Tarrytown, NY: Marshall Cavendish, 2010. 207p. ISBN 9780761457152. **J** **H**

This cookbook for teens sets out recipes in nine sections divided by meal, starting with breakfast and working through to desserts. In what will be a welcome feature in a teen cookbook, there are additional groupings for snacks, salads and dressings, soups, sides, sandwiches and burgers, and pizzas coast-to-coast. Novices will welcome the introductory note about safety in the kitchen and the clear preparatory instructions in the recipes. Readers confused by the imperial measurements can find a conversion table at the back as well as a glossary of "kitchen essentials" and a picture dictionary of tools.

Keywords: Cooking • Recipes

Raab, Evelyn.

Clueless in the Kitchen: A Cookbook for Teens. Richmond Hill, ON; Buffalo, NY: Firefly Books, 2011. 216p. ISBN 9781554078240. **J** **H**

Raab's updated edition of her cookbook is an even more user-friendly guide for novice and nervous cooks than her first book. She starts out by giving more detailed instructions about the basic equipment and staples to keep in a kitchen, then provides readers with a shopping guide that answers questions about how and what to buy in parts of the store as diverse as meats, cheeses, herbs, spices, and vegetables. The recipes are presented clearly, with readers having been recommended to read through the entire narrative and gather all ingredients and tools before starting. Supplementary information is often included, such as suggestions for what to do with the leftovers or alternative cooking methods. Inexperienced cooks will particularly appreciate supplementary pages that demonstrate "how to chop any vegetable" or "how to cut up a chicken" and "how to cook rice." The chapters are organized in the following order: breakfast, salads and sides, meats, pastas, desserts, fish, vegetarian dishes, snacks, and a final section that explains how to plan a meal.

Keywords: Cooking • Meal planning • Recipes

Stern, Sam.

Get Cooking. Somerville, MA: Candlewick Press, 2009. 143p. ISBN 978076363926. **J** **H**

The third book from England's teen chef is divided into eight sections, each devoted to recipes for the favorite food of one of Stern's best mates: tomatoes, cheese, pasta, vegetables, meat, potatoes, chocolate, and sweets. Introductions to each section explain the appeal of the main ingredient, and every page of the book has pictures of the dishes, Sam, and his friends. All of the recipes have clear directions, and most of them feature sidebars that offer either variations for ingredients or serving options.

Keywords: Cooking • Recipes

Now Try: Though it is always nice to see what professional chefs come up with in their cookbooks, it is equally refreshing to see reminders that they can make mistakes. A collection of those errors makes for compulsive reading in Jen Yates's *Cake Wrecks: When Professional Cakes Go Hilariously Wrong*, wrecks gathered from her popular blog, cakewrecks.blogspot.com. This highly appealing title was chosen for the 2011 Quick Pick for Young Adult Readers.

Real Food, Real Fast. Cambridge, MA: Candlewick Press, 2008. 128p. ISBN 9780763635336 pbk. **J H**

British teen Sam Stern's sophomore entry into the cookbook field organizes recipes by cooking time. Aspiring chefs will find "healthy and delicious" offerings grouped according to how long it takes Stern to prepare them, ranging from five to thirty minutes. The dishes often feature pictures of the finished product or Stern and his friends, as well as clear directions and suggestions for ways to vary the recipe and "time tricks" to speed up the cooking process.

Keywords: Cooking • Recipes

Zinczenko, David, with Matt Goulding.

Eat This, Not That! 2010: Thousands of Simple Food Swaps That Can Save You 10, 20, 30 Pounds—or More! New York: Rodale; distributed to the trade by Macmillan, 2008. 304p. ISBN 9781594868542. **H**

If the term "functional food" is unfamiliar to you, unlike "convenience food," let these authors introduce you to some simple exchanges and tricks that can save you and your waistline from thousands of calories. Where are the hidden traps in menus, grocery store aisles, and particular restaurant chains? This updated edition reflects changes that were made to restaurant menus after they were named to the authors' "worst" lists in the 2007 edition.

Keywords: Convenience foods • Dieting • Nutrition

Now Try: David Zinczenko and Matt Goulding wrote *Eat This, Not That: Supermarket Survival Guide* specifically to help educate readers on becoming smarter shoppers. The supermarket guide includes nutrition information and tours readers through every section of the grocery story to help them buy the best possible products.

Technology

Technology offers today's young adults ample opportunities for creative outlets. The books in this section go beyond providing basic introductions to equipment and software. The authors provide suggestions on how to put the knowledge covered to use. For example, readers can use the instructions in *Programming Video Games for the Evil Genius* to write their own games for any Mac or PC. Let the fun begin!

Ang, Tom.

Digital Photography: An Introduction. New York: Dorling Kindersley, Limited, 2010. 224p. ISBN 9780756658373. **H** **A/YA**

Amateur and professional photographers are introduced to the art of digital photography, digital cameras, and what can be done with them. Readers will find not only chapters on the fundamentals of taking pictures, but also on manipulating images and printing and publishing images and creating a Web site, as well as a buying guide.

Keywords: Digital cameras • Digital photography

Cinnamon, Ian.

Programming Video Games for the Evil Genius. New York: McGraw-Hill, 2008. 319p. ISBN 9780071497527. **H** **A/YA**

Ian Cinnamon was fifteen when he wrote this instruction manual for programming games to run on any Mac or PC. Readers with a computer and access to the Internet may follow along with the projects in this book, using Java and C++ to learn the fifty-seven gaming projects, starting with a compiler and working through to becoming a true evil genius. Styles of games include racing, board, space destroyers, strategy, and retro.

Keywords: Computer programming • Java • Programming • Video games

Jenisch, Josh.

The Art of the Video Game. Philadelphia, PA: Quirk Books, 2008. 160p. ISBN 9781594742774. **H** **A/YA**

After a short history of video game artwork, intended to introduce readers to the extent to which its quality has improved in current games, Josh Jenisch looks at concept, development, and in-game video art. Each game examined not only provides an opportunity to showcase how the artists have used their talents for the purposes of the game, but also gives Jenisch a chance to provide additional background information about the games. Each game is shown to advantage, with several illustrations that help to show how the artists emphasize mood and tone. Gamers and artists alike will appreciate the wide range of images and styles covered in this book. **QP**

Keywords: Computer animation • Computer art • Computer graphics

Games

The books in this subgenre provide readers with information about specific games, whether from a historical perspective or to help them learn about, participate in, and get ready to play the game. Readers will also find information about great players and where to play, such as Daniel King's *Chess: From First Moves to Checkmate*. Look for information about creating gaming software in the technology section.

King, Daniel.

Chess: From First Moves to Checkmate. New York: Kingfisher, 2010. 64p. ISBN 9780753419304. **J** **H**

This introduction to the game of chess from an International Grandmaster provides a history of the game as well as an explanation of each piece, exercises, and suggestions for strategies that will help even experienced players improve their game. The illustrations are clear, and supplemental information includes a glossary and Web sites listing chess organizations and further information. While the "ultimate match" remains Gary Kasparov's 1997 game against Deep Blue, it is interesting to note that this updated edition includes information about chess databases and a 2006 world championship contest in which a contestant was accused of using computer assistance.

Keywords: Chess • Games

Lipkowitz, Daniel.

The LEGO Book. New York: Dorling Kindersley, 2009. 200p. ISBN 978075665623. **M** **J**

When the LEGO© brick was patented in 1958, it revolutionized the company's "System of Play," creating a form of interactive play that would reach around the globe and across generations. This colorful book introduces readers to the design elements, themes, sets, and evolving technology that continue to make LEGO© such an enduring form of creative play and education. **QP**

Keywords: LEGO©

Survival Skills

We live in a dangerous world—so it's lucky for readers that books can help prepare them for the many treacherous situations in which they might find themselves. The titles in this subgenre are intended to help readers cope with problems or hazards that are a part of everyday life (*The Worst-Case Scenario Survival Handbook: Middle School*) or those that are beyond our control (such as the situations covered in the volumes of the <u>Prepare to Survive</u> series). Some places on Earth provide such extremes that creatures have adapted to survive there; humans have been able to develop either phenomenal skills or technology to enable them to visit these areas, whether on land, on sea, or in outer space. Although the experts and skills used as sources in these books are legitimate, the skills are generally outside the realm of possibility for the average reader and offer instead either practical advice or a humorous reading experience.

Borgenicht, David, Ben H. Winters, and Robin Epstein.

The Worst-Case Scenario Survival Handbook: Middle School. San Francisco, CA: Chronicle Books, 2009. 128p. ISBN 9780811868648. **M** **J**

Middle school can present teens with many dangers, from the daunting unknowns of the first day to the myriad risks associated with being popular (or not), bullying, homework, and the choices they need to make. The authors offer advice for situations that readers will likely find both amusing and reassuring.

Keywords: Humor • Middle school • Survival skills

Now Try: Readers who enjoy the humorous aspect of the "Worst-Case" guides will flock to the authors' compendium of possible disasters, the junior edition of the *Worst-Case Scenario Survive-o-pedia*. From flu pandemics to mudslides and the Bermuda Triangle, this book covers a wide variety of dangers, along with guidance on how to handle things when they can't be avoided, such as turbulence.

Edge Books.

Prepare to Survive. **RR**

The six slim books in this series look at different dangerous situations and present the best ways to deal with them. Where possible, readers are also presented with ways to be prepared, knowing that chances for survival may be greatly increased if they have survival kits and are aware of potential dangers. These are books that appeal both to reluctant and ESL readers, as the language is not difficult but the subjects are interesting and include a number of examples and photographs of people surviving tragedies. All of the books offer suggestions for further reading and Web sites.

Doeden, Matt.

How to Survive a Flood. Mankato, MN: Capstone Press, c2009. 32p. ISBN 9781429622776. **M**

Did you know that floods may be categorized as flash floods or storm surges, which can be caused by hurricanes or tsunamis? All categories are potentially life threatening, and they are one of the most common forms of natural disaster in the United States. Because they can happen anywhere, it is important to be prepared for them. Floods bring with them other dangers, including downed power lines, rushing water, and lingering troubles in the aftermath that may include frightened animals such as snakes, low food supplies, and high bacteria counts in flood water. Matt Doeden offers many tips for how to best prepare for as well as survive an actual flood, and true tales of survivors.

Keywords: Floods • Survival skills

Martin, Michael.

How to Survive a Tornado. Mankato, MN: Capstone Press, c2009. 32p. ISBN 9781429622783. **M**

Tornadoes occur all over the planet, but they are more common in the United States than anywhere else on the planet, having killed more than 10,000 people there since 1900. There is even an area in the centre of the country, encompassing parts of Oklahoma, Kansas, and other nearby states, that scientists call Tornado Alley. The dangers from a tornado are not only the destructive powers of the winds, but also collateral damage, whether people are hurt by collapsing buildings or lack food and water. Michael Martin offers readers advice on how best to be prepared and stay safe from these extremely dangerous storms, whether caught in a house, mobile home, school, or mall.

Keywords: Survival skills • Tornadoes

Montgomery, Heather.

How to Survive an Earthquake. Mankato, MN: Capstone Press, 2009. 32p. ISBN 9781429622790. **M**

Earthquakes can happen at any time, but they are usually small enough not to be felt. The earth's plates are constantly in motion, and it is only when the motion stops that tension builds up and the plates slip, causing an earthquake, usually at a fault where two plates meet. This is why there are more earthquakes in some places than in others. Scientists use a rating system called the Modified Mercalli Intensity Scale to measure the effects of an earthquake. This volume gives readers advice on what to put in a survival kit as well as how best to survive an earthquake in a number of situations. Several survivors' stories illustrate how to be prepared and stay safe.

Keywords: Earthquakes • Survival skills

O'Shei, Tim.

How to Survive Being Lost at Sea. Mankato, MN: Capstone Press, c2009. 32p. ISBN 9781429622806. **M**

In this volume of the <u>Prepare to Survive</u> series, Tim O'Shei tells readers that the key to survival at sea is to remember that although one may be surrounded by water, none of it is potable; and drinking saltwater will dehydrate and adversely affect the body. Having a survival kit on a boat ensures that in the event of an accident, one may at least have water or a desalination kit at hand. Survivors also need to prepare to deal with problems such as temperature, predators such as sharks, and gathering food and water. Tips for ways to stay warm and ration food and then advice for gathering food and water are included in the guide, along with suggestions for further reading and Web sites.

Keywords: Survival after shipwrecks • Survival skills

How to Survive in the Wilderness. Mankato, MN: Capstone Press, 2009. 32 p. ISBN 9781429622813. **M**

This guide for surviving and thriving in the great outdoors provides not only information about what to pack in a survival kit to be prepared to face possible dangers, but also illustrations and instructions for a number of things that future *Survivor* competitors would enjoy, including preparing shelters, making fire, finding water, facing dangerous animals, and looking after yourself in the wild. Readers are given suggestions for further reading, a Web site to find more information, and true tales of wilderness survivors.

Keywords: Survival skills • Wilderness survival

How to Survive on a Deserted Island. Mankato, MN: Capstone Press, 2009. 32p. ISBN 9781429622820. **M**

Surviving on an island poses many unique problems. For example, survivors may need to deal with extremes in temperature. The water that surrounds them is likely to be saltwater and undrinkable, and their inhospitable surroundings could include inclement weather or quicksand. Tim O'Shei offers survival advice that includes hunting and fishing tips, as well as tales from a rescued U.S. fighter pilot and reminders of the people on television's *Survivors*, who maroon themselves willingly.

Keywords: Desert island survival • Survival skills

Piper, Ross.

Surviving in the World's Most Extreme Places. Fact Finders. Extreme Explorations. Mankato, MN: Capstone Press, 2009. 32p. ISBN 9781429645607. **M**

Finding ways to survive in a hostile environment is something that needs to be done on much of the planet, whether because of temperature extremes or the necessity to deal with living in the watery climes that cover 70 percent of the earth's surface. This book presents the ways in which various life forms have adapted to thrive in some of the harshest climates around—from fish with antifreeze chemicals in their blood, found in the waters around the poles, to giant tube worms, which depend on the gases in magma for their survival. Of course, the fact that pictures of these animals were all taken by people is a testament to humans' adaptability, epitomized by a photograph of an astronaut taking a space walk.

Keywords: Adaptation • Animal adaptation • Survival skills

Towell, Colin.

The Survival Book: Essential Skills for Outdoor Adventure. New York: DK Publishing, 2009. 320p. ISBN 9780756642792. **H**

This comprehensive guide to surviving in the outdoors is divided into seven main sections. "Before You Go" considers preparations, the environment, and what to take; "On the Trail" looks at everything you need to know about weather and maintaining your bearings en route; and "Camp Craft" provides directions for organizing a site and making a fire. These are followed by "Taking Shelter," "Water and Food," "In an Emergency," and "First Aid." The author's two thorough appendices on wild food and natural dangers, though not illustrated and unlikely to be taken into the backcountry, do provide an abundance of useful information. In addition, readers will find a glossary and a list of resources in North America.

Keywords: Camping • First aid • Outdoor adventures • Survival • Survival skills

Turner, Tracy.

🎗 *Deadly Perils and How to Avoid Them.* New York: Walker & Company, 2009. Unpaged. ISBN 9780802787385. **M**

The world is full of dangers, although not all of them pose the same level of threat. Admittedly, tortoise-dropping birds do not pose quite the same level of menace to one's existence as a tsunami, but this amusing guide still gives readers the good and bad news, should they find themselves confronted with either of these perils, among many others. Each peril is rated on a scale from 1 to 10, as well as given a written summary that provides facts and instructions to help the reader avoid these potentially threatening situations. **QP**

Keywords: Dangers • Humor • Survival

Now Try: Readers interested in finding out about some of the dangers or horrors that humans have dealt with will be drawn to *Danger!*, DK Publishing's collection on plants, animals, viruses, and other toxic things. This colorful, highly illustrated volume is divided into seven sections, on nature's nasties, precarious planet, spooky space, scary science, human body horrors, petrifying places and killer culture, and past perils.

Consider Starting with . . .

These titles are suggested as an introduction for readers new to the genre.

Abel, Jessica, and Matt Madden. *Drawing Words & Writing Pictures: Making Comics: Manga, Graphic Novels, and Beyond.*

Brown, Bobbi, with Rebecca Paley. *Beauty Rules: Fabulous Looks, Beauty Essentials, and Life Lessons for Loving Your Teens and Twenties.*

Fagerstrom, Derek, and Lauren Smith. *Show Me How: 500 Things You Should Know - Instructions for Life from the Everyday to the Exotic.*

Nicolay, Megan. *Generation T: Beyond Fashion: 110 T-shirt Transformations for Pets, Babies, Friends, Your Home, Car, and You.*

Oldham, Kristen. *Seventeen Presents . . . 500 Beauty Tips: Look Your Best for School, Weekend, Parties & More!*

Peot, Margaret. *Inkblot: Drip, Splat and Squish Your Way to Creativity.*

Stern, Sam. *Real Food, Real Fast.*

Fiction Read-Alikes

- **Bauer, Joan.** *Close to Famous.* When Foster McFee and her mother Rayka wind up in Culpepper after fleeing Rayka's Elvis-impersonator boyfriend, Foster initially holds out little hope for the town. Little does she know that she will find a place to sell all of the muffins and cupcakes inspired by Sonny Kroll, her idol and favorite TV chef, as well as a friend in the town's most famous inhabitant, former movie actress Miss Charleena. Miss Charleena's offer to teach Foster how to read in exchange for cooking lessons opens up a world of new possibilities for Foster.

- **Bray, Libba.** *Beauty Queens.* When the contestants in the Miss Teen Dream Pageant find themselves on what they think is a deserted island, having survived a plane crash, they are determined to do whatever is necessary not only to stay alive until help comes, but to thrive in the process, although they soon find themselves surprised not only by large reptiles on the island but also by television actors, a corrupt corporation, and just how resourceful they can prove to be. This satirical novel provides a clever and witty look at politics as well as popular culture, in a package that allows all of the girls to show that there is a great deal underneath their very pretty veneers.

- **Dessen, Sarah.** *Whatever Happened to Goodbye.* McLean Sweet, named for the winningest coach in DiFriese University history, and her dad have had three new starts since her parents' divorce, and they are about to get a fourth. McLean, distraught over the scandal when her mother left her father for his idol, the coach for whom she had been named, chose not only to go with her dad, a restaurant consultant, but to keep herself out of any spotlight at all by using a diminutive of her middle name, Elizabeth, around which to create a new persona for herself in each of their new towns, so that she could slide in and out of town seamlessly. She isn't sure who she will be in Lakeview, and somehow she winds up finding a place where it's okay to be McLean, along with several previous denizens of Dessen's novels, an added bonus for Dessen's fans. McLean finds out that things are not always as they initially seem, including grown-up relationships, and gets a chance to do a lot of growing up *of her own as she finds a home in which she and her dad find a place in which she might actually just be okay as herself.*

- **Sachar, Louis.** *The Cardturner.* All Alton Richards knows about his "favorite" great-uncle Lester is that he is old, sick, and very, very rich, all things that combine to ensure that his parents want him to stay in his uncle's good graces. So when an opportunity arises for Lester to become the cardturner for the bridge games his uncle attends several times a week, his parents are thrilled. Initially Alton is not nearly as excited, but finds himself becoming fascinated by his uncle and his amazing computer-like ability with the game.

- **Wolitzer, Meg.** *The Fingertips of Duncan Dorfman.* Duncan Dorfman initially disagrees with his mother that he has an actual "power," because being able to read things with your fingertips while your eyes are closed just makes you weird; it's not like it would let him save a little old lady. Yet it brings him to the attention of the coolest kid in his school, who understands how Duncan's ability could come in handy at the national Youth Scrabble Tournament. At this tournament Duncan will also meet April Blunt and Nate Saviano, who have been preparing for Scrabble glory for most of their lives. This book is a fun mixture of characters and gamesmanship, as all three determine what really matters to them as they come closer to the final tournament, where Duncan will have to decide for himself if he will use his power or try to win the tournament on his own.

References

Carter, Betty. 1987. "A Content Analysis of the Most Frequently Circulated Information Books in Three Junior High Libraries." Ed.D. thesis, University of Houston.

"DIY." 2006. *Wikipedia.* Available at http://en.wikipedia.org/wiki/DIY (accessed August 30, 2007).

"Do-it-yourself, n." n.d. *OED Online.* Oxford University Press. Available at http://www.oed.com.elibrary.calgarypubliclibrary.com/view/Entry/56544 (accessed October 30, 2011).

Chapter **10**

The Arts

Definition

This chapter covers books about the arts, including artists, art history and appreciation, music, musicians, film, and literature.

Appeal

The arts are a great means of self-expression. Although art is a product of the mind and imagination of the artist, the product itself is tangible. Reading books about art and creative people from around the world is one way to find inspiration for one's own work. (Biographies *about* creative people are listed under "The Creative Life" in chapter 4. Readers looking for instruction about drawing, or craft ideas, will find them in chapter 9.)

Art conveys emotions, thoughts, and ideas. It is up to the audience to interpret what they see and experience, and their perceptions may change as they mature. As our knowledge of culture, the world, and its denizens increases, we often better appreciate literature and popular culture.

Recent books not only introduce readers to art and artists in novel ways, such as Bob Raczka's novel introductions to artists and forms, but also provide a wide enough variety of formats and reading levels to ensure that every reader may find something interesting.

Chapter Organization

The first section, "Visual Arts," includes the subheading "Art and Artists," containing books meant to introduce readers to styles of art, artists, and their works. This is followed by "All about Music," which is divided into "Music" and "Musicians." The next section is "Film." The section "Literature and Language" is divided into two subsections, "Grammar and Writing" and "Books and Authors," which contain books about English, its development, writing, and the great writers and discussions of their lives, times, and works. The section "Poetry" is next, divided into three subsections: "About Poetry and Poets," "Poetry Collections and Anthologies," and "Verse Biographies." The chapter finishes with the section "Folklore, Myths, and Legends."

Visual Arts

Art and Artists

Artists are some of the most influential and visionary people in society. Their stories demonstrate creativity, drive, and frequently difficulties, given that artists tend not to be singled out for recognition during their lives. These books cover art history and art appreciation and provide novel ways to introduce readers to artists and their works, such as Bob Raczka's interviews with Vermeer's paintings.

Ball, Heather.

Astonishing Women Artists. The Women's Hall of Fame Series. Toronto: Second Story Press, 2007. 122p. ISBN 9781897187234. **M** **J**

Portraits of successful female artists include Emily Carr, Georgia O'Keefe, and Frida Kahlo. Readers will learn that though not all of the women were taken as seriously or given the same respect as their male counterparts, their works demonstrate their passion, originality, and achievements. This volume of The Women's Hall of Fame Series also includes pictures and links to online examples of the artists' works.

Keywords: Art • Artists • Women artists

Christensen, Bonnie.

Fabulous! A Portrait of Andy Warhol. New York: Christy Ottaviano Books/Henry Holt & Company, 2011. Unpaged. ISBN 9780805087536. **M**

Andy Warhol's journey from a shy, sickly, spindly boy to the "Prince of Pop Art" and one of America's best-recognized painters is presented by Bonnie Christensen in a smoothly told picture-book biography that covers the pertinent points of the interim journey. Learn about his art classes, his training, the famous Campbell's Soup cans, and his studio, known as "The Factory." A complete timeline and some further resources will lead interested readers to more information about this complex artist.

Keywords: Art • Artists • Pop art • Warhol, Andy

Herrera, Nicholas.

High Riders, Saints and Death Cars: A Life Saved by Art. Toronto: Groundwood Books, 2011. 56p. ISBN 9780888998545. **J** **H**

New Mexican Nicholas Herrera admits that his life started down the wrong path by the age of twelve. Undiagnosed dyslexia and behavioral problems, including early drinking and drugs, led to him being placed in special education classes and becoming involved in violent confrontations in his community. At the same time, he found himself trying to lead a life that wasn't entirely dangerous, but was unable to join the military because of his dyslexia. His mother's lifelong interest in art, its influence on him, and how it became his salvation after a head-on collision left him in a coma is a story that demonstrates how this artist has not only learned from his past but also used it to show how his personal history and culture are part of his art. Herrera's artwork, many pieces of which are discussed in the book, may be found in the permanent collection of the Smithsonian American Art Museum.

Keywords: Artists • Folk art • Folk artists • Herrera, Nicholas

Raczka, Bob.

Name That Style: All About Isms in Art. Minneapolis, MN: Millbrook Press, 2009. 32p. ISBN 9780822575863. **M/J**

Intending to explain artistic styles, Bob Raczka covers fourteen key stylistic movements in Western art, starting with naturalism and ending with photorealism. Each is presented in a double-page spread, with a reproduction by one of the most famous painters on the left-hand side. Answers to questions about the styles are found on the right-hand side and include the key elements of the style, when and where it was popular, some of the most famous artists who painted in that style, and key characteristics of the style. Readers will also find an answer to why the included painting is a good example of that style and definitions of any potentially puzzling terms, making this a valuable tool for looking at any kind of art.

Keywords: Art • Art movements • Painting

The Vermeer Interviews: Conversations with Seven Works of Art. Minneapolis, MN: Millbrook Press, 2009. 32p. ISBN 9780822594024. **M J**

This book introduces the reader to an artist and his art in a completely novel way. After providing a short introduction to Vermeer and his techniques, Raczka proceeds to "interview" seven of the subjects of Vermeer's most famous paintings, including *The Milkmaid*, *The Artist in His Studio*, *Woman in Blue Reading a Letter*, and *The Sphinx of Delft*. The questions are often humorous and are accompanied by reproductions of the works and photographs of Vermeer's tools. This allows the reader to examine the paintings and get enough information about Vermeer to be enticed into further reading on the subject.

Keywords: Art • Painting • Vermeer, Johannes

Reich, Susanna.

Painting the Wild Frontier: The Art and Adventures of George Catlin. New York: Clarion Books, 2008. 160p. ISBN 9780618714704. **J** **H**

George Catlin gave up his career as a lawyer to devote himself to his artwork, gaining permission to travel in the American West to paint American Indians, depicting their daily lives. There is no denying that he was a product of his times: he shared its prejudices, and the author illustrates that his motives were not always noble, yet he was a consistent friend to the Plains tribes and left behind a legacy that remains even today. This volume contains a large number of reproductions of Catlin's paintings, as well as a long list of further resources.

Keywords: Catlin, George • Native Americans • Plains Indians

Say, Allen.

Drawing from Memory. New York: Scholastic Press, 2011. 64p. ISBN 9780545176866. **M** **J**

Caldecott Award–winning artist Allan Say presents a combination memoir/history that recounts his early years in Japan, as his love of art flourished under the tutelage of Noro Shinpei, Japan's leading comic artist. The inclusion of original artwork by both artists, as well as a large number of photographs, helps to transport readers to Japan in the 1940s as well as give them a sense of Say's life from the ages of twelve to fifteen, when he immigrated to America.

Keywords: Artists • Say, Allan

All about Music

Representing an overwhelming number of genres and styles, the books in this section provide information about music that may be of interest to prospective musicians as well as music lovers of all kinds. It covers many styles of music, contemporary and from past eras, followed by books about some of the great musicians who helped define those eras.

Music

The titles in this section are general books for readers interested in music or those wanting to learn more about its history. A popular recent title also presents readers with advice for starting their own band, including quotes from some of rock's legends.

Heatley, Michael.

The Girl in the Song. Chicago: Chicago Review Press, 2010. 144p. ISBN 9781569765302. **H**

This short volume introduces readers to the inspirations behind fifty of the most popular and enduring songs in music history. Each song is given an entry that provides its story, along with some biographical information about the person for whom the song is named as well as the songwriter, the musician or musicians who performed it, and their relationship. The entries cover a number of genres, from the rock classic "Layla" to the enduring "Girl from Ipanema." Each biography also includes an update on the careers of both the muse and the musician.

Keywords: Music • Musicians • Rock songs

Now Try: P. Craig Russell takes opera and makes it accessible rather than intimidating or daunting to readers in *The P. Craig Russell Library of Opera Adaptations. Volume 3, Adaptations of "Pelleas and Melisande"; "Salome"; "Cavalleria rusticana."* This graphic adaptation of three operas may entice readers who have never listened to or seen an opera to try both the book and the music. The operas in this story include a story of doomed lovers and the tale of Salome, the enchantress refused by St. John the Baptist.

Hopper, Jessica.

The Girls' Guide to Rocking: How to Start a Band, Book Gigs, and Get Rolling to Rock Stardom. New York: Workman Pub., 2009. 229p. ISBN 9780761151418. **J H**

This book answers all of the questions that could possibly come up when someone is thinking about forming or being part of a band, from buying and caring for equipment to writing songs, going on tour, and making a recording. Jessica Hopper offers plenty of advice, quotes from music legends, sets out fairly realistic expectations, and bases this fun and very entertaining guide on lots of her own experience.

Keywords: Music • Musicians • Rock bands • Songwriting

Now Try: A more lighthearted take on starting a band can be found in Travis Nichols's combination text and graphic nonfiction introduction for future rock stars, *Punk Rock Etiquette: The Ultimate How-To Guide for DIY, Punk, Indie and Underground Bands*. Providing instruction on everything from forming a band to touring with it, this title, chosen for the Popular Paperbacks for Young Adults, provides realistic advice with a humorous tone.

Hudson, Noel.

The Band Name Book. Erin Mills, ON: Boston Mills Press, 2008. 336p. ISBN 9781550464870. **J H**

This entertaining volume is great for browsing, providing hometowns and background information for the band members as well as the CD artwork for thousands of band names. Readers looking for a particular band will find an index at the back of the book; those more interested in general pop culture may be guided by the thematic groupings, which include broad headings such as "Love & Lust" and "Horror Chiller Monster Thriller." **QP**

Keywords: Bands • Music • Musicians

Musicians

What makes a musician great? These books explore singers, pianists, and composers who have left lasting musical legacies. The titles in this area provide a wide range of possibilities, from Ann Angel's award-winning biography of Janis Joplin to Richard Kleist's graphic biography of Johnny Cash. Readers will find even-handed takes that do not overlook any of the singers' foibles or tragedies and share why these musicians' songs are still hot ticket items on iTunes.

Angel, Ann.

Janis Joplin: Rise Up Singing. New York: Amulet Books, 2010. 120p. ISBN 9780810983496. **J H**

Forty years after her death, Janis Joplin remains a music icon, one of the premiere women of rock music. This visually arresting biography and balanced portrait of the singer shows Joplin's insecurities and drug problems as well as her artistic successes. As noted in the timeline, she was inducted into the Rock and Roll Hall of Fame twenty-five years after her untimely and unfortunate death at the age of twenty-seven. **AENYA**

Keywords: Joplin, Janis • Musicians

Crease, Stephanie Stein.

Duke Ellington: His Life in Jazz with 21 Activities. Chicago: Chicago Review Press, 2009. 148p. ISBN 9781556527241. **M J**

This biography of one of the twentieth century's greatest jazz musicians also introduces readers to the entertainment industry, showing how it changed as swing and jazz became popular. Ellington's career as a composer and bandleader illustrates not only his achievements but also the changing face of the music industry and America, as his own story is set against the backdrop of momentous events such as the Great Depression and World War II. Readers will also find activities intended to help them become familiar with jazz interspersed throughout the text, such as learning how to improvise rhythms or designing an album jacket.

Keywords: Ellington, Duke • Jazz • Musicians

Golus, Carrie.

Tupac Shakur. Lifeline Biographies. Minneapolis, MN: Twenty-First Century Books, 2011. 112p. ISBN 9780761354734. **J H**

Tupac Shakur had a career that lasted just six years before his death at the age of twenty-five in 1996. In that remarkable short time, which included eleven months in jail, he left a legacy that continues to influence rap and hip-hop artists and entertain film and music fans. This biography features articles from *USA Today* alongside a text that shares the highlights of this multitalented artist's short life as well as the difficulties in it.

Keywords: Hip-hop • Rap music • Shakur, Tupac

Kleist, Reinhard.

Johnny Cash: I See a Darkness. New York: Abrams ComicArts, 2009. 221p. ISBN 9780810984639. **H** **GN**

This portrayal of the Man in Black covers Cash's life from his upbringing picking cotton in Arkansas to his famous Folsom Prison recording in 1968. It does not flinch away from either his run-ins with the law or his drug dependency. His influence on American music cannot be denied, and the starkness of the artwork in this graphic novel highlights his journey and will likely draw readers unfamiliar with it to his music.

Keywords: Cash, Johnny • Country music • Country musicians • Graphic nonfiction

Rubin, Susan Goldman.

Music Was IT: Young Leonard Bernstein. Watertown, MA: Charlesbridge Publishing, 2011. 178p. ISBN 9781580893442. **M** **J**

Lenny Bernstein, best known as the composer of *West Side Story* and other Broadway shows, always loved music. As a two-year-old he often shouted out for more "Moynik," and he started piano lessons at the age of ten, determined to make music his life. Yet until he stepped onto the stage of Carnegie Hall for his triumphant conducting debut at the age of twenty-five, his father still hoped that he would go into the family beauty supply business. This moving portrait presents a young, American Jewish musical genius studying in the United States at a time when every major conductor had studied in Europe. Lenny's struggles to pay for his schooling while studying with the best teachers of the day demonstrate not only his skills and determination, but also the path he paved for future musicians. His eminent career is further illustrated in an ample timeline and backmatter. **ALA**

Keywords: Bernstein, Leonard • Conductors • Musicians

Spitz, Bob.

Yeah, Yeah, Yeah: The Beatles, Beatlemania and the Music That Changed the World. New York: Little, Brown, 2007. 234p. ISBN 9780316115551. **J** **H**

Spitz starts this adaptation of his adult biography of arguably the world's most famous band with a mutual friend introducing John and Paul. Readers are given a background for each of the Beatles, in addition to the band's history before they actually became the Beatles. The narrative follows through to the band's breakup and is complemented by a large number of sidebars and photographs, making this a great book for browsing. While it chronicles the effects that the Beatles' music had on popular culture, a particular strength of this book is that it also reflects on how that popularity took its toll on the Beatles: the difficulties in the musicians' personal lives are given equal attention.

Keywords: Beatles • Musicians

10

11

Watson, Cindy.

Out of Darkness: The Jeff Healey Story. Toronto: Dundurn Press, 2010. 132p. ISBN 9781554887064. **J** **H**

There is no denying that jazz and blues guitarist Jeff Healey was an unusual musician: he was a phenomenal talent from an early age. He wanted to be remembered as a talented musician, rather than a blind musician; and as this book reminds us, he left a tremendous legacy. Readers are given a complete and balanced portrait of the artist, his life, and his career, including the things that influenced him and how his blindness affected his growth as an artist, his friends, and his family. The latter were a very important part of Jeff Healey's life, and their thoughts help paint a picture of him that readers will appreciate.

Keywords: Blues • Guitarists • Healey, Jeff • Jazz guitarists

Film

Movies remain one of North America's most popular forms of entertainment. Books in this section help readers find movies, give them information about films and the cinema, and provide film buffs with light reading that allows them to expand their cinematic knowledge. A current trend in this genre is to provide an inside look at a recent film, often from the point of view of the director or writer, showing how adaptations are made to take a book from the page to the screen, such as Catherine Hardwicke's *Twilight: The Director's Notebook: The Story of How We Made the Movie.*

Hardwicke, Catherine.

Twilight: The Director's Notebook: The Story of How We Made the Movie. New York: Little, Brown, 2009. 163p. ISBN 9780316070522. **J** **H**

The director of *Twilight* provides an insider's point of view on her creative process for the adaptation of Stephenie Meyer's novel. This book chronicles all of her decisions and provides readers with information about such moviemaking processes as wardrobe and storyboarding. Her journal illustrates each step with photographs from the set, providing readers with a timeline and giving them further information about how a movie is made as well as insight into this particular pop culture phenomenon. **QP**

Keywords: Movie making • Movies • *Twilight*

Maltin, Leonard.

Leonard Maltin's 151 Best Movies You've Never Seen. New York: HarperCollins, 2010. 323p. ISBN 978006173248. **H**

The 151 movies reviewed in this guide provide something for almost any movie lover, from classics to zombies to the downright silly. Readers will find out not only what led Maltin to include each "unsung" film, but also the movie's stars and a synopsis, among other pertinent information about the movie and its stars—all meant to entice the reader into watching the movie.

Keywords: Movie reviews • Movies

O'Connor, Mimi.

Reel Culture: 50 Classic Movies You Should Know About (So You Can Impress Your Friends). San Francisco, CA: Zest Books, 2009. 176p. ISBN 9780981973319. **H**

Actors and actresses have always been admired, but what is surprising is how many movies have remained a part of popular culture, decades after their release. This examination of fifty great movies gives readers a synopsis of each film, along with sidebars entitled "Why All the Fuss?" and "What People Still Talk About." These present a justification for the movie's inclusion in the overall list and will act as an enticement for readers to seek out the films, which cover a wide range of types, from classics such as *Citizen Kane* to scarier movies like *Silence of the Lambs* or *Jaws* and humorous movies like *Airplane!*

Keywords: Movie reviews • Movies

Selznick, Brian, with Additional Material by Martin Scorsese and David Serlin.

The "Hugo" Movie Companion: A Behind the Scenes Look at How a Beloved Book Became a Major Motion Picture. Photography by Jaap Buitendijk. New York: Scholastic Press, 2011. 255p. ISBN 9780545331555. **J H**

This book will provide insight to fans of both *The Invention of Hugo Cabret* and *Hugo*, presenting both Brian Selznick's original inspirations for the story and a bird's-eye view of the translation of the Caldecott-winning book into a wonderful movie from the point of view of key people such as the director, Martin Scorsese, and the casting director. Readers will enjoy the layout, which includes photographs from the movie and pages with short explanations of the duties of people on set, such as the dialect coach and the on-set magician.

Keywords: *Hugo* • Movies

Literature and Language

This subgenre is divided into two subsections, "Grammar and Writing" and "Books and Authors." Readers will find titles that can help them improve their writing and that look at great writers.

Grammar and Writing

The books in this section discuss the craft of writing and give readers tools to help them hone their skills. They range from books that offer a better understanding of the history of the English language to those intended to improve their grammar to those containing creative suggestions meant to inspire budding writers.

Barry, Lynda.

🎗 *What It Is.* Montréal, QC: Drawn & Quarterly, 2008. 209p. ISBN 9781897299357. **J** **H** **GN**

Barry asks readers a question on the cover, "Do you wish you could write?" Inside, readers find pages of vivid and imaginative art made up of collage, drawings, and comics. Into this background are woven autobiographical thoughts and musings meant to teach and inspire readers to become writers. **BBYA**

Keywords: Creative writing • Graphic nonfiction • Writing

Budzik, Mary.

Punctuation: The Write Stuff. Illustrated by Simon Basher. New York: Kingfisher, 2010. 64p. ISBN 9780753464205. **M**

This short, sprightly volume introduces readers to the major punctuation marks and how to use them correctly. Writers and their teachers will appreciate the concrete examples that help them construct sentences; use commas correctly to avoid run-ons; and learn how and when to use parentheses, dashes, colons, and semicolons with confidence.

Keywords: Grammar • Parts of speech • Punctuation

Dubosarsky, Ursula.

The Word Snoop. Illustrated by Tohby Riddle. New York: Dial Books, 2009. 272p. ISBN 9780803734067. **J** **S**

A "Word Snoop" introduces readers to the fun and unusual characteristics and conventions that can be found in English and other languages, from acronyms to tongue twisters. The historical survey of the language goes from cuneiform through the evolution of spelling and punctuation to a discussion of texting.

Keywords: Acronyms • English • Language • Wordplay

Fogarty, Mignon.

Grammar Girl Presents the Ultimate Writing Guide for Students. Illustrated by Irwin Haya. New York: Henry Holt & Company, 2011. 294p. ISBN 9780805089431. **M** **J** **H**

Writers just beginning to navigate the seas of parsing sentences will find this guide a welcome introduction; those already familiar with the parts of speech, their uses, and the rules of punctuation but looking for a refresher in them will find this a useful and understandable resource. Fogarty, known as the Grammar Girl from her iTunes podcast and the www.quickanddirtytips.com Web site, has fashioned a welcome and readable volume with concrete examples and pop quizzes.

Keywords: Grammar • Rhetoric • Sentence structure • Writing

Gorrell, Gena K.

Say What? The Weird and Mysterious Journey of the English Language. Toronto: Tundra Books, 2009. 146p. ISBN 97800887768781. **M** **J**

Gena Gorrell's introduction to the evolution of the English language shows readers how the language we now speak has evolved and changed throughout history, as it was affected by Sanskrit, Greek, Latin, and Old English, with spelling and pronunciation changing along the way. There are exercises that will delight readers from the most reluctant student to devoted logophiles, from clear explanations for apostrophe usage to useful games and riddles that reference Harry Potter and would be useful for any upper-level spelling bee.

Keywords: English • Grammar • Spelling

Mazer, Anne, and Ellen Potter.

Spilling Ink: A Young Writer's Handbook. Illustrated by Matt Phelan. New York: Roaring Brook Press, 2010. 275p. ISBN 9781596435148. **M** **J**

Two authors offer a lighthearted and interesting guide to writing in short chunks of practical ideas and humorous suggestions. They also address potential pitfalls of the writing process. Readers will be encouraged to learn from these published authors that writer's block can happen, and that it is permissible to break rules if there is a good reason for doing so, bearing in mind that one should know the rules before breaking them. The illustrations complement the text, and sidebars entitled "I Dare You" tempt readers into improving their skills in various areas from subplots to trying a springboard exercise with friends.

Keywords: Writers • Writing

Books and Authors

The titles in this subgenre offer readers a chance to become better acquainted with their favorite genres, authors, and formats, as well as to discover worthy new ones. Readers who enjoy these titles may also enjoy the books in the section "Humorous Memoirs" in chapter 3.

Fleischman, Sid.

 The Trouble Begins At 8: A Life of Mark Twain in the Wild, Wild West. New York: Greenwillow Books, 2008. 224p. ISBN 9780061344329. **M** **J**

The posters announcing Mark Twain's speaking engagements let people know that the "Doors open at 7 o'clock. The Trouble begins at 8 o'clock." Twain wasn't sure that people would come to listen to a journalist speak, but he ended up launching a new career, becoming the man who "made laughing out loud as respectable as afternoon tea." Find out how Samuel Clemens began as a steamboat pilot and evolved into a newspaperman, novelist, and public figure, travelling from the Mississippi River to San Francisco to the Sandwich Islands while gathering the stories that he used to create some of America's greatest literary masterpieces. **BBYA**

Keywords: Authors • Clemens, Samuel • Humorist • Twain, Mark

Now Try: Readers new to Mark Twain's works who would like to find out more about the man himself will be delighted with Robert Burleigh's *The Adventures of Mark Twain by Huckleberry Finn*. This rather deceptive informational picture book, accompanied by Barry Blitt's cartoon-like illustrations, presents Twain's story from Finn's point of view. An additional highlight is a "warning" and assurance to the reader from "the editors" that they will be able to figure out the "special ways Mr. Finn speaks," including using "ain't," dropping the "g" from the end of words, and using many expressions in place of common words.

Hinds, Gareth.

King Lear: A Play by William Shakespeare. Somerville, MA: Candlewick Press, 2009. 123p. ISBN 9780763643430. **J H GN**

Hinds leaves the majority of the play intact in this graphic adaptation of Shakespeare's tragedy, and all changes are explained in accompanying notes, making this both an appealing introduction to the story and an enticing addition to the canon. Readers will find their comprehension aided significantly by the beautiful illustrations, which darken substantially throughout the volume to reflect dramatic mood as Lear descends into madness.

Keywords: Graphic nonfiction • King Lear • Shakespeare, William • Tragedy

Now Try: Readers looking for more information about the Bard of Avon will find it in a colorful and inventive package that combines literary, biographical, and historical information, Kristen McDermott and Ari Berk's *William Shakespeare: His Life and Times*. The foldout pages, of various sizes, contain stories about Shakespeare, his contemporaries, his works, or some kind of supplementary information. The intricacies of the packaging, added to the information they contain, make this more of a book for older readers, and it will likely not last long in a public library.

Madden, Kerry.

Harper Lee: A Twentieth Century Life. Up Close. New York: Penguin/Viking, 2009. 223p. ISBN 9780670010950. **J H**

Writing a biography of a living person is difficult under the best of circumstances; to do so convincingly and authoritatively without the participation of the subject is extraordinary. To present this very readable biography of Harper Lee, a notoriously publicity-shy person, Kerry Madden, did an amazing amount of research, accommodating Ms. Lee's wish for privacy while still presenting a complete portrait of the beloved author. Readers are given a portrait of Lee's childhood in Monroeville, her life in New York, and the transformation her life underwent after writing *To Kill a Mockingbird*.

Keywords: Authors • Lee, Harper • Writers • Writing

Marcus, Leonard S., ed.

Funny Business: Conversations with Writers of Comedy. Somerville, MA: Candlewick. 2009. 214p. ISBN 9780763632540. **M J H**

In this guide readers will find out about authors' and humorists' lives and work and perhaps be introduced to someone whose work they haven't yet had a chance to read, such as Norton Juster, Hilary McKay, or Dick King-Smith. The authors discuss their quirks, how they came to be published, or where they first found their published works, all of which offer chances for laughs of their own. Daniel Handler, who as a child had a large vocabulary, delighted in his readers' vocabulary; he points out that in meeting his readers, the "children who read the book are more likely to look up the word or figure out its meaning, whereas adults are more apt to fake it" and goes on to say that when meeting his readers he has heard "an eight-year-old explain *ersatz* to an adult who has heard the word a million times but never gotten a grip on it."

Keywords: Authors • Humor • Writing

Reef, Catherine.

Ernest Hemingway: A Writer's Life. Boston: Clarion Books, 2009. 183p. ISBN 9780618987054. **J H**

This chronological account of the famous and oft-studied American journalist and author introduces readers to Hemingway's famous declarative style and shows how his globe-trotting life influenced his works. It is a balanced portrayal of the man, supplemented with photographs and quotations not only from Hemingway but also from those who knew him best, including editors, family, authors, and filmmakers.

Keywords: Authors • Hemingway, Ernest

Jane Austen: A Life Revealed. Boston: Clarion Books, 2011. 208p. ISBN 978054737217. **J H**

Austen, who died at the age of forty-one, is best known for books that have provided a window into nineteenth-century English society. Her work has been read for generations around the world, translated into television and film. As very few of Austen's own letters have survived, readers are given a portrait of her culled from details gathered from family records and a few remaining letters, along with a portrait of the time in which the novels were set. A complete list of resources will help in cases where further research is warranted.

Keywords: Austen, Jane • Authors • Writers

1

2

3

4

5

6

7

8

9

10

11

Silvey, Anita, ed.

Everything I Need to Know I Learned from a Children's Book: Life Lessons from Notable People from All Walks of Life. New York: Roaring Brook Press, 2009. 233p. ISBN 9781596433953. **M** **J** **H**

This collection introduces readers to a wide variety of children's books, varying from picture books to novels to nonfiction, from the point of view of the life lessons that they imparted. Jay Leno points out that performing better for a larger audience, as Mike Mulligan and Mary Anne did, "made sense" to a young show-off, whereas Maureen Taylor traces the roots of her adult career to Madeleine L'Engle's *A Wrinkle in Time*, which taught her to "engage in scientific enquiry."

Keywords: Authors • Children's books • Memoirs

Poetry

Defined by its sounds, meaning, and rhythm, with various types dependent on the use of a specific number of lines, poetry covers a broad span of topics and forms. Readers are introduced to poetry in Paul Janeczko's *A Foot in the Mouth: Poems to Speak, Sing, and Shout*; his poems beg to be read aloud. Ellen Paschen organizes 100 poems by theme. Poetry—writing and reading—is very popular with teens.

This section is organized into three subsections. "About Poetry and Poets" includes works that help provide background and understanding of poetry and poetic forms. This is followed by "Poetry Collections and Anthologies" and "Verse Biographies." The latter examines the recent trend of composing biographical tributes in verse, which continue to serve as read-alikes for the many verse novels found in school and public libraries.

About Poetry and Poets

This section lists works that help readers understand poetry and poetic forms.

Agard, John.

The Young Inferno. Illustrated by Satoshi Kitamura. London: Frances Lincoln, 2009. 80p. ISBN 9781845077693. **J** **H**

In this graphic retelling of Dante's *Inferno*, Aesop leads a twenty-first-century hero in a hoodie through the nine circles of hell. Other updates include turning the Furies into a street gang and adding some political commentary, along with some still recognizable politicians, into the mix. This is a valid pairing with the original *Inferno* and useful for a discussion about poetic forms or revisions.

Keywords: Dante • Graphic nonfiction • Poetry

Janeczko, Paul B.

A Foot in the Mouth: Poems to Speak, Sing, and Shout. Illustrated by Chris Raschka. Somerville, MA: Candlewick Press, 2009. 61p. ISBN 9780763606633. **M J**

> Paul Janeczko presents a collection meant to introduce readers to great poetry by giving them poems that beg to be read aloud. As in his earlier books, the illustrations complement the poems beautifully. A wide variety of poems illustrate the oral history of poetry, from Arnold Spilka's six-word "Gigl" to Lewis's "Twas brillig, and the slithy toves," made more familiar by the recent remake of *Alice in Wonderland*, to the inclusion of Sandra Cisnero's "Good Hot Dogs," which is presented in both Spanish and English.
>
> **Keywords:** Poetry • Poetry anthologies

Poetry Collections and Anthologies

> This section covers both collections by one poet and anthologies of works by more than one poet.

Franco, Betsy, ed.

Falling Hard: 100 Love Poems by Teenagers. Cambridge, MA: Candlewick Press, 2008. 144p. ISBN 9780763634377. **J H RR**

> One hundred poems explore love and all that goes along with it, from desire to disdain and heartbreak. The poets range from thirteen to eighteen years of age and represent both genders and a diverse range of experience and sexual orientations. The collection is arranged in a whimsical fashion that encourages browsing and will likely have readers reaching for their own pens and paper. **QP**
>
> **Keywords:** Feelings • Love • Poetry anthologies • Writing
>
> **Now Try:** Readers interested in exploring love have ample opportunities to benefit from other people's experiences by perusing Bill Shapiro's collection *Other People's Love Letters: 150 Letters You Were Never Meant to See*. This title, which was selected as a Quick Pick for Reluctant Young Adult Readers, shares cards, notes, letters, diagrams, and even e-mails that all have in common the expression of honest emotions by the sender.

Paschen, Ellen, ed.

Poetry Speaks: Who I Am. Naperville, IL: Sourcebooks, 2010. 161p. ISBN 9781402210747. **M J**

> This anthology has gathered together more than 100 poems covering themes that appeal to teenagers, such as friendship, identity, and loneliness. As an added bonus, many of them have been recorded on the accompanying audio CD: hearing poetry adds meaning, whether you are listening to

Marilyn Nelson or Robert Frost. This is a book that may be browsed or read and will encourage budding poets to pick up their pens. The track number for each poem included on the CD is listed next to the title in the book.

Keywords: Poetry • Poetry anthologies

Rosen, Michael J.

The Cuckoo's Haiku and Other Birding Poems. Illustrated by Stan Fellows. Somerville, MA: Candlewick Press, 2009. Unpaged. ISBN 9780763630492. **M** **J** **RR**

This beautiful picture book introduces readers to haiku as well as to twenty common North American birds. The haikus are presented in a seasonal arrangement and accompanied by full-color, double-page watercolors of the birds in their natural environment. Readers will also find facts about the birds interspersed throughout the illustrations. Each poem from the avowed birder is evocative, presenting a fact about the particular bird that makes it unique.

Keywords: Birds • Haiku • Poetry • Poetry collections

Verse Biographies

Books of poetry continue to be a popular format for authors to use as a way to present a life in an intriguing way. Readers who enjoy reading about people's lives will be able to find a number of alternatives in chapters 3 and 4.

Bernier-Grand, Carmen T.

🏅 *Diego: Bigger Than Life.* Illustrated by David Diaz. New York: Marshall Cavendish, 2009. 64p. ISBN 9780761453833. **J** **H**

Carmen Bernier-Grand presents the story of Diego Rivera, the Mexican muralist and Frida Kahlo's husband, in spare, chronological poems accompanied by David Diaz's artwork. The complex personality of the subject, including his art, liaisons, and infidelities, are all included and are given more depth in an added biographical piece, notes, and an "in his own words" item that leads interested readers to further information. This title was chosen as a Pura Belpré honor book (see appendix A) for illustration in 2010.

Keywords: Poetry • Rivera, Diego

Engle, Margarita.

🏅 *Hurricane Dancers.* New York: Henry Holt & Company, 2011. 143p. ISBN 9780805092400. **J** **H**

Margarita Engle presents a fictionalized verse account of historical figures. Through the addition of fifth figure and intertwining stories, readers are shown the 1509 ship on which the pirate Bernardino de Talavera has captured former conquistador Alonso de Ojeda. The former slave Quebrado, who works as a translator on the ship for Talavera, is washed ashore with the men when a hurricane sinks the ship, but he is the only one able to make himself understood by the native Ciboney Indians, including the fisherman Naridó, who rescues him. The other thread in the story is a forbidden love between Naridó and Caucubú, a chieftain's daughter. Quebrado is a fictional character used by Engle to tie together narrative threads and present the other, historical figures, who are introduced in a long author's note. This title was a Pura Belpré honor book. **ALA**

Keywords: Caribbean history • Pirates, history • Shipwrecks • Verse novel

Nelson, Marilyn.

The Freedom Business: Including a Narrative of the Life and Adventures of Venture, a Native of Africa. Illustrated by Deborah Dancy. Honesdale, PA: Wordsong, 2008. 72p. ISBN 9781932425574. **J H**

In a unique pairing, readers find both Venture Smith's narrative, first published in 1798, and poems by Marilyn Nelson, which keep pace with, respond to, and expand upon the narrative. Deborah Dancy's watercolors make a lovely background for the amazing story of Broteer, prince of Dukandarra, Guinea, who admittedly "paid an enormous sum/for my freedom" but bought not only himself but also his family from slavery.

Keywords: Poetry • Smith, Venture • Verse biography

Sweethearts of Rhythm: The Story of the Greatest All-Girl Swing Band in the World. Illustrated by Jerry Pinkney. New York: Dial Books, 2009. 80p. ISBN 9780803731875. **M J**

Through instruments languishing in a pawnshop, readers are introduced to the "greatest all-girl swing band in the world." The instruments reminisce about their former owners in poems by the former poet laureate of Connecticut and with accompanying illustrations by Caldecott winner Jerry Pinkney. Marilyn Nelson's poetry captures the swing tones of the music as well as the times, which are reflected as well in Pinkney's illustrations. Readers will learn about the era of the 1930s and 1940s, when the white musicians had to wear dark makeup because it was illegal to play on the same stage as black musicians, which could be very dangerous when playing under hot lights. Readers will follow the Sweethearts, via their instruments, through the years and up to the time just before Hurricane Katrina hit. This title was chosen for the Amelia Bloomer list. **ALA**

Keywords: Musicians • Sweethearts of Rhythm • Swing band

Weatherford, Carole Boston.

Becoming Billie Holiday. Illustrated by Floyd Cooper. Honesdale, PA: Wordsong, 2008. 116p. ISBN 9781590785072. **M J**

This BBYA and Coretta Scott King author honor award title looks at the youth and adolescence of one of America's greatest jazz musicians, Billie Holiday, born Eleanor Fagan. Information is included about her troubled childhood, which included a rape, reform school, jail, and the racism she endured even as she worked to overcome both color and gender barriers when touring with notable musicians of the day. The book finishes with Holiday's first performance of "Strange Fruit," tied to the text of a 1969 lynching. Readers will find an abundant list of further sources, supplemented in the text. Most of the poems are headed by Holiday's song titles and complemented by Floyd Cooper's illustrations.

Keywords: Holiday, Billie • Jazz • Music

Folklore, Myths, and Legends

The books in this section contain traditional tales, myths, or retellings of traditional myths and legends. They have either been adapted for older readers, such as Susan Berner Rotraut's *Definitely Not for Little Ones*, or have been integrated into a format that would be unsuitable for small hands, such as Matthew Reinhart and Robert Sabuda's incredibly beautiful and intricate pop-up books.

Encyclopedia Mythologica.

These beautiful pop-up books are just as complex as any of their predecessors from Reinhart and Sabuda's <u>Encyclopedia Prehistorica</u>. Readers will find the same breathtaking center spread, supplemented by up to several additional spreads per page and enough information on the subject to fulfill the expectations of a reader looking for material in the area. The combination of their own ephemeral nature and the wonder of their layouts means that though these books are unlikely to be found in libraries, they would be ideal gifts for someone with an interest in the subject.

Reinhart, Matthew, and Robert Sabuda.

Dragons & Monsters. Somerville, MA: Candlewick Press, 2011. Unpaged. ISBN 9780763631734. **M**

The concluding volume in Reinhart and Sabuda's trilogy is just as breathtaking as its predecessors. Readers will be captured from the opening spread, with the snakes from Medusa's head breaking free from the top and sides of the pages, a prime example of "monsters of antiquity." As will all the other books in the series, each item features up to several integrated pages of additional pop-outs and information pertinent to the subject being illustrated, from dragons and leviathans to cryptids. This is a book that would not last long in a collection or with young readers; but for devotees of the subject matter, it will remain a favorite.

Keywords: Dragons • Monsters • Mythology • Pop-ups

Fairies and Magical Creatures. Cambridge, MA: Candlewick Press, 2008. 12p. ISBN 9780763631727. **M**

The introductory volume of the <u>Encyclopedia Mythologica</u> introduces readers to fairies from around the world, as well as literary sprites ranging from Shakespeare's Titania to Perrault's Fairy Godmother and mythological creatures such as Pegasus. Although the delicate nature of this book renders it more of a gift book than one that will last in circulation, readers will return to it again and again for the intriguing information and stunning renditions, in addition to the remarkable engineering of the multiple pop-ups on every page.

Keywords: Fairies • Mythology • Pop-ups

Gods and Heroes. Somerville, MA: Candlewick Press, 2010. Unpaged. ISBN 9780763650858. **M**

The second volume in the Encyclopedia Mythologica goes far beyond touring readers through the pantheon of Greek gods and heroes, although the flip version of Hercules's twelve impossible tasks is truly stunning. Introductions are also provided, with the series' trademark delicate and imaginative pop-ups, to Norse, Asian, and even New World mythology, from Aztec to Iroquois legends.

Keywords: Greek gods • Greek mythology • Norse mythology • Pop-ups

Mazan, Cecile Chicault, and Philip Petit.

Tales from the Brothers Grimm. Translation by Joe Johnson. Classics Illustrated. New York: Papercutz, 2008. 130p. ISBN 9781597071000. **M J GN RR**

This graphic nonfiction collection presents four thorough retellings of Grimm's tales: "Hansel and Gretel," "Learning How to Shudder," "The Devil and the Three Golden Hairs," and "The Valiant Little Tailor." The stories are faithful to the original, showing the ghosts and devils as suitably scary and providing definitions in the margin for the occasional word likely to be unfamiliar to readers.

Keywords: Fairy tales • Graphic nonfiction • Grimm

Napoli, Donna Jo.

Treasury of Greek Mythology: Classic Stories of Gods, Goddesses, Heroes and Monsters. Illustrated by Christina Balit. Washington, DC: National Geographic Society, 2011. 191p. ISBN 9781426308444. **J**

This volume provides introductions to twenty-five classic characters in Greek mythology, starting with Gaia and Uranus, working through the pantheon of the major gods and goddesses, and then telling the stories of some of the great heroes. Readers will find out why Perseus is sent after Medusa's head and how he succeeds in his quest, as well as the legend of Helen, the "Lethal Beauty." Each story is told succinctly but completely in a few pages and is accompanied by large, full-color illustrations. A supplementary section at the back includes a map of Greece today; timeline; and cast of characters that summarizes the pertinent information for all of the included characters, with their Greek and Roman names, title, symbol, birthplace, generation, and parents.

Keywords: Greek mythology • Greek myths • Perseus

O'Connor, George.

Athena: Grey-Eyed Goddess. Olympians. New York: Neal Porter Books/First Second, 2010. 78p. ISBN 9781596436497. **J** **GN**

> Here is the story of Pallas Athena, the warrior goddess who sprang fully grown, fully clothed, and fully armed from her father's head. How she had come to be there is explained, along with how she adopted her moniker and obtained and added to her aegis by taking on the gigantes, advising Perseus in his quest with Medusa, and demonstrating her wisdom in a final competition with Arachne. Readers will enjoy the attractive graphic presentation that propels the story. The extensive supplementary information includes further details about Athena, Perseus, and Medusa; a bibliography with further resources; discussion questions; and an author's note.
>
> **Keywords:** Athena • Graphic nonfiction • Greek mythology • Pallas Athena • Perseus • Zeus

Hera: The Goddess and Her Glory. Olympians. New York: Neal Porter Books/First Second, 2011. 76p. ISBN 9781596437241. **J** **GN**

> Hera, the Greek goddess most often remembered as Zeus's wife and for her more negative character traits, is shown here being first wooed and then repeatedly cheated on by her husband. Who wouldn't be bitter after finding her husband in the company of several mortals and then being asked to raise the resulting offspring? Surely this explains Hera's hatred of Herakles, which resulted in his being assigned tasks difficult enough to kill him. Of course, he managed to accomplish those ensuing twelve tasks, which resulted in his becoming a hero for all time instead of being killed by the effort. O'Connor's artwork is colorful and engaging and brings the stories of Hercules and Hera to life, including discussion questions and suggested titles for further reading.
>
> **Keywords:** Graphic nonfiction • Greek mythology • Hera • Hercules

🏵 *Zeus: King of the Gods.* Olympians. New York: Neal Porter Books/First Second, 2010. 76p. ISBN 9781596436251. **J** **GN**

> The first volume of the Olympians series presents the chronology of the gods of Olympus, starting from the beginning. Readers are presented with a very helpful family tree on the endpapers, showing that Gaea, Earth, was the mother of the Titans as well as the Cyclopes, then are told that Kronos swallowed all of his children, having heard that one of his children would overthrow him. That child, Zeus, and his rise to power are shown in colorful panels that depict the soon-to-be king of the gods as a blond, Thor-like figure determined to fulfill his destiny. In addition to an interesting story, O'Connor has included information about Zeus, Metis, and Kronos; a bibliography; discussion questions; and a section entitled "G[r]eek Notes" that explains pertinent details about particular panels in the book. This title was chosen for the Great Graphics Novels for Teens list.
>
> **Keywords:** Graphic nonfiction • Greek mythology • Mythology • Zeus

Regan, Sally.

🎗 *The Vampire Book.* New York: DK Publishing, 2009. 96p. ISBN 9780756655518. **J** **M** **H**

Vampires have developed an undeniable allure through their appearances in literature and the movies. They weren't always portrayed as the brooding, haunted, and enticing creatures that draw fans; for centuries they were bogeymen in cultures around the world. This comprehensive guide presents information in four sections. The first introduces vampires, their powers, and how to stay safe from them; the second looks at various myths and legends from around the world; the third looks at the rise of the vampires and their beginnings in the folklore of eastern Europe through the 1600s; and the final section looks at the vampire on screen, the evolution of the form in literature, and the subsequent increase in their popularity in literature. **PP, QP**

Keywords: Folklore • Vampires

Rotraut, Susanne Berner.

Definitely Not for Little Ones: Some Very Grimm Fairy Tale Comics. Translated by Shelley Tanaka. Toronto: Groundwood Books, 2009. Unpaged. ISBN 9780888999573. **M** **J** **GN**

This darkly humorous graphic picture book presents several fairy tales, ranging from "Little Red Cap" to "Tom Thumb," with a sarcastic tone that is matched in both pictures and words; for example, they "would still be alive today . . . if they hadn't died, that is."

Keywords: Fairy tales • Graphic nonfiction • Humor • Picture-book nonfiction

---

Consider Starting with . . .

Angel, Ann. *Janis Joplin: Rise Up Singing.*

Fleischman, Sid. *The Trouble Begins At 8: A Life of Mark Twain in the Wild, Wild West.*

Gorrell, Gena K. *Say What? The Weird and Mysterious Journey of the English Language.*

Marcus, Leonard S., ed. *Funny Business: Conversations with Writers of Comedy.*

Mazer, Anne, and Ellen Potter. *Spilling Ink: A Young Writer's Handbook.*

Nelson, Marilyn. *Sweethearts of Rhythm: The Story of the Greatest All-Girl Swing Band in the World.*

Raczka, Bob. *The Vermeer Interviews: Conversations with Seven Works of Art.*

Rubin, Susan Goldman. *Music Was IT: Young Leonard Bernstein.*

Say, Allen. *Drawing from Memory.*

Silvey, Anita, ed. *Everything I Need to Know I Learned from a Children's Book: Life Lessons from Notable People from All Walks of Life.*

Fiction Read-Alikes

- **Benway, Robin.** *Audrey, Wait.* "Audrey, WAIT!" were the last, extremely pathetic words that Audrey Cutler heard her wannabe musician ex-boyfriend Evan calling after she dumped him. Little did she know that she'd soon be hearing those words over, and over, and over again, along with the rest of the country, when Evan turned them into the chorus of a surprisingly catchy song that rose very quickly up the charts. Her life would never be the same when she was identified by the paparazzi as the heartbreaker of pop radio's new darling.

- **Green, John, and David Levithan.** *Will Grayson, Will Grayson.* While Will Grayson and Will Grayson might realistically have gone their whole lives without ever meeting, fate had other things in store. The two Wills' lives end up intertwined and on a new course halfway through this dual novel, which they narrate. Their stories revolve around the fabulous Tiny Cooper, "the world's largest person who is really, really gay, and also the world's gayest person who is really, really large." Tiny writes and directs a high school musical based on his life and works to affect the friendships and romances of his friends.

- **Gulledge, Laura Lee**. *Paige by Paige.* When a shy teenager moves from Virginia to New York, her artwork serves as her companion. At first, sketching in her notebook is the only thing that keeps Paige from feeling totally lost. Starting slowly, she opens up to a small group of friends by sharing her drawings, which leads to an online sketchbook, confronting her perfectionist mother, and learning a lot about her own identity.

- **Marillier, Juliet**. *Wildwood Dancing.* The popularity of both vampires and fairy tale adaptations will attract readers to Marillier's first book for young adults. Jenna has always looked after her four sisters, making sure that they follow the rules that allow them to travel into the Wildwood and safely enjoy the dancing and celebrations that happen there. After her father goes away, everything seems to go wrong: her cousin starts taking over Piscul Dracului; her sister Tati starts ignoring the rules, even taking up with one of the dark ones; Gogu, her best friend and companion, is acting very strangely; and her cousin sets out to destroy everything, even the Wildwood itself, in this Best Book for Young Adults.

- **Poe, Edgar Allan.** *Nevermore: A Graphic Adaptation of Edgar Allan Poe's Short Stories.* Readers interested in short stories or adaptations of modern literature will enjoy this one by Sterling Publishing. Nine artists reimagine Poe's best known stories for a modern audience, with art that maintains all of their spooky qualities while adding touches to appeal to teenagers, such as setting the story in the future or adding a rock star main character.

- **Schmidt, Gary.** *The Wednesday Wars.* During his seventh-grade school year in 1967, Holling Hoodhood spends the Wednesday afternoons when his classmates are all either studying their catechism or at Hebrew School under the watchful eye of his teacher, Mrs. Baker. During the school year he will have a wide variety of adventures, from reading and gaining an appreciation for Shakespeare, to learning the consequences of the Vietnam War, to hunting some very large rats, in this bittersweet Newbery honor–award winning and BBYA title. The war is still going on in the companion novel, *Okay for Now*, in which Doug Swieteck and his family move to small town Marysville, New York. Doug finds refuge from his abusive father in a delivery job that introduces him to his local library and the other denizens of the town. His friendship with the town's librarian not only introduces him to reading but also allows Doug to discover his talent as an artist, reinforced in the book by the inclusion of Audubon paintings.

- **Werlin, Nancy.** *Impossible.* Upon finding out that not only is she pregnant after being raped at the age of seventeen, but her pregnancy is also a curse and she is destined to go mad, one in a long line of females to do so in her family, Lucy Scarborough has little hope. Committed to keeping both her baby and her sanity, her only hope lies in solving three unsolvable riddles from a version of "Scarborough Fair." With the support of her boyfriend, now her husband, and her foster parents, Lucy sets out to save herself and her unborn child.

1

2

3

4

5

6

7

8

9

10

11

Chapter 11

Understanding and Changing the World

Definition

This chapter includes books about popular culture, the media and how they have affected consumer culture, social concerns and issues, and religions. What these books have in common is that they help teens better understand the world in which they live.

Appeal

It is not surprising that with the increasing prevalence of the modern media and the Internet, the number of books published about advertising and consumerism has increased. Many of these books provide background about both sides of relevant issues in our society, showing how people are affected by portrayal of these subjects, fostering debate, and offering the chance to see how other people live. Many also provide readers with objective presentations of topics that are often misunderstood or shown in a one-sided manner; religions, the paranormal, and human rights are such subjects.

Chapter Organization

The sections in this chapter give readers a broader exposure to the world in which we live, as well as showing them how teenagers live today and how teenagers' lives today differ from the past. The initial section, "Popular Media and Culture," looks at advertising and media. This is followed by the section "Social Concerns and Issues" and a final section, "Religion."

Popular Media and Culture

This category includes books that explore the advertising that helps to make up the foundation of our informal popular culture, as well as a title that examines the history and development of the media. Readers are provided with information about several different media, as well as photographs that purport to be of psychic phenomena. Readers will also find a series that considers how women have been presented in twentieth-century media.

Gladstone, Brooke.

The Influencing Machine: Brooke Gladstone on the Media. Illustrations by Josh Neufeld. New York: W.W. Norton and Company, 2011. 170p. ISBN 9780393077797. **H**

> This entertaining and enlightening graphic novel history of the media allows Gladstone to point out that all of the problems of the modern media have been present since their inception and in all their incarnations. The format provides a novel review of pertinent moments of reporting in U.S. history and includes discussions of journalistic ethics, bias, objectivity, and technology before looking at the media's ability to influence the public.
> **Keywords:** Broadcast journalism • Graphic nonfiction • Journalism

Gourley, Catherine.

🎗 **Issues and Images of Women in the Twentieth Century.**

> Catherine Gourley's five-volume series examines how women have been portrayed in the media and offers readers a lens through which to view both the evolution of popular culture in the twentieth century and women's changing roles. It gives readers examples of both the stereotypical expectations of the times and real-life examples of women who lived with, surpassed, and reshaped them. This series was chosen for the Amelia Bloomer list, discussed in appendix A.
>
> *Flappers, and the New American Woman: Perceptions of Women from 1918 through the 1920s.* Minneapolis, MN: Twenty-First Century Books, 2008. 144p. ISBN 9780822560609. **J** **H**
>
> > **Keywords:** Gender • Media • Popular culture • Portrayals of women in the media
>
> *Gibson Girls and Suffragists: Perceptions of Women from 1900 to 1918.* Minneapolis, MN: Twenty-First Century Books, c2008. 144p. ISBN 9780822571506. **J** **H**
>
> > **Keywords:** Gender • Media • Popular culture • Portrayals of women in the media

Gidgets and Women Warriors: Perceptions of Women in the 1950s and 1960s. Minneapolis, MN: Twenty-First Century Books, c2008. 144p. ISBN 9780822568056. **J** **H**

> **Keywords:** Gender • Media • Popular culture • Portrayals of women in the media

"Ms." and the Material Girls: Perceptions of Women from the 1970s through the 1990s. Minneapolis, MN: Twenty-First Century Books, c2008. 144p. ISBN 9780822568063. **J** **H**

> **Keywords:** Gender • Media • Popular culture • Portrayals of women in the media

Rosie and Mrs. America: Perceptions of Women in the 1930s and 1940s. Minneapolis, MN: Twenty-First Century Books, 2008. 144p. ISBN 9780822568049. **J** **H**

> **Keywords:** Gender • Media • Popular culture • Portrayals of women in the media

Rockcliff, Mara.

Get Real! What Kind of World Are You Buying? Philadelphia, PA: Running Press Book Publishers, 2010. 112p. ISBN 9780762437450. **J** **H**

This fascinating look at consumerism in North America today is accompanied by discussions of renewable resources, as well as a look at current practices in advertising, production, fast food, labeling, garbage, and recycling. A chapter on "frankenfoods" looks at the use of chemicals in food production. Readers are given recommendations about how their shopping practices can contribute positively to the environment, from buying or working for local stores to reasons why it is better to pay more for a fair trade product.

Keywords: Consumerism • Environmental writing • Shopping

Willin, Melvyn.

🎗 *Paranormal Caught on Film: Amazing Photographs of Ghosts, Poltergeists and Strange Phenomena.* Cincinnati, OH: David & Charles, 2008. 140p. ISBN 9780715329801. **J** **H**

This collection of photographs presents five groups of anomalies, including ghostly figures, simulacra, back from the dead, the unexplained, and strange lights and apparitions. Each photograph is accompanied by background information from the owner and possible explanations of the cause or presence of the particular phenomenon, such as a double exposure. **QP**

Keywords: Curiosities • Ghosts • Phenomena • Photographs

11

Social Concerns and Issues

The books in this category examine some of the social and political issues of the world we live in today, the lives of teenagers and the world in which they are living, and the possibility of bringing about change in the world.

Bellows, Melina.

🏅 *NatGeo Amazing! 100 People, Places and Things That Will Wow You.* Washington, DC: National Geographic Society, 2010. 192p. ISBN 9781426206498. **H**

The collection of wonders gathered here will astound, touch, and amaze readers. There is something for everyone: the table of contents groups the subjects into fourteen large categories that include the animal kingdom, survival stories, global cultures, and planet in peril. Amazing photographs will capture a reader's attention, while short essays provide background information and a reason for the subject's inclusion in the book. This companion to the television series takes full advantage of National Geographic's astounding photography collection and provides a captivating book that can be browsed or read straight through. **QP**

Keywords: Cultures • Photographs • Places • Wonders

Bowman, Robin.

🏅 *It's Complicated: The American Teenager.* New York: Umbrage Editions, Inc., 2007. 155p. ISBN 9781884167690. **H**

To present this portrait of the American teenager, Robin Bowman took a number of road trips across the country, photographing and presenting 419 teenagers with the same questions, including: What is your biggest fear?; What is the toughest thing about being a teenager?; What is the easiest thing about being a teenager?; What is your ethnic background?; Is money important to you?; and Who do you respect the most, and why? Answers to these questions are summarized and presented beside pictures of the interview subjects, along with their pictures and demographic information. The answers represent a wide sample of the seventy-seven million teenagers in America, including ages thirteen to nineteen, as well as teens from a range of socioeconomic groups and ethnicities. Discussions about sexuality demonstrate the common ground among today's teenagers. **QP**

Keywords: Adolescence • American life • American teenagers • Photography • Sociology • Teenagers

Edge, Laura B.

From Jazz Babies to Generation Next: The History of the American Teenager. Minneapolis, MN: Twenty-First Century Books, 2011. 112p. ISBN 9780761358688. **J**

Given the ubiquity of teenagers in the world today, it is difficult to believe that the word only came into usage in the second half of the twentieth century. Laura Edge traces the evolution of the teenager, which has changed significantly since the eighteenth century, depending on whether a thirteen- or eighteen-year-old child's "labor was essential to the survival of the family," which would then in turn affect his or her schooling and leisure activities. The evolution of teenagers' pursuits over the years, and the growing impact youths have had on economy and culture, as they now spend billions of dollars annually on technology and entertainment and are increasingly targeted by advertisers, makes fascinating reading.

Keywords: Advertising • Consumers • Teenaged consumers • Teenagers

Every Human Has Rights: A Photographic Declaration for Kids Based on the United Nations Universal Declaration of Human Rights. Foreword by Mary Robinson. Washington, DC: National Geographic, 2009. Unpaged. ISBN 9781426305115. **M J**

With clearly labeled photographs, complemented by poetry from the ePals Human Rights Writing Contest community, this book eloquently communicates the meaning behind the thirty principles of the Universal Declaration of Human Rights, which is itself reprinted in full at the end of the book. An example is number seventeen, the right to own property, which shall not be taken away, illustrated by a photograph of a Mongolian woman and her yurt, a house that can be taken apart and moved when needed. An additional note informs readers that Mongolia's constitution "guarantees women equal rights, including the right to own property." Rights and freedoms are by no means equal or guaranteed around the world, and this book provides an important and welcome reminder to be thankful for the liberties we have.

Keywords: Human rights • Universal Declaration of Human Rights

Kaye, Cathryn Berger, and Philippe Cousteau.

Going Blue: A Teen Guide to Saving Our Oceans & Waterways. Minneapolis, MN: Free Spirit, 2011. 151p. ISBN 9781575423487. **M J**

This informative guide contains a wealth of information about water and the various waterways on the planet. Readers are presented with information about service learning and ways to find out about water usage globally and locally, followed by examples from communities around the world. Facts and stories are spread throughout the book, along with an initial call to arms from Philippe Cousteau that urges readers to consider using the material in the book, whether the historical material or numerous examples of "teens in action," as a spur for their own activities.

Keywords: Environmentalism • Marine ecology • Marine pollution

Smith, David.

If America Were a Village: A Book about the People of the United States. Toronto: Kids Can Press, 2009. 32p. ISBN 9781554533442. **M**

If it is a given that understanding statistics can be complicated and trying to picture particularly large numbers is difficult, then this book provides a simpler metaphor for many difficult conceits about the more than 306 million people living in the United States, presenting them as a village of 100. Not only are readers given breakdowns for nuclear families, languages spoken, and income, but some questions, such as age, are answered with comparative numbers against a comparable world "village." This makes the book particularly useful as a starting point for a discussion about the United States and its people.

Keywords: Demographics • Ethnic origins • People and places • Social science

Taylor, Tannis.

31 Ways to Change the World: We Are What We Do. Somerville, MA: Candlewick Press, 2010. Unpaged. ISBN 9780763645069. **M** **RR**

The thirty-one actions in this book are, above all, simple, and are laid out in an enticing, colorful, and attractive style; they present the possibility for change. Small things add up, and most of the different ways and methods offered here to change our behaviors do not require money, time, or any physical effort, whether it is being nicer to people, turning off the light when you leave a room, teaching your granny how to text, or recycling your toys. The last action requests readers to add their own initiative, thereby continuing the chain and adding to the efforts. This charming, funny, and inspiring book presents quick and clever ideas about changing how we think and treat first ourselves, then the world around us.

Keywords: Activism • Behavior • Recycling

Now Try: Readers interested in simple ways to change the world for the better will find them, as well as short, contemplative essays that range from contemplative to humorous to plaintive, in *Recycle This Book: 100 Top Children's Authors Tell You How to Go Green*. Well-known authors provide ways to help the environment, whether home, school, community, or the planet. Readers who are attracted to the idea of simple ways to make the world a more environmentally friendly place will find a plethora of ideas in *True Green Kids: 100 Things You Can Do to Save the Planet*. In this book authors Kim McKay and Jenny Bonnin start in a reader's room and work outward, presenting painless, effective ways in which readers can make a difference.

Warren, Frank.

A Lifetime of Secrets: A PostSecret Book. New York: William Morrow, 2007. Unpaged. ISBN 9780061238604. **J** **H** **RR**

The fourth volume in Frank Warren's series of postcards presenting people's secrets is organized by age. This gives readers not only a glimpse into the lives of other people but also a chance to appreciate the universality of the feelings expressed, as they are just as likely to find fear, despair, and hope expressed by a child, teen, adult, or senior. While the format of the book allows for browsing, the material makes it compulsively readable. Information about the original project and touring art is available at http://postsecret.blogspot.com. **QP**

Keywords: Feelings • Letters • Postcards

Now Try: Readers who enjoy a glimpse into other people's lives and letters may also enjoy the compiled entries at Kerry Miller's Web site Passiveaggressivenotes.com. Photographs transmit emotions ranging from frustration to rage, in tones from amusement to outrage. The writers' reasons for their communications are evident and make it easy to understand why Miller's *Passive Aggressive* Notes: Painfully Polite and Hilariously Hostile Writings: * and Just Plain Aggressive* was chosen as a Quick Pick for Reluctant Young Adults. Readers who have found themselves intrigued by the PostSecret books may enjoy Davy Rothbart's *Requiem for a Paper Bag: Celebrities and Civilians Tell Stories of the Best Lost, Tossed, and Found Items from Around the World*. Rothbart follows up his earlier volume, *Found*, with an entertaining collection of essays that describe notable discoveries people have made. The articles and the impacts the subjects have had on the authors vary widely, from Seth Rogan's coming across an issue of *Playboy* at a young age to a Kalashnikov bullet dug from the grille of author Mohsin Hamid's car in Pakistan, which became his lucky bullet.

Religion

In this section are books that explore various spiritual beliefs, beliefs about faith and the afterlife, and the religions practiced around the world, and include a moving look at what faith means to teens.

Noyes, Deborah.

Encyclopedia of the End: Mysterious Death in Fact, Fancy, Folklore, and More. Boston: Houghton Mifflin, 2008. 143p. ISBN 9780618823628. **J H**

This A-to-Z compendium of all things related to death includes a very wide range of topics, from rituals and ceremonies to famous people, events, and discussions of the literal and spiritual possibilities about what happens after one dies. The informational aspects of this book are well chosen and complete; quotes and literary references are explained within the text and often given cross-references to provide context for the casual reader, making this a useful book for reports as well as an interesting book for recreational reading.

Keywords: Curiosities and wonders • Death and dying

Now Try: Georgia Bragg's *How They Croaked: The Awful Ends of the Awfully Famous* chronicles the deaths of some very famous historical personages, noting how each subject lived and was treated (or not) by medical doctors or other practitioners when nearing death, and what handling the body received after death. The writing is presented in a casual style that offsets the gory subject matter and will appeal to junior and senior high students. It's all complemented by Kevin O'Malley's cartoon illustrations. Readers interested in the rather gross supplemental facts added to the material, such as the dangerous treatments of the day and common uses for mummies, will find further reading in the sources.

Pogue, Carolyn.

A World of Faith: Introducing Spiritual Traditions to Teens. Kelowna, BC: CopperHouse/Wood Lake Publishing, Inc., 2007. 191p. ISBN 9781551455549. **J** **H**

> This introduction to nine religions is unique in that it not only considers a practice that is largely known through archaeological study, but also begins each chapter by introducing the religions practiced around the world through the words of a teenager of that faith. Readers are encouraged to learn tolerance by becoming more familiar with other faiths. They are provided with a considerable amount of information, including an overview, a glossary of terms, rituals and ceremonies, and stories for each faith.
>
> **Keywords:** Aboriginal spirituality • Baha'I • Buddhism • Christianity • Goddess tradition • Hinduism • Islam • Judaism • Religion • Sikhism

What Do You Believe? London; New York: DK Publishing, 2011. 96p. ISBN 9780756672287. **M** **J**

> This book provides a basic and interesting comparative introduction to the world's six major religions: Buddhism, Christianity, Hinduism, Islam, Judaism, and Sikhism. The editors look at the main beliefs and tenets of these faiths, introducing readers to their rites, festivals, and customs, without ever forgetting that there are people in the world who adhere to other beliefs or to none at all. Starting with timelines and introducing questions from philosophy and science, this is a great overview of the world's differing views.
>
> **Keywords:** Buddhism • Christianity • Hinduism • Islam • Judaism • Religion • Sikhism

World Religions.

> The volumes in Compass Point's <u>World Religions</u> describe the origins and practice of five major religions: Buddhism, Christianity, Hinduism, Islam, and Judaism. There are similarities among the texts, which cover each religion's founders, difficulties faced by followers of the faith, sacred texts, and rituals, and provide readers with illustrations of modern challenges, such as a 2007 Burmese protest and the subsequent arrest of thousands of monks.

Nardo, Don.
Buddhism. Mankato, MN: Compass Point Books, 2010. 48p. ISBN 97807 56542368. **M** **J**

> **Keywords:** Buddha • Buddhism • Siddhartha

Christianity. Mankato, MN: Compass Point Books, 2010. 48p. ISBN 97807 56542375. **M** **J**

> **Keywords:** Bible • Christianity • Pope

Raatma, Lucia.

Islam. Mankato, MN: Compass Point Books, 2010. 48p. ISBN 97807 56542399. **M** **J**

> **Keywords:** Islam • Qur'an

Rosinsky, Natalie M.

Hinduism. Mankato, MN: Compass Point Books, 2010. 48p. ISBN 9780756542382. **M J**

> **Keywords:** Hinduism

Judaism. Mankato, MN: Compass Point Books, 2010. 48p. ISBN 9780756542405. **M J**

> **Keywords:** Judaism • Torah

Consider Starting with . . .

> Bellows, Melina. *NatGeo Amazing! 100 People, Places and Things That Will Wow You.*
>
> Bowman, Robin. *It's Complicated: The American Teenager.*
>
> Rockcliff, Mara. *Get Real! What Kind of World Are You Buying?*
>
> Taylor, Tannis. *31 Ways to Change the World: We Are What We Do.*
>
> Warren, Frank. *A Lifetime of Secrets: A PostSecret Book.*

Fiction Read-Alikes

- **Abdel-Fattah, Randa**. *Does My Head Look Big in This?* When sixteen-year-old Amal decides to wear the hijab, the Muslim headscarf, full time as a badge of her faith, she may not know quite what she is getting into. An Australian-born Muslim Palestinian with a lot of hyphenates treats readers to a dose of humor with both faith and culture.

- **Dominy, Amy Fellner.** *OyMG.* Ellie Taylor knows that the key to her future lies in attending Benedict High School. Her best chance to attend the school is a scholarship awarded by Mrs. Yeats, the benefactor of the summer Christian Society Speech and Performing Arts camp, in her best event, oratory. Complicating matters somewhat is Ellie's relationship with Devon Yeats, especially when Ellie finds out that Mrs. Yeats is anti-Semitic, and Devon recommends that Ellie hide the fact that she is Jewish. Ellie must decide how badly she wants the scholarship and whether to choose between her faith and her dreams.

- **Green, John.** *The Fault Is in Our Stars.* Hazel Lancaster needs to haul around an oxygen tank because of the tumors in her lungs and knows she is living on borrowed time. Augustus Waters is an amputee because of his osteosarcoma and feels immediate sparks when he sees Hazel across the room at a cancer support group meeting. Their relationship leads to pondering questions about the meaning of life, love, and loss.

- **Ness, Patrick.** *A Monster Calls.* There isn't much right with thirteen-year-old Conor's life. Bullies pick on him daily at school; his father has a new family in America; he doesn't get along with the grandmother who has been looking after him and his mother, who is undergoing medical treatments for cancer; and he has been having a recurring nightmare. He has so much going on that when an actual monster comes to him in the middle of the night, it hardly fazes him. The monster, which visits him in the shape of a yew tree, comes back again to tell Conor three stories in exchange for one of Conor's, stipulating only that it must be the truth. Conor must face his greatest fear, which will give him the chance to say good-bye to his mother and learn a truth at the same time, in this sad and beautiful ALA Notable title based on an idea from the late Siobhan Dowd.

- **Zusak, Marcus.** *The Book Thief.* This lyrical, Printz Honor–winning book tells the story of Liesel Meminger, narrated by Death himself and set in Nazi Germany before and during the Second World War.

Appendix A

Nonfiction Readers' Advisory Resources for YA Librarians

Although there are few readers' advisory or reviewing resources devoted solely to young adult nonfiction, there are sources that can help with both readers' advisory and collection development.

Reference and Readers' Advisory Sources

Cords, Sarah Statz.

The Real Story: A Guide to Nonfiction Reading Interests. Westport, CT: Libraries Unlimited, 2006.

> The first readers' advisory guide solely devoted to nonfiction contains definitions of the genres; thoughtful, detailed annotations; and read-alikes for the titles that older teens will appreciate.

Fraser, Elizabeth.

Reality Rules: A Guide to Teen Nonfiction Reading Interests. Westport, CT: Libraries Unlimited, 2008.

> The first volume of this guide contains over 500 titles in the genres considered here, published since the year 2000.

Gillespie, John T., and Catherine Barr.

Best Books for Middle School and Junior High Readers: Grades 6–9. Westport, CT: Libraries Unlimited, 2009.

Best Books for High School Readers: Grades 9–12. Westport, CT: Libraries Unlimited, 2009.

> These two guides contain entries for virtually every subject, including fiction and nonfiction. This edition of the guides includes graphic novels and audio versions. Supplements to these editions were released in 2011, covering books released between 2009 and 2011.

Holly, Pam Spencer.

Quick and Popular Reads for Teens. Chicago: American Library Association Editions, 2009.

> Readers are given annotated bibliographies and themed lists based on YALSA's Quick Pick for Reluctant Readers and Popular Paperback lists. The nonfiction titles are pulled out.

Wyatt, Neal.

The Readers' Advisory Guide to Nonfiction. Chicago: American Library Association. 2007.

> This general introduction to readers' advisory for adults provides a good overview of the types of nonfiction, its appeal, and the main genres. Readers will find lists of the main authors and title suggestions, as well as suggestions for ten books from each area as a starting point.

Review Journals

Booklist. PO Box 607, Mt. Morris, IL 61054-7564. Phone: 1-888-350-0949. Web site: www.booklistonline.com.

> *Booklist* is a critical collection development and review journal, which reviews more than 2,500 children's titles annually, with both a print and an online component. Booklistonline offers access to a database of more than 130,000 reviews.

Horn Book. 7858 Industrial Parkway, Plain City, OH 43064. Web site: www.hbook.com.

> The *Horn Book*'s Web site includes subscription information for the long-running bimonthly magazine; the semiannual *Horn Book Guide*, which provides readers with 2,000 reviews; and access to 80,000 more through the *Horn Book Online*. Additional enticements include Roger Sutton's blog and coverage of the Boston-Globe Horn Book awards.

School Library Journal. 160 Varick Street, 11th Floor, New York, NY 10013. Phone: 646-380-0700. Web site: www.schoollibraryjournal.com.

> Subscriptions to *School Library Journal* may be obtained through its Web site, which also offers an archive of the magazine and some of the strongest, most

interesting blogs around, authored by subject specialists. Readers will find Angela Carstensen's Adult Books 4 Teens, and nonfiction titles discussed in time for the ALA's Youth Media Awards in the Heavy Medal blog. It is also the home of the wonderful Battle of the Kids Books.

Voice of Youth Advocates (VOYA). E L Kurdyla Publishing LLC, Bowie, MD. Web site: www.voya.com. E-mail subscriptions@voya.com.

VOYA includes nonfiction titles in each bimonthly magazine. Its August issue features a Nonfiction Honor list.

Online Sources

Many review journals have developed strong Web presences, with notable blogs that are updated on a daily basis. In addition, several bloggers and libraries post interesting discussions about books in the months before the Youth Media Awards.

Cybils (Children's and YA Bloggers' Literary Awards). http://www.cybils.com.

The Cybils Award had its sixth anniversary in 2011. Of its eight categories, with nominations open to the reading public, three highlight nonfiction.

Fuse8. http://www.schoollibraryjournal.com/afuse8production/.

Elizabeth Bird's blog is a window on the book world. It is made up of a mix of items, which may include reviews, comments on trends or upcoming events, and links to other blogs and items of note. It is always fascinating.

The Hub. http://www.yalsa.ala.org/thehub/.

The Hub is a one-stop shop "to find out about great teen reads," with content created by librarians and teens.

Reading Rants. http://www.readingrants.org.

Jennifer Hubert Swan's blog contains well-written and thoughtful reviews of new titles that will appeal to a wide variety of readers.

Discussion Lists

Although there are no discussion lists specifically for young adult nonfiction, nonfiction titles are discussed on YALSA-BK and Adbooks. Subscription information is available here:

- **Adbooks** (http://groups.yahoo.com/group/adbooks/). Adbooks was created in 1998 as an e-mail list for the discussion of adolescent literature by people of all ages. It became a Yahoo group in 2009.

- **YALSA-BK** (http://lists.ala.org/wws/info/yalsa-bk). YALSA-BK is an open book discussion group of the Young Adult Library Services Association. Participants are invited to discuss specific titles, as well as any topic in the area of reading.

Book Awards and Selection Lists

The increasing amount of quality nonfiction for young adults is well reflected in the recognition these books receive. YALSA's Award for Excellence in Nonfiction for Young Adults, first awarded in 2010, is a prime example of this. Following is an explanation of the awards and book lists cited in this book and the organizations that award them.

- The **Young Adult Library Services Association (YALSA)** has several committees that work to find the best books for teens aged twelve to eighteen. These annual lists have the specific purpose of choosing the following:

  1. The Best Books for Young Adults, which were chosen through 2010 by a selection committee under the direction to select a list that considered both literary quality and popularity. After 2010 this committee's purview was changed, as was its name, to reflect YALSA's new nonfiction award.

  2. Quick Picks for Reluctant Young Adult Readers, pleasurable books for teens who do not like to read.

  3. Popular Paperbacks, pleasurable reading in a variety of accessible themes and genres.

  4. Great Graphic Novels for Teens.

- The **Michael L. Printz Award** is given annually by YALSA to the book that exemplifies literary excellence in young adult literature. As many as four Printz honor books may be chosen annually.

- The YALSA **Award for Excellence in Nonfiction for Young Adults,** awarded for the first time in 2010, honors the best in nonfiction published for an audience between the ages of twelve and eighteen. A shortlist of five titles is published annually in November, and the full list of the committee's nominated titles is published after YALSA's media awards are announced at the Midwinter meeting in January.

- The **Alex Awards** are chosen by YALSA and are given annually to the best adult books for young adults. The awards are sponsored by the Margaret A. Edwards Trust, which is named after Margaret Edwards, who was called "Alex." Since 2010 the committee also publishes its full list of nominated titles after the Youth Media Awards announcement at the ALA Midwinter meeting.

- **The Coretta Scott King Book Awards** commemorate the life and works of Dr. Martin Luther King Jr. and honors Mrs. Coretta Scott King with the Coretta Scott King Award. These titles promote understanding of the cultures of all people and their realization of the American dream. The Coretta Scott King Award and the John Steptoe New Talent Award, which celebrates the beginning of a career, are given to African American authors and illustrators for outstanding inspirational and educational contributions.

- The **Bologna Book Fair** is held annually for children's publishers in Bologna, Italy. At the fair an international panel chooses the Bologna Ragazzi award winners in fiction and nonfiction in four age categories, including young adult.

- The **International Reading Association** (http://www.reading.org/Resources/ Booklists/TeachersChoices.aspx) is a professional organization for people involved in teaching reading to any age group. Their annual Teachers' Choices include fiction and nonfiction books in primary, intermediate, and advanced reader categories. The goals of the project include choosing books that may be used across the curriculum and that will encourage young people to read more.

- The **Robert F. Sibert Informational Book Medal** is awarded annually by the ALA's Association for Library Services to Children (ALSC) at its Midwinter meeting in January. The Sibert award is given to the author, author/illustrator, coauthor or author, and illustrator of the most distinguished informational book published in the United States during the preceding year. Honor books may also be awarded.

- The **Norma Fleck Award for Canadian Children's Nonfiction** (http://www. bookcentre.ca/awards/norma_fleck_award_canadian_childrens_nonfiction) is overseen by the Canadian Children's Book Centre. It was established in 1999 to recognize the high quality of informational literature available to children and young adults.

- The **Boston Globe-Horn Book Award (**http://www.hbook.com/bghb/default. asp) is cosponsored by the *Boston Globe* and *Horn Book Magazine*. Nonfiction is one of the three categories of the award, which is judged by three children's literature professionals.

- The **Lane Anderson Award** (http://www.laneandersonaward.ca/) honors the best science writing in Canada in both young adult and adult categories. The award was established in 1987 and is administered by the Fitzhenry Family Foundation.

- The **National Book Award for Young People's Literature** (http://www .nationalbook.org/nba.html) has been celebrating "the best in American literature" since 1950.

- The **Orbis Pictus Award** (http://www.ncte.org/awards/orbispictus) for Outstanding K–8 nonfiction is chosen by the National Council of Teachers of English.

- The **Red Maple Award** (http://www.bookcentre.ca/awards/red_maple_award) is administered by the Ontario Library Association and is one of its annual Forest of Reading awards. A young reader's choice award intended to honor the best books for readers in grades seven and eight, it has included a nonfiction book category in alternate years since 2005.

- **ALSC Recommended Titles** (http://www.ala.org/ala/mgrps/divs/alsc/awards grants/index.cfm). The Association for Library Service to Children (ALSC), which serves children up to the age of fourteen, makes available its annual Notable Book Lists as well as information about the Newbery Award and the Pura Belpré Award.

- **Amelia Bloomer Project** (http://www.libr.org/ftf/bloomer.html). The Feminist Task Force of the Social Responsibilities Round Table of the American Library Association creates an annual book list of the best feminist books for young readers, for children from birth through age eighteen. A list of the criteria used to choose the books is available on the task force's Web site.

Appendix B

Bibliography

"Adolescence." 2007. *Encyclopædia Britannica*. Available at http://search.eb.com. elibrary.calgarypubliclibrary.com/eb/article-9003766 (accessed September 8, 2007).

American Psychological Association (APA). 2008. *Shared Risk Factors for Youth Obesity and Disordered Eating*. Available at http://www.apa.org/about/gr/pi/ advocacy/2008/shared-risk.pdf (accessed October 29, 2011).

Aronson, Marc. 2003. "Biography and Its Perils." In *Beyond the Pale: New Essays for a New Era*. Lanham, MD: Scarecrow Press.

Barnett, Rosalind, and Caryl Rivers. 2011. "No Blank Slates." *Women's Review of Books* 28, no. 3: 23. MasterFILE Premier/Web (accessed February 23, 2012).

Carter, Betty. 1987. "A Content Analysis of the Most Frequently Circulated Information Books in Three Junior High Libraries." Ed.D. thesis, University of Houston.

Cords, Sarah Statz. 2006. *The Real Story: A Guide to Nonfiction Reading Interests*. Westport, CT: Libraries Unlimited.

Fraser, Elizabeth. 2008. *Reality Rules: A Guide to Teen Nonfiction Reading Interests*. Westport, CT: Libraries Unlimited.

Hill, Rebecca. 2012. "All Aboard!" *School Library Journal* 58, no. 4: 26.

Isaacs, Kathleen T. 2011. "The Facts of the Matter: Children's Nonfiction, from Then to Now." *Horn Book Magazine* (March 1): 10.

Partridge, Elizabeth. 2011. "Narrative Nonfiction: Kicking Ass At Last." *Horn Book Magazine* (March 11): 69.

Reisner, Rosalind. 2010. "Listen to My Life's Story." *Library Journal* (October 1): 41.

Wyatt, Neal. 2007. *The Readers' Advisory Guide to Nonfiction*. Chicago: American Library Association.

Author/Title Index

Subject Index

About the Author

ELIZABETH (BETSY) FRASER is currently selector for the Calgary Public Library system in Calgary, Alberta. She is a reviewer for *VOYA* and *School Library Journal*. She has served on several committees for the American Library Association, including the Michael L. Printz Award and the Award for Excellence in Nonfiction.